ECONOMIC
APARTHEID
in AMERICA

Also by Chuck Collins

Wealth and Our Commonwealth:
Why America Should Tax Accumulated Fortunes
with Bill Gates Sr.

Robin Hood Was Right: A Guide to Giving Your Money for Social Change
with Pam Rogers and Joan Garner

The Wealth Inequality Reader (co-editor)

ECONOMIC APARTHEID IN AMERICA

A PRIMER ON ECONOMIC INEQUALITY & INSECURITY

CHUCK COLLINS AND FELICE YESKEL

WITH UNITED FOR A FAIR ECONOMY AND CLASS ACTION

THE NEW PRESS

NEW YORK
LONDON

Nick Thorkelson

DOWNSIZED RESTRUCTURED OUTSOURCED

Requests for permission to reproduce selections from this book should be mailed to:
Permissions Department,
The New Press, 38 Greene Street, New York, NY 10013

Published in the United States by The New Press, New York, 2005
Distributed by W. W. Norton & Company, Inc., New York

LIBRARY OF CONGRESS CATALOGING-IN-PUBLICATION DATA

Collins, Chuck, 1959–
    Economic apartheid in America: a primer on economic inequality
& insecurity / Chuck Collins and Felice Yeskel; with United for a Fair Economy
and Class Action.—Rev. and updated ed.
    p.   cm.
ISBN 1-59558-015-8 (pbk.)
        1. Income distribution—United States. 2. United States—
    Economic conditions—1981– 3. Poverty—United States 4. Wealth—
    United States. I. Yeskel, Felice. II. United for a Fair Economy.
    III. Class Action (Organization) IV. Title.

HC110.I5 C586 2005
330.973—dc22   2005043850

The New Press was established in 1990 as a not-for-profit alternative
to the large, commercial publishing houses currently dominating the book
publishing industry. The New Press operates in the public interest
rather than for private gain, and is committed to publishing, in innovative ways,
works of educational, cultural, and community value that are often deemed
insufficiently profitable.

www.thenewpress.com

Printed in Canada

2 4 6 8 10 9 7 5 3 1

Contents

4. Building a Fair Economy Movement

5. Actions to Close the Economic Divide

John Jonik

BOOMING ECONOMY

Acknowledgments

For Nora Collins and Shira Ma'ayan Yeskel-Mednick,
our wonderful daughters,
in the hope that they grow up in a world with greater equality

This second edition of *Economic Apartheid* is the outgrowth of ten years of work and two lifetimes of commitment to building a more equitable economy. In 1994, we co-founded United for a Fair Economy (UFE) to draw attention to the dangers of growing income and wealth inequality and support grassroots organizing efforts to close the precarious divide.

In 2002, Class Action started to raise consciousness about issues of class and money and their impact on our individual lives, our relationships, organizations, institutions, and culture. Class Action aims to heal the wounds of classism and support the development of cross-class alliance-building, and to support the movement of resources to where they are most needed to create equity, justice, and sustainability for all.

Thanks to all who have contributed to this project.

Major thanks to Amy Hackett, Chris Hartman, and Christina Strong, who provided significant research help. We would like to especially thank Ellen Reeves at The New Press, who was our editor for both editions, and Liz Polizzi, Maury Botton, and Jessica Colter, who brought this edition to print.

Thanks to the artists and photographers who generously contributed their work. These include: John Lapham, Dan Wasserman, Ted Rall, Matt Wuerker, Laura Wulf, Bulbul, Lindsay Roberts, Nick Thorkelson, Mike Konopacki, Carole Simpson, Gary Huck, and Kirk Anderson.

A few people read the whole manuscript and helped set us straight on a number of counts. Thanks to Meizhu Lui, who read the second edition. And thanks to several people who helped shape the first edition: Nancy Folbre, James Heintz, Tami Geicek, Julie Greenberg, Joanne Jones, Felicia Mednick, Mike Miller, Scott Klinger, Mike Lapham, Jean Phillips, Donnie Roberts, and Genevieve Melford.

Mike Prokosch, John Cavanagh, and Lisa McGowan helped with the global-economy sections. Tom Schlesinger assisted with the sections on the Federal Reserve. Heather Booth helped with the section on action.

Chuck's thanks: Thanks, Tricia! Thanks to the UFE gang and other sources of inspiration, including Daniel Moss, Jim Driscoll, Naomi Swinton, Holly Sklar, Jim Wallis, Charlie Derber, Julie Schor, and the Hampstead Road Neighborhood.

Felice's thanks: I want to thank Felicia Mednick, my partner, who has been a loving supporter of this work and who has done more than her share of childcare, and my daughter, Shira, who reminds me to play on a regular basis. I also want to thank the wonderful community of friends who have talked with me late into the night about issues of class, justice, and changing the world—in particular, Jenny Ladd, a founder of Responsible Wealth and Class Action, who models moving outside her comfort zone with grace. Thanks too to my late mother, Phyllis Yeskel, who taught me to stand up for what I believe and fostered the chutzpah necessary to do so, and my late father, Harry Yeskel, who reminded me to have fun while working hard.

We are both unspeakably appreciative of the many, many wonderful people we have met in the course of doing this work. They inspire us to keep believing that creating a fair economy is possible.

Foreword

In February 1996, in the elegant Alpine village of Davos, Switzerland, I attended the World Economic Forum's annual week of global-ruling-class gabbing and deal-making. As usual, the topic was globalization. One evening, after plenty of wine, speaker after speaker stood up for self-congratulations on having won the world over to the cause of global free markets. A mere twenty-five years ago, the opinion that an unregulated, corporate-dominated market should reign supreme was held by only a minority. Today, they exulted, only extremist and decidedly fringe opposition to this worldview remains.

As one of those fringe opponents, perhaps the only one in the room, I remember smiling silently to myself. The moment of declaring such a victory is often the beginning of the end. And so may it be for the latest surge toward free-market globalism. The participants in that evening's dinner were conveniently forgetting the French general strike which had just ended, and they did not foresee the demonstrations which were to rock Bonn a short time later. Nor did they anticipate the powerful street protests to take place in Indonesia, or farmers and workers on the march in poor countries around the world. No surprise, then, that they were all blindsided by the "Battle of Seattle."

With the 1999 protests in Seattle, this struggle did finally reach the shores of the United States. Demonstrators demanded that powerful economic actors become accountable to democratic forces, that the processes which are generating inequality and environmental degradation be stopped, and that we revisit basic questions about the purpose of economic activity: Is the economy to serve the people who make it up, or is their labor for the sake of lining the pockets of the rich and powerful? Seattle has put this basic question back on the table.

This wonderful book goes a long way toward explaining why opposition to an unregulated global free market is now surfacing. It details, in an innovative and accessible way, the growing gap between those who are prospering in the global economy and those who are not. It shows that increased levels of inequality in income, wages, wealth, and power are creating an apartheid society.

The paradox of increased inequality has been the failure of large numbers of Americans to speak out or act forcefully against it. The work of United for a Fair Economy is beginning to change that. They were a major force in Seattle. And they are beginning to catalyze a new movement for economic justice in the United States. This book may well be the roadmap.

—Juliet B. Schor

Introduction:
ECONOMIC BOOM FOR WHOM?

Then again, from below, in the great heavy stack
Came a groan from that plain little turtle named Mack.
"Your Majesty, please . . . I don't like to complain,
But down here below, we are feeling great pain.
I know, up on top you are seeing great sights,
But down at the bottom, we, too, should have rights.
We turtles can't stand it. Our shells will all crack!
Besides, we need food. We are starving!" groaned Mack.
    —DR. SEUSS, *YERTLE THE TURTLE*

The Amazing U.S. Economy?

Since the first edition of *Economic Apartheid in America* was published in 2000, a lot has changed—but a lot has stayed the same. The problem of growing wage and wealth inequality has only worsened after a slight improvement at the end of the 1990s.

How well you think the economy is working depends on which end of the inequality spectrum you are on. For some, these are the best of times. But it is important to look at a wide variety of signs of the times. What are the indicators of economic health? What's working? What are the signs that all is not well?

Inflation has been flat. Unemployment as a national average is relatively low. Yet the much-touted prosperity brought on by the economic boom of the late 1990s was not evenly shared. The economy of the last fifteen years has been particularly rewarding if you own a lot of assets such as real estate, stocks, or bonds.

However, if you are on a fixed income or depend on a job to bring home wages or a salary, things have been a bit rough. If you're not part of the 40 percent of the population that has $5,000 or more in the stock market,[1] then all the media hoopla about an improving economy doesn't help. In fact, you're invisible. The economy is not working for everyone. And the gap between the very wealthy and everyone else is growing dangerously wide.

Being poor in America has always been a rocky road, worsened in recent years by social scapegoating and the erosion of living standards as a result of cuts in social programs. But many people in the American middle class also share a growing sense of precariousness.[2] "We have the impression from television and the media that our prosperity is huge, but that is not the middle-class experience," observed the late Marc Miringoff, a Fordham University expert on social indicators.[3]

The signs of the economic times present two divergent pictures. Some of these signs include:

$ **Stretch limousines are longer, yet more people are homeless. There are more "statement house" mansions being built, yet fewer affordable apartments to be found.**

$ **Unemployment figures are low, yet 2002 and 2003 were record years for worker layoffs.**

$ **Stores that serve the middle class have gone out of business—or have remade themselves into either bargain-basement outlets targeted at working families or luxury retailers to appeal to the nation's richest shoppers.**

$ **Consumer spending and borrowing have gone up while personal savings have plummeted.**

$ **Top corporate chief executive officers (CEOs) pay themselves megamillions while the wages of over half the U.S. workforce have remained flat or fallen.**

$ **A growing number of new jobs are temporary or part-time and do not offer health insurance, retirement, or vacation benefits. Two out of three new private-sector jobs are in the "temporary employment" category, with median wages at about 75 percent of those of full-time salaried workers. One of America's largest employers is now Manpower, Inc., a temporary employment agency, with over 2.3 million workers globally.**

$ **Thirty zip codes in America have become fabulously wealthy. Meanwhile, whole urban and rural communities are languishing in unemployment, crumbling infrastructure, growing insecurity, and fear.**

$ **In the final month of each year, the juxtapositions become more ironic. Newspaper articles that chronicle the lavish bonuses that go to a handful of Wall Street financiers are placed next to stories of destitution and insecurity and exhortations to "Remember the Neediest!"**

WARNING: Entering New Global Economy— PROCEED WITH CAUTION

Welcome to the new global economy, designed by and for America's largest corporations and wealthiest individuals. From their point of view, this is the biggest bash of the century. The economy at the beginning of this century makes the Reagan Revolution of the 1980s look like a sedate card party.

The people who own America are working overtime to convince you that the economy is improving. Look at that climbing stock market, even when it's on a roller coaster. Check out the growing number of millionaires and people invested in the stock market with do-it-yourself Internet brokerages. The message seems to be, "Hey, Jack (or Jane), what's your problem? How come you ain't rich? Get off your duff!"

But the reality is that many people are working extremely hard and facing growing economic uncertainty. Personal debt and bankruptcies are rising. While "keeping up with the Joneses" in our high-tech, advertising-driven, consumer society accounts for some of this, a large percentage of workers, particularly those in their twenties and thirties, have two jobs with no benefits. A growing number of people are living without health insurance and postponing necessary medical treatment. In the last thirty years, an increased number of people have little or no retirement or job security.

People are being told, "You are on your own"; "Security is an illusion"; "Don't expect anything from your employer"; "Don't expect anything from the government (especially as we dismantle it)"; "Get out there and become an entrepreneur!" All these messages are shaped by the most rich and powerful people in our country, people who have left nothing to chance in terms of their own personal economic security and comfort.

Meanwhile, the media gives us a skewed picture of the economy. We do not see many news stories about economic insecurity and growing inequality in America. Perhaps FOXNews, Viacom (the new owner of CBS), General Electric (the owner of NBC), Disney (the owner of ABC), and Time Warner (with its controlling interest in CNN) do not believe that the widening gap between rich and everyone else is a worthy story. We have to get the real story about our economy from somewhere else.[4]

The mass media encourages us to look up the economic ladder and fantasize about and identify with the superrich, while unscrupulous politicians encourage people to direct their blame and anger toward people one or two rungs down the economic ladder. The scapegoats for the polarized economy include women on welfare and new immigrants. Alternatively, they distract us with other "wedge" issues like same-sex marriage.

During economic hard times, we have experienced periods of both progressive and regressive populism. The rural Populist movement of the 1880s and 1890s was mostly progressive as it

WHO OWNS THE MEDIA?

GENERAL ELECTRIC

OWNS

OWNS

VIACOM

OWNS

TIME WARNER

OWNS

encouraged people to look at large corporations and concentrated wealth as the source of their insecurities. However, during the 1980s and 1990s, we experienced a wave of regressive populism as people were encouraged to look down the economic ladder to blame those below them.

The Trends: Rising Tide, Sinking Boats

The larger economic trends of the past three decades help to explain many of the signs of the times we currently observe. Each of the following trends will be examined in more depth in Chapter 2.

FALLING WAGES. There has been an overall growth in income, but virtually all income growth has gone to the highest-earning fifth of the population, with the biggest gains flowing to the richest 1 percent. For the bottom 60 percent of the population, real wages, the actual spending power of people's paychecks, have stagnated or fallen. There is some good news: since 1997, median real wages began to climb back to where they were in the 1970s, but this hardly qualifies as an economic success story. And since 2002, real wages for the bottom half of wage earners have started to dip again.[5]

WEALTH INEQUALITY. The overall wealth pie has grown, but almost all of the gains have gone to the wealthiest 1 percent of households. The top 1 percent of households currently have more wealth than the bottom 95 percent combined.

WIDENING GAP BETWEEN HIGHEST- AND LOWEST-PAID WORKERS. While real wages have fallen for half of U.S. workers, compensation to top managers and CEOs has skyrocketed. Inequality in wages is at an all-time high.

LOSING GROUND AT WORK. During the last twenty-five years, three out of four U.S. wage-earners have lost ground on the job. In real terms, this means that people's wages have not kept up with inflation or that workers have lost some portion of the benefits they previously had. Instead of having a pension or 100 percent health care coverage, many workers now have no retirement security or pay some or all of their health care costs. Many workers are now temporary or part-time workers with no benefits. Some have lost their jobs and have not been able to find a comparable paying job or any job at all.[6]

PRECARIOUS AND STRESSED MIDDLE CLASS. These trends mean a lot of people are feeling the sands shifting beneath their feet. A generation ago, people were more likely to know where they would be working in five years. Today, half the population says they feel no employer loyalty or job security.[7] The *silent depression* of falling wages is masked by two trends we shall discuss in detail later: rising consumer debt and an increase in the number of hours worked per family in the paid workforce. These trends put enormous stress on working families.

THE RISING TIDE LIFTS ONLY THE YACHTS. Since the late 1980s, there has been an expansion in the economy and an increase in productivity.[8] Yet unlike previous periods of economic growth, the rising tide has not lifted all the boats. Inequality has grown, with the rising tide lifting up only the yachts while the smaller boats rock in the wake. Unlike the post–World War II years, when economic growth was shared more equitably,[9] there has been a dramatic pulling apart in the last twenty-five years between the small number of "haves" and everybody else.

Despite these uncertain conditions, recent polls show that almost a third of the population is happy about the performance of the economy.[10] After all, many people seem to be driving bigger cars, living in bigger houses, and taking vacations on airplanes. Yet this may be a false sense of comfort, as many people's current standard of living is largely based on personal debt, money borrowed upon the assumption of future growth and prosperity. On one hand, this borrowing spree has buoyed the economy with increased consumer demand; on the other hand, there are falling savings rates, rising costs of health care and college education, increasing bankruptcies, and other signs of economic insecurity. For many in the middle class, there is a precarious undercurrent to this prosperity.

The "perpetual motion" economy at the turn of the century is chugging ahead based on a number of factors that can't go on forever. Some homeowners have seen their home values grow faster than their wages. This leads people to borrow money against their homes and against anticipated stock earnings. Mortgage and home-equity loans have been the fastest-rising form of consumer debt since 1999, though there has also been a tremendous run-up in other types of debt as well, such as credit card debt.[11] This is just one factor that points to instability. When the social fabric pulls so far apart, it begins to rip. Our society's response has been to put record numbers of people in prison and build more gated communities. Any bump in the road, any economic downturn, will reveal the hidden dangers of growing inequality.

We Can Build a Fairer Economy

Most of us experience our daily lives in terms of family, work, friends, and our local community. We do not always see the connections between the personal struggles we may be facing and changes in the larger economy, such as longer working hours, having multiple jobs, and the inability to save money. In fact, we are encouraged to see our problems as personal. Even when we understand the link between the larger economic forces and our daily lives, we do not necessarily believe that we can do anything to improve our circumstances. Often we simply hear, "That's just the way things are" or "There is no alternative." However, this is not true.

There are alternatives—and there were recent times in our country's history when we were not so economically divided. The U.S. economy was significantly fairer in the thirty years following World War II. Prosperity, while elusive for some, was better shared among a majority of people in society than it is today. There is no reason why this should no longer hold true in the present. During the last few decades the rules of the economy have been changed by wealthy individuals and corporations—and they can be changed back by people like us. In the 1930s, the New Deal ushered in an era of greater economic security and a rising standard of living for seniors and working families. In the 1960s, we launched a War on Poverty that improved health care for seniors and the poor and provided a "Head Start" to low-income children. Today, at the beginning of a new century, we need a new set of policies and priorities to ensure a more broadly shared prosperity. We need to revive the values of concern for the common good. We also need to expose the assumptions and myths that are used to justify economic inequality.

There have also been cycles of great inequality in our country's past that we can learn from today. In the 1880s, as the United States went through the industrial revolution, there was grotesque inequality as the richest 1 percent owned an estimated 50 percent of all private wealth.[12] The ostentatious fortunes of the robber barons were built on the backs of impoverished workers and

"Thanks to the economic boom...
we only have to cut your wages 10% this year."

by extracting wealth from the natural environment. The industrial workforce was subject to enormous dangers and sweatshop conditions. Children worked in factories. Cities were crowded and disease thrived in unsanitary conditions.

In the face of these challenges, a coalition of workers, farmers, and urban reformers created a social movement pushing for fundamental reforms to make the economy fairer and the distribution of income and wealth more equitable. The Populist movement united farmers and urban workers across racial lines to build a powerful political movement that became a countervailing force to the agenda of big corporations and wealth-holders. The Populists pushed for democratic reforms such as the direct election of U.S. senators. They fought for reforms like antitrust legislation and a constitutional amendment for the first income tax to break up overconcentra-

tions of wealth. They established alternative economic institutions, including a national network of agricultural producer cooperatives. They pressed for reforms in tariffs and cuts in special subsidies for the big trusts, a nineteenth-century version of cutting corporate welfare. The Populists and their reforms changed the political and economic face of the United States.

Today, we find ourselves in a world similar to that of the farmers and workers in the 1880s before the peak of the Populist movement. Inequality is on the rise. Power has shifted into the hands of fewer wealthy individuals and corporations, and economic insecurity is growing for most. It is time to build an economic fairness movement to counteract the power of concentrated wealth and large corporations. Indeed, the seeds of this movement already exist. We hope this book will prove a useful tool for expanding such a movement.

About the Book

This book is designed to be a primer about growing economic insecurity and inequality in the United States. It is for students, religious people, workers, and ordinary people who want to have a better understanding of the economic forces shaping our lives. The problem is important and complicated. There are already a number of excellent books and academic studies that help explain dimensions of inequality. This book attempts to consolidate and summarize many of them; we attempt to explain economics in an understandable and user-friendly way. Our bias

in this book is that people and communities matter. We agree with the U.S. Catholic Bishops who wrote in their 1986 pastoral letter on the economy, "the economy should serve people; people should not serve the economy."[13]

Growing inequality is not caused by some natural phenomenon, like sun spots. "We the people" can exercise much more control over our destiny and the type of economy we want to have. Economics is essentially about values. We believe that an economy should be organized around the values of strengthening communities and supporting families. The economy should be in harmony with the environment and should foster greater democracy. We think the values of possessive individualism and greed, the values that now underlie our economy, have brought our country to a dangerous point. We need to rebuild our economy in a more equitable and sustainable manner.

The problem of inequality is, in part, a problem of democracy. The growing role of big money in politics is only one aspect of the decline of democracy. The vast majority of people in this country have been excluded from decision-making about some of the most important rules determining our shared economic lives. Economics has been mystified, so that we have become less able to understand how to protect ourselves. This book is designed to give you the tools to participate in the building of a fairer economy for everyone. We don't believe economics is a science to be discussed and handled only by the "experts." Ordinary people need to become engaged in dialogue and action on one of the most significant issues of our time.

This book does not offer a sweeping alternative vision to the current economic order. We hope it will lay the groundwork for broader discussions about alternatives to unbridled free-market capitalism. But we don't need to have a comprehensive blueprint for change to point out the fundamental problems with the current economic system. We know that too much inequality is bad for our economy, democracy, and culture. We know that the private market lacks an ethical compass and that civic institutions need power in order to bring moral values into the marketplace.

We know that the excesses of the private market must be tamed to protect human values and our quality of life. We don't need a countervision or blueprint to stop the worst harms threatened by the current economic order.

We believe that we are at a dangerous juncture. As wealth concentrates in the hands of a few, so does the power to change the rules that govern our economy. Rules like who pays taxes, who benefits from global trade agreements, and whether there will be an increase in the minimum wage are increasingly decided by fewer and fewer people, who have a vested interest in keeping an economic order that benefits only themselves.

This is a vicious cycle. As corporations gain more power, they use their power to buy lobbyists and pay to elect candidates who will change the rules in their favor. They buy the media and utilize complex tactics to influence and shape public opinion and culture. As a result, the power of corporations increases, and the cycle continues.

We believe that we can address the problems of concentrated corporate wealth and power—and the growing inequalities in our country—through organized people power and the revitalization of our democracy. The seeds of an emerging social movement are now being planted, and it is our hope that this book will help accelerate its formation.

The focus of this book is on the United States, though we provide an introduction to the ways in which global inequality and globalization contribute to growing inequality in the United States. We believe that inequality cannot be addressed in this country without addressing the engine of the new global economy and its impact on people worldwide.

The basic questions this book examines are: Why should we care about inequality? What is the inequality picture? What has caused the growth of inequality? And what can we do to change it?

CHAPTER 1, "The Dangerous Consequences of Growing Inequality," examines the negative effects of growing inequality and how it affects our daily lives and contributes to a multitude of other social problems. It speaks to the question of why we urgently need to address the problem of growing inequality.

CHAPTER 2, "The Picture: Growing Economic Insecurity and Inequality," explains the economic trends that affect us, including what has happened to our income, wages, savings, and wealth.

CHAPTER 3, "The Causes of Inequality," examines what has happened in the last several decades to worsen inequality and to keep the economy from working for most people.

CHAPTER 4, "Building a Fair Economy Movement," examines some of the strategic considerations in building a fair economy movement and the lessons from previous movements that are relevant today.

CHAPTER 5, "Actions to Close the Economic Divide," looks at how we can reduce inequality and suggests actions we can take. You can skip directly to this section if you are eager for action ideas, but each previous section provides an analysis that helps inform this action program.

Because this book looks primarily at problems through the lens of class, it is limited in its explanation of the fundamental intersection between race, gender, and economic inequality. The impact of economic inequalities fall heaviest on women and people of color, and the remedies to economic inequality must be devised to focus on broadly inclusive solutions. We hope this book will stimulate continued discussion about the interweaving of analysis and interventions to address the racial and gender manifestations of economic inequality. Watch for the complementary book by United for a Fair Economy, *The Color of Wealth* (The New Press), which looks at the legacy of racial discrimination in wealth-building.

Are we advocating class war or blaming rich people for our country's woes? Our experience is that there are many people in the richest 5 percent of this country who are opposed to the way in which the current economy is worsening inequality. Many are working hard to change things. We do think it is important to talk directly about the class divide in this country. We realize that simply by raising the issue, some will perceive us to be "against rich people" rather than opposed to the structures of the economy that create grotesque inequalities. We do believe, however, that individuals are responsible for their actions. Top managers who raise their own pay while laying off thousands of workers are responsible for the suffering they cause, as are investors who press to maximize their investment returns without asking about the conditions degrading the workers. We believe that those who have benefited from this system have a special responsibility to repair the damage it causes and prevent it from causing further harm.

This book is by no means a comprehensive economics textbook. Nor does it do justice to some of the excellent intellectual work that has been done on the issue of inequality, its causes, and its solutions. However, we hope that this book will be an entry point into further reading, discussion, and agitation about these concerns. At the end of the book, we provide a list of additional recommended reading and action organizations. Our apologies in advance for any omissions.

If you are like us, you can only suffer so much of the bad news before you want to consider strategies for action (or just take a break to look at the cartoons). Too many books are laden with problem analysis but weak in terms of solution. We are indebted to those who have helped us provide the research and analysis necessary to raise and explain these issues. At the same time, our work is dedicated to those who are inspired to take action to build a fairer economy.

Chapter 1

THE DANGEROUS CONSEQUENCES OF GROWING INEQUALITY

You can have wealth concentrated in the hands of a few, or democracy. But you cannot have both.

—LOUIS BRANDEIS

How wealthy the wealthy are does matter. If we allow great wealth to accumulate in the pockets of a few, then great wealth can set our political agenda and shape our political culture—and the agenda and the culture that emerge will not welcome efforts to make America work for all Americans.

—SAM PIZZIGATI

Some people argue that inequality is a relative problem. We should not be so concerned with the gap as with the overall improvement in our standard of living. Someone living in the bottom half of the income spectrum today has a much higher standard of living than someone in the bottom half of the income spectrum forty years ago. Apologists for inequality point to mobility and the notion that people move up the economic ladder over their lifetimes.

Others might say that *poverty* is the problem that we should address. We should not concern ourselves with the top end of the income and wealth ladder because it is irrelevant. In the words of one commentator, "How rich the rich are doesn't matter."

Robert J. Samuelson writes that our real problem is that we have come to expect too much. Our expectations after the economic prosperity of the 1950s and 1960s have grown unrealistically, and we have come to feel entitled to ongoing economic security. He states,

> It's true that growth has slowed, but stagnation hardly describes the explosion of new products that has benefited millions of Americans since 1970: the profusion of VCRs, personal computers, cable T.V., microwave ovens. Since 1970, air travel has roughly tripled, an increase 10 times the rise in population. In the same period, the share of adults who are college graduates doubled, from 11 to 22 percent. Indeed, for all our angst, the economy is doing fairly well.[1]

Is Samuelson right? Does the increased availability of consumer goods, twenty-four-hour communications and entertainment networks, cheap air travel, and more college graduates add up to a great economy for all? Or have we paid too great a price for this "prosperity" by tolerating a surge in economic inequality, a hollowing-out of the economic and social middle?

Much of the picture that Samuelson and others paint is accurate. Yet there are a variety of other signs that point to current suffering, continued insecurity, and future volatility. We believe that growing inequality underlies these indicators. Economic inequality does matter and is the critical issue of our time. Too much inequality undermines many of the professed values upon which the United States was founded. In this section, we will examine the consequences of inequality and the dangers it poses to our democracy, economy, culture, and social order.

We will look at how economic inequality...

$ **undermines the security of our families,**
$ **is bad for the economy,**
$ **threatens our democratic institutions,**
$ **is bad for public health, and**
$ **contributes to a breakdown in social cohesion.**

Pressures Facing Our Households

Let's start by looking at the impact of the changing economy close to home. There are new pressures and some alarming trends facing a growing number of households in this country. These include

$ **less free time and more working hours,**
$ **fewer households with health insurance,**
$ **rising personal debt,**
$ **declining personal savings,**
$ **diminishing retirement security,**
$ **growing number of temporary jobs, and**
$ **rising college costs.**

THE DECLINE OF LEISURE TIME AND THE BREAKDOWN OF CIVIL SOCIETY. One powerful consequence of growing inequality is an erosion in the amount of free time that families have. As individuals and families struggle to stay afloat and remain secure in the changing economy, they are spending more hours at work.

Falling wages in the 1970s and early 1980s were masked by the entry of a second wage earner in many households—usually a woman—into the workforce. Families now have to work longer hours to make up for falling wages. At the same time, temporary and part-time workers generally do not have paid vacations, and their numbers in the workforce are growing. The number of overall hours worked, per household, has increased since 1972. The number of hours worked per person each year has increased 4 percent, from 1,905 in 1980 to 1,966 in 2001.[2] This may not seem dramatic, but at the same time the average two-earner middle-income family saw its annual paid workload grow from 3,331 hours to 3,719.[3] An extra 388 hours per year translates into ten more weeks a year in the paid economy. This has left parents with a dramatic 11 percent decrease in their free time and leisure time in the last several decades.[4]

In the aftermath of a string of school shootings in relatively affluent suburban high schools, a few commentators wondered if our supercharged economy might be partly to blame, since it leaves so little time for family suppers and informal, unscheduled parent-child contact. Pat Wechsler wrote in *BusinessWeek*, "With every step in this march toward a 24-hour economy, there is a cost: less time for things beyond the realm of getting and spending. Most important, a 24-7 economy squeezes the time a healthy society needs for its parents to spend time with their families."[5]

The Family and Medical Leave Act was passed in 1993 to give working families unpaid time off to deal with family emergencies and new children. But very few families can afford to use it because they can't live for long without their paychecks.[6] In May 1999, President Bill Clinton proposed altering federal regulations to allow workers to collect unemployment benefits while on leave to care for newborn or newly adopted children. He cited a 1999 study by the Council of Economic Advisers showing that the percentage of married mothers in the workforce has nearly doubled over the last thirty years, from 38 percent in 1969 to 68 percent in 1996.[7] As of 2003, 72 percent of women who had a child aged one year or older participated in the workforce.[8] Unfortunately, since married fathers didn't start staying home in equal numbers, the increase in work hours per household directly means less time parents have with children.

Technological advances in the workplace, instead of increasing the amount of free time, are having the opposite effect. Productivity has been steadily increasing, but these gains have not translated into higher wages or increased free time. Blue-collar and service workers have experienced a veritable "speed-up" in the workplace as employers squeeze productivity gains into increased profits. Not only are people working longer hours, but in many cases the tempo and scope of their jobs have become more harried and stressful.

For middle-class service and white-collar workers, technological advances like computers, pagers, faxes, and electronic mail can contribute to a breakdown of leisure time and an erosion of vacation time. Today's modern white-collar worker goes on summer vacation for a much-needed break, but brings along a cell phone, a computer with Internet access, and a portable fax machine. Employers may even encourage the ways in which technology breaks down the division between work and leisure.

U.S. vacations are among the shortest in the industrialized world, averaging only two weeks. They are also not legally mandated, as they are in many Western European countries, where workers get between four and six weeks of vacation.[9] During the years 1965 to 1985, Canadian and

Western European vacations expanded, largely as result of union clout and collective bargaining, while U.S. vacations shrank. In Canada, annual paid vacation time increased from 2.9 weeks in 1965 to 4.3 weeks in 1985.[10] In 2002, as U.S. annual work hours approached 2,000, French workers only worked 1,545 hours and German workers only 1,444.[11] Sixty-five percent of American white-collar workers say they would take a salary reduction to get more time off.

This loss of leisure time has a direct impact on the quality of people's lives. As people have less free time, they have less time available to care for children and elders, less time to be involved in schools and education, and less time to volunteer to help others. This dramatically increases stress, particularly on women, whose unpaid labor is largely performed in this non-monetary "caring economy." Stress leads to increased illness and the unraveling of communities, the breakdown in voluntary mutual-aid systems, and the fragmentation and isolation of people. It leads to "latchkey" children and a lack of support for the next generation, with serious consequences.

Overwork feeds the breakdown of civil society and civic institutions. A free democratic society depends on strong voluntary institutions, such as religious congregations, political parties, neighborhood block clubs, fraternal or women's organizations, nonprofit service organizations, and other nongovernmental, nonbusiness organizations. A number of sociologists have pointed to the decline of the "social capital" that comes from strong voluntary institutions as contributing to the erosion of democracy.[12] As these institutions weaken, so does the power of ordinary citizens to defend their interests as consumers, workers, and communities. As we will discuss later, this contributes to the power imbalance that underlies growing inequality.

FEWER HOUSEHOLDS WITH HEALTH INSURANCE. Conspicuously absent from Samuelson's statistics on the lower prices for consumer goods is the explosion in health care costs over the last forty years. Between 2000 and 2004, the cost of health care coverage grew by 35.9 percent, while average earnings only grew 12.4 percent. Over the same period, the number of households paying more than one-quarter of their earnings on health care rose by 23 percent, from 11.6 million to 14.3 million.[13] Over 45 million people in the nation lack health insurance, up from 31 million a decade ago.[14] This makes the United States the only industrialized nation that views health care as a privilege, not a basic human right.[15]

Having a job does not guarantee health insurance. The percentage of Americans under the age of 65 covered through employer-sponsored health insurance declined from 70.4 percent in 1999 to 63 percent in 2003. Among low-income Americans, the share of those with employer-sponsored health insurance fell from 40.3 in 1999 to 35.0 percent in 2002.[16] Twenty-four million of those without insurance are employed, 17 percent of whom are in the temporary or contingent workforce. In 2003, 83 percent of part-time employees had no access to health care benefits through their employers.[17]

Even as the unemployment rate declines, the rate of workers without health insurance increases. Even with a sustained decrease in unemployment, current trends indicate that the number of uninsured nonelderly Americans is growing by 1 million a year and will exceed 47 million by the year 2006, equal to one in five Americans under the age of 65. Thirty-four percent of the nation's 37.4 million Hispanic people have no health insurance, compared to 22 percent of blacks and 12 percent of non-Hispanic whites.[18]

RISING PERSONAL DEBT. Another way families continue to make up for falling wages in order to maintain (or in some cases attain) a certain standard of living is by going deeper into debt. Approximately 60 percent of all American households carry credit card balances, unable to pay their full month bill.[19] In 2004, the credit card industry claimed that the average household consumer debt was approximately $9,000. Yet, when the roughly 40 percent of households that pay their balances each month were taken out of the equation, average household consumer debt was closer to 13,000[20] and late payments are at a five-year high.[21] Total credit card debt increased from $243 billion in 1990 to $735 billion in 2004.[22] Some of this is rooted in consumerism, but a central reason for growing debt lies in declining or stagnant wages. People are now using credit cards for things like food and medicine—items previously paid for with cash. One downside of growing personal indebtedness is the increasing number of personal bankruptcies, which are now at an all-time high. In 2003, 1.6 million individuals filed for

U.S. SAVINGS RATE, 1983–2003

*Rising health care, education, and child care costs—
not frivolous spending—are putting the squeeze on families.*

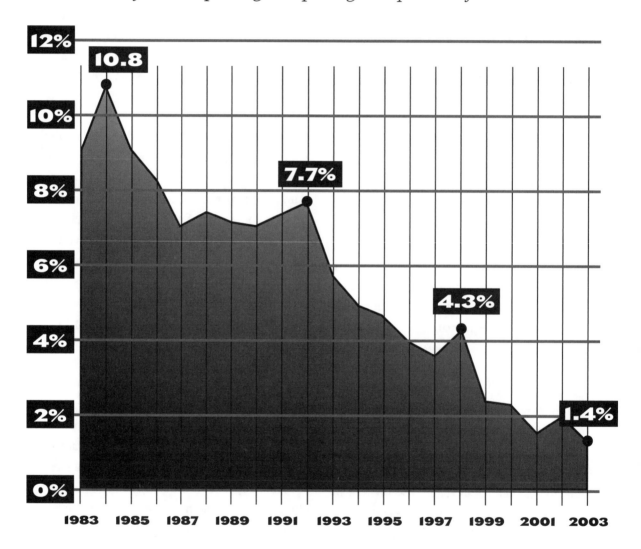

Source: U.S. Department of Commerce, Bureau of Economic Analysis. Personal savings as a percentage of disposable personal income.

personal bankruptcy, up from 1.4 million in 2002 and almost triple the 661,000 who filed in 1990.[23]

DECLINING PERSONAL SAVINGS. The flip side of greater debt is less savings. The savings rate is the percentage of annual income that is actually saved each year. Since 1980, the savings rate has generally fallen. The United States has the lowest savings rate of any industrialized country. In 2003, the U.S. savings rate was 1.4 percent, down from 4.5 percent in 1997 and 10.8 percent in 1984.[24] In contrast, the savings rate in 2003 in Japan was 7 percent and in Germany it was 10.8 percent.[25]

Why does the United States have such a low savings rate? It is *not* because the average person has no personal restraint or will to save. According to researchers from the Boston Federal Reserve, the main reason for the lower savings rate is linked to the rising cost of health care and the increase in other involuntary costs such as day care and bank-service fees.[26]

DIMINISHING RETIREMENT SECURITY. Those employees lucky enough to have pensions have ones that are less secure. The percentage of workers in the private labor force in monthly pension plans (where companies bear the risk of falling markets) has declined from 38 percent in 1980 to 25 percent in 1998.[27] These are called "defined-benefit plans," which are better for workers because they are federally insured and provide a guaranteed monthly pension amount. More workers now have "defined-contribution plans," like 401(k) plans, in which the benefit amount depends on how well the underlying investments perform. This growth in private 401(k) pension plans has failed to broaden overall pension coverage. In fact, there is more inequality in 401(k) plans than in defined-benefit plans, as they tend to be held by higher-income workers. The decline in both savings and guaranteed pensions are two concrete indicators of growing insecurity.

Retirement planners suggest that Social Security should be only one leg of the three-legged stool of retirement security. Personal savings and an employer-funded pension fund are the other two legs. But as personal savings plummet and fewer and fewer workers have pension funds, the prospects for a large percentage of people retiring into poverty grows. Worse yet, people will never be able to stop working, even as they go into their seventies.

GROWING NUMBER OF TEMPORARY JOBS. The greatest percentage of new jobs in the workforce are filled by temporary and part-time workers. Currently about 30 percent of the workforce is what is called "contingent," including temporary, part-time, contract, and day laborers.[28] Some of these workers are *voluntarily* part-time. But a growing number are *involuntarily* part-time, often holding two to three jobs to pay their bills. According to the Bureau of Labor Statistics, two-thirds of contingent workers would like traditional permanent jobs. As we will discuss later, the "temping of America" is part of a larger economic restructuring that is changing the nature of work and contributing to economic inequality.

The growing number of temporary and part-time jobs is a depressing trend for many younger people entering the workforce after high school or college. Only 11 percent of female and 15 percent of male full-time temporary workers have health insurance provided through their employer.[29] In fact, fewer than 30 percent of all contingent workers have health insurance, and only 11 percent have pensions.

HIGHER EDUCATION, HIGHER REACH. The cost of going to college has risen, while government support to ensure access to higher education has failed to keep pace. Going to college is more of a privilege than it was twenty years ago.

Federal college loans have now replaced college grants, rising from 41.4 percent of student financing in 1982 to 58.9 percent in 2001.[30] Student debt between 1991 and 1997 totaled $140 billion—more than the total combined student borrowing for the 1960s, 1970s, and 1980s.[31] Student debt has dramatically increased from an average of $8,200 per student in 1991 to $18,900 in 2003.[32] Many students will still be paying off college loans in their mid-thirties.

The rising cost of college affects who gets to go to college. The country's poorest families are increasingly underrepresented in higher education, particularly at four-year schools. Only 20 percent of all community college students nationally

Kirk Anderson

come from families with annual income under $25,000, only 11 percent at public four-year colleges, and just 8 percent at private four-year colleges.[33] In 1995, 83.4 percent of high school students in the top fifth of income-earning households went to college, compared to 56.1 percent of students in the middle three quintiles and 41.3 percent in the bottom quintile.[34] As of 2001, 29 percent of whites had completed four years of college compared to 17 percent of blacks and 11 percent of Hispanics.[35] Higher education is becoming much more class-segregated than it was a decade ago.

Because of economic pressures, students have become more career-focused earlier. A liberal-arts education with time for critical thinking has become a privilege among the privileged.

Some of these stresses on families are invisible and not widely discussed or shared. Nor do we often think of them as the result of a more polarized society. Many of us experience them as a result of our individual failing. In the next several sections, we will examine the effects of inequality on other aspects of our lives that undermine our basic sense of well-being.

Inequality and the Threat to Prosperity

Economic inequality is bad for the economy and for economic growth. Inequality means that some people have too much money burning holes in their pockets while some people don't have enough. As the stable middle class in this country loses savings and security, inequality has a downside for everyone, particularly smaller businesses. Small-business owners should be alarmed about the economic divide because it directly affects their consumers. Unless you're a Lexus car dealer or a diamond jeweler, inequality is a threat to your prosperity—as well as to the wider prosperity of our economy.

The polarization of income and wealth distorts our economy and ultimately undermines its health and sustainability. Some economists have argued that past economic depressions are in part rooted in the concentration of wealth, as working people lack spending power and are unable to meet debt obligations. At the same time, wealthy people have so much surplus money that they begin gambling on risky, high-return investments. This speculation can be destructive and destabilizing for the economy, as investment is diverted from truly productive sectors of the economy.[36]

Since 1980, there has been a visible stratification in the retail market. Stores that used to serve the middle class are going out of business. Retailers must either remake themselves as bargain outlets to compete in the low-end market with stores like Wal-Mart or Kmart, or they must become upscale, like Bloomingdale's, Neiman Marcus, or Brookstone, to chase the plentiful but concentrated cash of the richest 10 percent of the population.

In 2004, the growing stratification of wealth led shoe and clothing marketer Jones Apparel

Group to jump into the luxury market with the purchase of the upscale clothier Barneys New York. Jones CEO Peter Boneparth told investment analysts that "America is getting poorer and richer at the same time. Catering to the truly wealthy people is a real opportunity for this company." Marketing to the rich, Boneparth continued, would help Jones Apparel Group get into an area that is not vulnerable to economic woes and is "bullet-proof."[37]

Pay Everyone Enough So They Can Buy Your Product

People often respond to the old saw that rich people create jobs. After all, have you ever gotten a job from someone poor? But nobody decides to sell things without people to buy them. Business leaders like Henry Ford understood that greater equality created a demand for his products. He publicly committed to pay *all* of his employees, not just top managers, enough so that they could all purchase Ford automobiles. He saw that his long-term self-interest was tied to shared prosperity. In the words of Henry Ford:

> And now take wages. An unemployed man is an out-of-work customer. He cannot buy. An underpaid man is a customer reduced in purchasing power. He cannot buy. Business depression is caused by weakened purchasing power. Uncertainty or insufficiency of income weakens purchasing power. The cure of business depression is through purchasing power and the source of purchasing power is wages.... Wages is more of a question for business than it is for labor. It is more important to business than it is to labor. Low wages will break business far more quickly than it will labor.[38]

In explaining lackluster sales at regular department stores during a recent Christmas season, the *Wall Street Journal* reported the observations of Carl Steidtman, chief economist at Management Horizons, a prominent management consulting firm. "Income groups seem to have become more polarized, with families struggling to get by at one end, while at the other end people are riding stock market gains to new wealth. That helps explain why both upscale retailers and value-oriented shops have done well this Christmas." According to this report, high-end retailers with big sales included Neiman Marcus, Nordstrom, and Saks Fifth Avenue, while value-oriented winners included Wal-Mart, Dollar General, and Costco warehouse stores.[39]

Products are now designed with this two-tier market in mind. Take the refrigerator market, for example. Manufacturers of refrigerators create a stripped-down basic model that they sell to working families. This no-frills model has a couple of shelves and plastic vegetable drawers. However, they also design, for the affluent, an upscale refrigerator that dispenses ice and mineral water and includes an audio message center that retails for 200 to 300 percent higher than the basic model.

The Atlanta-based Affluent Market Institute predicted that by the end of the decade millionaires will control 60 percent of the nation's purchasing dollars.[40] Yet is organizing the economy to serve the needs of the very rich a good use of society's resources? Knocking down mansions on eastern Long Island and building new megamansions might create jobs, but what are the opportunity costs to the economy of so many human, financial, and natural resources devoted to the pursuits of a few wealthy people? Might these resources have been even more productive if directed to other sectors? In the words of economist Randy Albelda, "Mink coats do not trickle down."

Ultimately, too much inequality is a threat to prosperity. Our "Titanic economy" may seem invincible, but in fact it is vulnerable to sinking on the iceberg of inequality.

Inequality and Democracy

**Plutocracy: I. The rule or power of wealth or the wealthy;
2. a government or state in which the wealthy class rules; 3. a class or
group ruling, or exercising power or influence, by virtue of its wealth.
—WEBSTER'S UNABRIDGED DICTIONARY[41]**

Americans spent a good part of the eighteenth century throwing off the rule of the British monarchy and establishing our own self-governing democracy. Yet we are now at risk of becoming subjects again in a plutocracy. Too much economic inequality is a fundamental threat to our democracy.

Once a household accumulates wealth in excess of $15 million, placing it in the richest 0.5 percent, it has moved beyond meeting the needs and wildest desires of itself and its heirs. As the character Bud Fox asked speculator Gordon Gekko in the classic film *Wall Street*, "How many yachts can you water-ski behind?" After a certain point, the accumulation of wealth is about amassing power—the power to influence society and the rules of our economy.

This influence, however, has not always been all bad. Carnegie's libraries and Rockefeller's national parks stand as testaments to how personal wealth has contributed to the commonwealth. Nonetheless, concentrated wealth can have great corrupting power when it extends to the ownership of the media and the power to mold public opinion, through the shaping of philanthropic priorities and through political contributions. Such concentrated power mocks democracy and undermines the power and participation of the broader society.

Large corporations use their concentrated wealth and power to lobby for rule changes in legislatures across the land. Corporate lobbyists, with millions in campaign contributions at their disposal, roam the halls of Congress, influencing the writing or unraveling of environmental regulations, tax laws, and health, safety, and consumer protections. After the 2000 elections, lobbyists from large chemical and manufacturing companies sat down with the new Republican majority to rewrite the environmental rules of the land. Corporations deploy their minions around the clock to "Gucci Gulch," the hallway outside the Senate Finance Committee, to advance their corporate interests and lobby for special tax breaks.

Corporations spend enormous resources manufacturing constituencies to support their policies. They hire professional public-relations firms to create bogus grassroots organizations, with campaigns run directly out of corporate lobby offices on K Street in Washington, D.C. John Stauber and Sheldon Rampton, the authors of *Toxic Sludge is Good for You*, document hundreds of examples of this "astroturf" lobbying: corporations orchestrating fake constituencies in an elaborate masquerade, in contrast to real "grassroots" citizen groups.[42] If corporations and wealthy individuals have the ears of Congress all to themselves, the average citizen is not being heard.

When It Comes to Big Money, Corporations are "Buy-Partisan"

BIG ALCOHOL MONEY KILLS DRUNK DRIVING LEGISLATION

In May 1998, the liquor lobby killed popular legislation that would have penalized states that refused to adopt tougher drunk-driving laws. A broad coalition including Mothers Against Drunk Driving (MADD) backed the legislation, with Congresswoman Nita Lowey (D–N.Y.) as prime sponsor. The measure enjoyed broad bipartisan support. President Clinton backed the legislation, and polls showed that the public overwhelmingly supported it. It passed easily in the U.S. Senate by a vote of 62 to 32.

But then beer, liquor, and restaurant lobbies went to work. "The death of the proposal to lower the blood-alcohol limit for drunk driving is a classic Washington story of big money, influential lobbyists, and questionable political tactics," observed journalist Michael Kranish. "There was a perception that if the measure passed, beer and liquor sales would decline as people consumed one less drink for the road."

Members of the House of Representatives did not want to go on record as voting against legislation to curb drunk driving. So they set out to kill it without a vote. The liquor lobby is one of the heaviest contributors to Congress, pouring in $5.8 million in the 1996 elections, with 67 percent going to Republicans and 33 percent going to Democrats. On the other hand, MADD hadn't contributed a dime. "We are a pitiful ragtag army up against a powerful industry," said Diane Riibe, then MADD's vice president.

Both former Minority Leader Richard Gephardt (D–Mo.) and then House Speaker Newt Gingrich (R–Ga.) received big contributions from the liquor lobby, along with Congressman Bud Shuster (R–Pa.), chair of the House Transportation Committee. All were instrumental in keeping the legislation from ever coming to a vote. The American Beverage Institute hired a new lobbyist, Ann Eppard, who had been Shuster's former chief of staff and remained his top campaign fundraiser. The late Joe Moakley (D–Mass.), the ranking Democrat on the House Rules Committee, let the bill die without a roll-call vote, which would have held representatives accountable. In the end, no one in the House ever voted on the bill, just as the liquor lobby wanted.[43] It was a buy-partisan victory!

In today's U.S. democracy, the cost of television advertising drives candidates toward big-money donors, be they individuals or political action committees. The cost of running for office continues to spiral upward. The average House winner spent $840,300 in 2000, up from $650,428 in 1996. The average winner for U.S. Senate spent $7.3 million in 2000, up from $5.2 million in 1996.[44] That translates into over $23,400 that the candidate senator needs to raise *each week* of his or her six-year term. If you needed to raise that kind of money, with whom would you spend your time every week?

The 2004 election cycle shattered all the records. In the presidential election, candidates George W. Bush and John Kerry spent a combined $548 million. This does not include the hundreds of millions spent by political parties or advocacy groups. Big money was the winner of the election across the board. The biggest spender was victorious in 415 of the 435 house races and 31 of 34 Senate races.[45]

Where Does the Money Come From?
2004 Spending on Federal Races[46]

Individual contributions to candidates and parties	$2.5 billion
PAC contributions to candidates and parties	$384 million
Candidate self-funding	$144 million
527 group spending (federal election)	$386 million
Public funding to presidential races and parties	$207 million
Convention host committee spending	$139 million
Other	$102 million
TOTAL	**$3.9 billion**

Voting rates differ greatly by economic class. Households with incomes over $75,000 are nearly twice as likely to vote as households with incomes under $25,000. The percentage of people registered to vote and actually voting climbs based on family income. Only 65 percent of households with incomes between $15,000 and $25,000 are registered to vote, and only 51.3 percent voted in 2000. Meanwhile, 82.1 percent of households with incomes over $75,000 are registered to vote, and 74.9 percent voted in 2002.[47]

As inequality grows, so does the dangerous imbalance of political power. Our democracy is predicated on the notion of "one person, one vote." However, the power of big money now renders irrelevant the votes of the majority of the U.S. population.

The Waltons: How Much Wealth and Power Should One Family Have?

Over the last decade, Wal-Mart has become America's biggest retailer and largest private employer, employing 1.2 million U.S. workers. Behind Wal-Mart stores is a family that we will hear much more about in coming years as they begin to flex the full muscle of their wealth and power. They are the Walton family, including Helen, the widow of the late Wal-Mart founder Sam Walton, and their four children, Alice, Sam, Jim, and John.

By all reports, the Waltons are decent people. They did not grow up with wealth, and they lead relatively simple lives, considering their vast treasure. Though they are the wealthiest family in America, you won't see photos of them in the tabloids dramatizing ostentatious displays of wealth. Paris Hilton they are not.

Yet there are reasons to be concerned when so much wealth, and the inevitable concentration of power that accompanies it, ends up in so few hands, regardless of their personalities.

The Walton family is worth over $90 billion, more than the net worth of Bill Gates and Warren Buffett combined. For all the publicity about the wealth of Teresa Heinz Kerry during the 2004 election, the Waltons have 117 times as much money. Their wealth is equal to the gross domestic product of Singapore and the annual revenues of IBM corporation.

The Waltons have enormous inherent economic power in the marketplace, as well as political power, as exercised through campaign contributions and charitable giving. For instance, the Waltons own 39 percent of Wal-Mart. Their estimated dividend income from this is $880 million a year, or $175 million for each of the Walton heirs. Wal-Mart's lucrative dividends are the result of continued growth internationally and within the United States.

Wal-Mart's slogan is "We Sell for Less." In order to deliver on this pledge, Wal-Mart must continually look for the lowest-cost goods and push producers to deliver products at the lowest possible price. Part of this is achieved through large-volume purchasing. However, it is also achieved by Wal-Mart vendors keeping wages low or producing products in sweatshops, both in the United States and abroad.

The Waltons also wield enormous clout in northwest Arkansas. The Waltons' holding company also owns several newspapers and the region's largest bank, Arvest. As *Fortune* magazine wrote: "Consider for a moment the power that Wal-Mart and the Walton family hold in the northwest corner of their state. It's not unlikely that an individual works at Wal-Mart, owns Wal-Mart stock in his 401(k), banks and has his mortgage at Jim Walton's Arvest, gets his news from the *Benton County Daily Record*, and perhaps even has a subscription to the Walton Arts Center."[48]

This does not include the influence of the Waltons' charitable giving, which is the biggest player in northwest Arkansas. What happens when the Walton Foundation swells to become the biggest foundation in the world, as is likely upon the death of Helen Walton? She has declared her intention to bequeath the majority of her fortune to charity.

The Walton family has two principal giving vehicles. One foundation is the Walton Family Charitable Support Foundation, whose board consists of family members and some outsiders. Its principal purpose is to give to public and private colleges in Arkansas. They recently made a $300 million matching grant to the University of Arkansas—the largest gift ever made to a public university.

The other entity is the Walton Family Foundation, which was created in 1987 and is entirely controlled by family members. It has a more open-ended mission, but is primarily concerned with education issues. In 2003, it made $106 million in grants, almost 80 percent toward education. Almost half the foundation's grants, totaling $45.5 million, went to school-privatization efforts. As Jim Hopkins reported in *USA Today*, the Waltons "have begun focusing more giving on private-school scholarships, charter schools and vouchers—revealing clues as to how they'll target giving as their family charitable foundations grow."49

But this is just the beginning. Since 1998, the Waltons' charities have given at least $701 million to education, compared to $1.05 billion given to education in the same period by the Bill and Melinda Gates Foundation. But as the Waltons shift more money into charity, their potential to fund their school-privatization efforts could grow to $1 billion a year. That is a mighty thumb on the scale of educational policy in this country.

The focus on public education reform reflects the outlook and activism of son John Walton, who is a school-privatization zealot. In 2000, he personally donated $100,000 to an election campaign to support back-to-basics education reform in San Diego. Many critics are alarmed at the potential impact $1 billion a year could have on public-policy debates on education.

Should any one family have so much economic and political power?

Inequality and Public Health

Inequality is not only bad for the economy and democracy, it's bad for your health as well. It comes as no surprise that as people's incomes rise, their health improves. But a growing body of international and U.S. research shows that inequality—the relative gap between rich and poor in a region—is an even more significant indicator of health than poverty rates. Once people reach a minimum standard of material security, they are better off living in a more economically equal community than not. Communities that have less inequality have lower infant mortality, longer life expectancy, and less violent trauma. A country or region with a high poverty rate but less inequality is a healthier place to live than a country or region with less poverty but greater inequality.

In the United States, people who live in states with greater inequality—for example, Louisiana, New York, Texas, Kentucky, and West Virginia—have more health problems. States with less inequality—including Utah, New Hampshire, Wisconsin, Iowa, and Minnesota—have better health, meaning longer life expectancy and lower incidence of infant mortality, infectious disease, cancer, heart disease, and homicide. The results were similar after factoring out differences in poverty, race, income levels, and smoking. Even the rich were healthier in states with more relative equality.

In our nation's capital of Washington, D.C., there are high levels of economic inequality. Twenty miles away, in Fairfax County, Virginia, there is a much smaller ratio between highest- and lowest-income residents. Men in Fairfax County have a 14.5-year longer average life span than men living in Washington, D.C.[50]

Why are communities with lower inequality healthier? Because inequality leads to the breakdown of communities and the social solidarity necessary for human health. According to a British researcher, Dr. Richard Wilkinson, communities with less inequality have stronger social compacts, more cultural limits on unrestrained individual actions, and greater networks of mutual aid and caring.

Looking at a number of different examples of healthy egalitarian societies, an important characteristic they all seem to share is their social cohesion. They have a strong community life. Instead of social life stopping outside the front door, public space remains a social space. The individualism and the values of the market are restrained by a social morality. People are more likely to be involved in social and voluntary activities outside the home. These societies have more of what has been called "social capital," which lubricates the workings of the whole society and economy. There are fewer signs of anti-social aggressiveness, and society appears more caring. In short, the social fabric is in better condition. The research tells us something very important about the way the social fabric is affected by the amount of inequality in a society.[51]

The fragmentation caused by economic inequalities leads to more social breakdown, violence, and disconnection, ultimately resulting in poorer public health. Healthy communities have higher levels of civic participation, voluntary organization, and neighbors who know and trust one another. These qualities are more likely to occur in communities without the tensions of severe income gaps.[52]

Kerula, India: The Benefits of Greater Equality

There are places on earth where we can get a glimpse of what a more equal society would be like. The Indian state of Kerula has been much studied because of its relatively small levels of inequality. In Kerula, the income disparity between the top 10 percent and the bottom 20 percent of the population is only 3.5 to 1. In the United States, the disparity is 12 to 1.

What does this mean for life in Kerula? Even though Kerula is materially much poorer than the United States and many other countries, it ranks very high in a number of quality-of-life indicators. Kerula is characterized by low crime rates, long life expectancy, and a lower infant mortality rate. It has the highest literacy rate in India, greater than 90 percent.[53] With approximately 32 million residents, Kerula is the size of California. While California has almost 200,000 people in prison, Kerula has only 5,000.

In Kerula there is a strong commitment to ensuring broad and affordable access to public services such as education and basic needs like electricity and food. Taxes are progressive and consumption is low.[54]

Social Polarization and the Withdrawal of the Haves

In 2004, Senator John Edwards ran for president with a stump speech decrying the polarization of our society as "two Americas." But almost a decade earlier, the private investment newsletter *Taipan*, published in Baltimore, began one of its issues with the following image:

An unstoppable wedge is about to be driven through the heart of America. It is a wedge of technology and culture that will divide this nation into two very different parts: the haves and the have nots … those who make the leap into the economy of the future and profit, and those who are left behind, trapped in dying neighborhoods and a dying economy.

In one part, crime will spread. Homes will be boarded up. Gangs of fatherless young men and boys will roam the streets. People will live shorter, meaner, poorer lives. Real estate prices will fall … entire areas will be abandoned.

Meanwhile, just a few hours' drive from these living nightmares will be some of the finest environments ever created on the planet. These enclaves of peace and prosperity will be protected by geography and electronic fortifications. And they will benefit from the technological breakthroughs that will totally transform our economy and our lives. They will have no factories and no smokestacks. But they will be centers of the new economy … and the upscale neighborhoods of the 21st century.

In our dying cities and declining suburbs, the life expectancy of the average American will drop to 40 years for males. Poor health habits, pollution, crime, a resurgence of tuberculosis and other diseases will contribute to a shortening life span. Infant mortality, which right now in our inner cities is about the level of Bangladesh, will rise even higher.

Meanwhile, in the lush enclaves of the new wealthy, many people will live to be 120 years old. Why? Because much of the secret to better health and longer life is in lifestyle. And these prosperous enclaves will have the highest standards of living in the world.[55]

This powerful depiction of two Americas is designed not to galvanize a movement for a fairer economy but to sell a product: in this case, a financial newsletter. If you felt a chill reading it, it had its desired effect. The newsletter manipulates people's fears about the real dangers of growing inequality so that they will subscribe, and increase their chances of joining the "haves."

When historian Arnold Toynbee analyzed twenty-one past civilizations that had collapsed, he determined that there were two common factors that led to their demise. The first was concentrated wealth and the second was inflexibility in the face of changing conditions. As employee-ownership expert Jeff Gates writes, concentrated wealth and societal inflexibility are "two sides of the same coin." Concentrated ownership leads to inflexibility when what societies need is greater cooperation, adaptability, and "locale-specific sensitivity."[56]

Unfortunately, the anti-utopian vision of two Americas is the direction in which our nation is moving. It is a likely picture of what our future holds when the wealthiest 10 percent of the population controls over 70 percent of the nation's wealth and an even greater share of political power.

What does it mean when this richest 10 percent have essentially privatized their personal needs and withdrawn to "prosperous enclaves"? What happens to public services like schools, parks, transportation, and so on? The richest 10 percent are less likely to send their children to public schools; they have private schools. And even when they do send their children to public schools, schools in wealthy areas are more attractive and well equipped because of the inequities in property taxes that fund public education in most jurisdictions.

The wealthy are less inclined to use public parks and recreation areas because they have private country clubs and summer homes. They do not rely on public transportation (though they drive on publicly financed highways). They do not need cities, except for downtown offices, the occasional sporting event, or high-culture performance. They do not always need public police and trash pickup, as many have private security forces and private trash-haulers. They don't need Social Security; they have private retirement funds. The wealthy have withdrawn from the institutions and public forms of shared common security that the majority of citizens depend on. They come to resent paying for public services they don't use. They lobby for reductions in money for public services, taking their resources and political clout with them, and build private societies separate from the majority.

Things are great. Just don't leave your room.

A visiting European official said during the G-7 economic summit in Denver in 1997: "Americans keep telling us how successful their economy is—then they remind us not to leave our hotel at night."

When the powerful no longer have a stake in the commonwealth, the common good suffers. This creates a "rush-to-the-door" phenomenon in our society as the withdrawal of the wealthy causes others to withdraw. When the quality of public transportation deteriorates, some people opt to drive their cars instead of fighting to improve bus service. Antigovernment attitudes become self-fulfilling, self-reinforcing prophecies as resources for public services and institutions decline.

As public services and the quality of life in nonwealthy communities deteriorate, those who can get out leave. Those choosing to withdraw include not only the richest 10 percent but anyone in the top half of the country's income earners who can afford to. They move to the suburbs, small towns, or gated communities. In some cases, they remove their children from public schools and enroll them in private schools. Such patterns further reinforce existing racial and class divides in America.

The problem is, however, that it is very expensive to privatize all of one's needs. For many in the middle class, the costs of moving to more expensive communities, commuting, parking, and sending their children to private school are out of reach. To attain these benefits, families increase the frenzy of their private lives, take on second jobs, increase personal debt, and isolate themselves from family and community. Just when they most need to be part of the community sphere and join civic institutions to improve their lives, they have no free time.

Even families in the top 20 percent—those with annual incomes over $94,000—sometimes feel economically and psychologically stretched like a drum.[57] They are paying the costs of private schools, long commutes, expensive houses in affluent communities, and exotic vacations to recover from their exhaustion. Maintaining a privatized lifestyle forces many people onto an economic treadmill, even though to judge from their housing and consumption patterns, Robert J. Samuelson and others might call them "successful."

The corollary is that a society with less polarization of income and wealth could invest more in the commonwealth and in our shared security. The need for privatizing security and other services would be reduced because the community institutions that provide for people's needs would be stronger.

You Are On Your Own: The New Individualism

This polarization has a dangerous psychological effect as well. If you cannot rely on society for any real security, then you and your family are on your own. There is an entire industry built on privately meeting people's individual security needs—private pensions, supplementary catastrophic health care insurance, disaster insurance. Put children into the mix and it adds another layer of worry and expense. These industries pepper us with advertisements to the effect of "What If... Disaster Strikes?" and "If You Die,

What Will Happen to Your Children?" In the years since the 2001 terrorist attacks, these feelings have only intensified.

All parents want the best for their children. If you want your child to go to college, we are told, start saving now. "Your child may only be two years old, but with the state of public higher education in jeopardy, it would be imprudent not to save up for a private college," advises one magazine for parents. The estimated four-year tuition total for an Ivy League University in the year 2016

"Hard work builds strong moral values.
Fortunately, I inherited my money."

will be $364,800 dollars. Four years at an average public college will cost $114,786.[58] Financial planners estimate that if you want your child to afford four years of tuition, fees, plus room and board, for an in-state public university, you must start saving $319 a month starting on your child's date of birth.[59] If we do not want our kids saddled with college debt, then we're stuck on the treadmill.

In an insecure world, where one's security depends on having access to wealth, there is tremendous pressure to accumulate wealth and pass it on to our children. This, of course, is virtually impossible for many people whose annual income barely covers their living expenses. But that doesn't stop people from literally killing themselves trying.

Low-income and working-class families make tremendous sacrifices for their children and work hard to leave them some escape from the economic treadmill. This includes working longer hours, taking dangerous jobs, and forgoing vacations and rest. Many people sacrifice time with loved ones in the present in the hope of giving them a better future. Being forced to make these trade-offs should be unacceptable.

Among the middle and upper-middle class, the drive for security pushes people into professions with high incomes but not necessarily high satisfaction. Who knows how many Picassos or cancer researchers are working as unhappy bankers or lawyers? In *The Cost of Talent*, Derek Bok, former president of Harvard University, describes the enormous cost to a society when talented people enter into high-paying careers in legal or financial services rather than choosing public-service professions. Bok shows how the income of professionals such as lawyers, stockbrokers, and business executives has outpaced incomes earned by teachers, social workers, researchers, government officials, and other professions concerned with the common good. This growing disparity leads to the drain of talent away from public-service vocations and further contributes to the growing economic divide.[60]

Will My Child Be the Next Oprah? Bobby Bonds? Michael Jordan?

A television advertisement for financial services shows a father and five-year-old son playing catch with a baseball. The young boy continually swings and misses the ball. Grounders roll through his legs. The message: You better start putting money into a trust fund for junior because he's not going to become a highly paid professional baseball star.

How many of us can risk the possibility that our children may not display the entrepreneurial, athletic, or artistic talent to rise to the top in our winner-take-all society? Sure, we hope they are hard workers who possess above-average intelligence, but that does not seem to be enough to be economically secure, let alone prosperous these days. We cannot even assume equality of opportunity, decent public education, or access to affordable higher education. The only assurance for the few who can afford it is to pass on private wealth.

Gated Communities and Bigger Prisons

Nothing symbolizes the fragmentation of community in the United States more vividly than the expansion of gated communities among the affluent alongside the burgeoning prison-industrial complex for the poor. Housing for all income levels is increasingly being built behind gates and walls with entrances patrolled by armed guards. According to 2001 Census data, there were 30,000 gated communities in the United States—a gated population of over 7 million people. In communities like San Antonio, Texas, one in three new homes being built is in a gated community. An estimated 40 percent of new homes in California are built behind walls.[61] The national number is expected to double in the next five years.

In many respects, the growth in gated communities is the latest chapter of the "white flight" that has led to the disinvestment of so many urban centers over the last four decades. The majority of gated communities are in Texas, California, Florida, and Arizona. All of these states have had large influxes of new Latino immigrants, propelling a new spate of racism and housing segregation. Most gated community dwellers are white and affluent, with incomes between $60,000 and $200,000 a year.[62]

The growth of gated communities often precedes tax battles, as inhabitants begin to resent paying for services that they themselves have privatized. Journalist Christopher Parkes observes:

> Most gated developments pay for their own private police patrols and security guards. Traditionally communal services such as schools, parks, entertainment facilities and even street cleaning and maintenance are often privatized within the enclaves. The inhabitants are ever more reluctant to pay higher taxes to maintain government and city services outside their walls.[63]

Not every gated community is a bastion of the privileged. According to Fern Shen of the *Washington Post*, "Electronic gates and guard shacks have long been features of the nation's wealthier communities and retirement developments. But in the last few years, gated communities have been mushrooming across the country and especially in the Sunbelt, offered at a wide range of prices." In metropolitan Washington, D.C., new home developers are finding a significant market for moderately priced homes in gated communities. Battered urban dwellers can escape their old neighborhoods to buy houses starting at $95,000.[64]

All this leads to a physical reinforcement of the growing economic divide in the structure of communities. In their book, *Fortress America: Gated Communities in the United States*, authors Edward Blakely and Mary Gail Snyder warn that behind the gated community trends of suburban separatism and the privatization of social needs lies a rejection of the sense of mutuality on which this country was founded.

There is another type of gated community that is proliferating in the United States due to growing inequality: prisons. The number of inmates in jails and prisons rose again in 2002 to over 2 million.[65] Between 1985 and 2003, the incarceration rate more than quadrupled from 313 inmates per 100,000 residents to 1,423 inmates per 100,000. Blacks, who make up 40.3 percent of jail inmates, are six times more likely than whites to be incarcerated.[66]

The prison-industrial complex now builds a new 1,000-bed jail every week to keep up with the demand for prison space. The stock price of Corrections Corporation of America, the nation's largest private for-profit prison corporation, has increased tenfold since 1994. Unions representing prison guards are one of the fastest-growing sectors of the union movement. Like any industry, the prison economy needs raw materials. In this case, the raw materials are prisoners. The prison-industrial complex can grow only if more and more people are incarcerated. Corporations have a vested interest in prison expansion and longer prison terms.

But the costs are extremely high, both in absolute dollars and in human costs. U.S. taxpayers pay an estimated $65 billion a year for incarceration. Sixty percent of the incarcerated population has substance-addiction or abuse issues, with a majority being nonviolent offenders. In California, it cost $3.5 billion in 2003 to run the state's prison system, but the costs are expected to rise to $1.3 trillion over the next two decades.[67] The annual cost of jailing someone is over $22,500.[81] A year in prison and a year at Princeton now cost about the same; only the curriculum is different.

A wide variety of evidence shows that when the social fabric is stretched too far, we can no longer successfully live side by side. Economic inequality is the single greatest factor that puts our nation's social cohesion at risk. We all have a stake, even the very wealthy, in building a society with greater equality and security for all. In the next chapter, we will examine the dimensions of economic inequality in the United States.

Chapter 2

THE PICTURE: GROWING ECONOMIC INSECURITY AND INEQUALITY

In the last chapter, we saw why inequality matters and how it touches each of us in a very personal way. You've likely heard that the rich are getting richer and the poor are getting poorer. But in this chapter, we will look at the economic indicators you may not see on the evening news. What's happened to the wages, incomes, savings, and net worth of everyone in the United States?

The Inequality of Income and Wages

What has happened to our incomes?

$ **Between 1979 and 2000, the average after-tax income of the wealthiest 1 percent of households went up 201 percent. The bottom fifth of households rose only 9 percent.**[1]

$ **In 2001, the top 5 percent of income-earners collected 27.5 percent of the national income; the bottom 20 percent collected 4.2 percent.**[2]

Sometimes an image tells the story best. In many of the workshops led by United for a Fair Economy, the following exercise is used to convey the facts about the overall trends in income and wage distribution.

Imagine that we are lining up all of the people in the United States, from those with the lowest income to those with the highest. Visualize all these people standing in a line as they are divided into five equal-size groups. Each fifth, or what economists call a "quintile," represents roughly 20 million U.S. families or households.

The lowest-income fifth includes people with household incomes between $0 and $24,100 in 2004 dollars. The people in this fifth likely have one income supporting their household. They are students, welfare recipients, and low-income retirees living on Social Security. They are low-paid service workers and new immigrant households working in minimum-wage jobs. They are disproportionately people of color. They are single mothers and their children, people with disabilities, and people without homes.

The second fifth are people with household incomes of between $24,100 and $42,100 (in 2004 dollars). These households include many low-wage workers and people working in service jobs. There may be one wage earner or two part-time or very-low-wage workers. The bottom two-fifths most likely rent their housing.

In the middle fifth, there are households with incomes between $42,100 and $65,000. This includes households with one service or professional income, with one unionized worker, or with two full-time lower-wage workers.

In the fourth fifth, household incomes range from $65,000 to $98,200. These could include teachers, nurses, electricians, managers, and households with two income earners.

The top fifth includes households with incomes starting at $98,200 and ranging up to the top income earners in the land.[3] The top fifth is diverse and could include a household with two schoolteachers all the way up to members of the Forbes 400 like George David, CEO of United Technologies, who was paid $70.4 million in 2003.[4]

Within this top fifth quintile, at the very top of the pyramid, is the wealthiest 1 percent of households. They are set dramatically apart from the rest of the income ladder, and the disparity even among this wealthiest 1 percent is enormous. The distance between the bottom end of the richest 1 percent, with incomes of $337,000 in 2003, and the top income earners is considerably greater than the spectrum of the entire income ladder.[5]

> **REAL INCOME:** The term "real income" refers to the measurement that shows the genuine purchasing power of people's incomes. Real income eliminates changes in income based on inflation.

What has happened to the incomes of each of these fifths in the last two decades? Whose income has grown and by how much? In our live illustration about incomes, we ask each person, who represents a fifth of the whole population, to take one step for each ten percent increase or decrease in real income. See the chart on page 41 to see this graphically. Since 1979, the bottom fifth takes a half step backward, reflecting a 2 percent decline in real income. The second fifth takes a full step forward, since their real income has gone up 8 percent. The middle fifth takes a full step and a half forward, reflecting a 15 percent increase in real income. The fourth quintile takes two and a half steps forward, since their real income rose 26 percent. Finally, the top quintile takes almost five steps ahead, reflecting a 51 percent increase in real income. The top 5 percent, with incomes exceeding $170,000, takes seven and a half steps forward, reflecting a 75 percent increase. When we examine the incomes of the top 1 percent, households with incomes of $337,000 or more, they move ahead ten and a half steps, reflecting a 106 percent gain in real income.[6]

The biggest leap in real growth in income over the last thirty years goes to households with incomes in the top 1 percent of households. The rich are getting richer, but it's not just the poor who are getting poorer. Half the population is either moving backward or holding what ground they have by working more hours.

The inequality of the last two decades becomes even more dramatic when we contrast the most recent twenty-five years to the thirty years after World War II (see chart on page 42). From 1947 to 1979, all of the quintiles saw their incomes increase 90 to 100 percent. The bottom quintile actually grew most rapidly, its income growing over 116 percent. Economic prosperity was shared; we grew together. However, in the last twenty-five years, we have grown dramatically apart.

RACE, GENDER, AND INCOME

The postwar years were by no means a utopia. Racism and sexism were powerful social forces constricting the lives of women and people of color. However, in the post–World War II years, people of color did share in the income gains of the society, though by no means equally. Incomes of blacks, Latinos, and other nonwhite groups still remain significantly lower than those of white households.

Because the U.S. Census has been tracking whites and blacks for decades, there are longer-term comparisons that can be drawn. There is less historical data for Latinos and other racial groups. In 1968, for every dollar of white income, blacks earned 55 cents. More than three decades later, blacks now earn 57 cents for every dollar of white income. At this pace, it would take 581 years for blacks to achieve parity with whites in terms of income.[7]

As we shall discuss shortly, the disparity of wealth and financial assets is great and diverging between whites and people of color. But trends in income disparity *within* black and Latino populations are similar to the patterns for the population

1979 TO 2003—REAL FAMILY INCOME GROWTH BY QUINTILE AND FOR TOP 5%

We Grew Apart

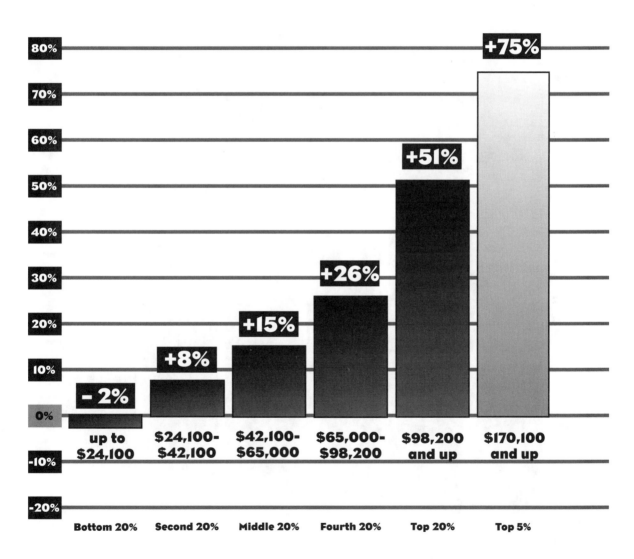

80%					+75%
				+51%	
			+26%		
		+15%			
	+8%				
-2%					
up to $24,100	$24,100-$42,100	$42,100-$65,000	$65,000-$98,200	$98,200 and up	$170,100 and up
Bottom 20%	Second 20%	Middle 20%	Fourth 20%	Top 20%	Top 5%

Source: U.S. Bureau of the Census, March 2004 Current Population Survey, Table F-3.

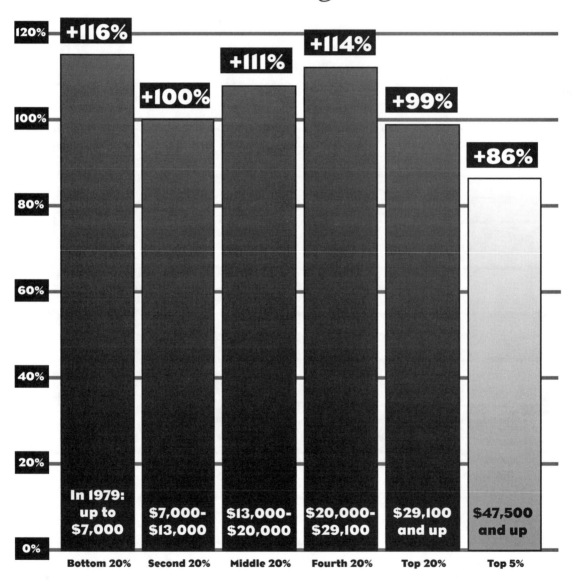

1947 TO 1979—REAL FAMILY INCOME GROWTH BY QUINTILE AND FOR TOP 5%

We Grew Together

+116%	+100%	+111%	+114%	+99%	+86%
In 1979: up to $7,000	$7,000-$13,000	$13,000-$20,000	$20,000-$29,100	$29,100 and up	$47,500 and up
Bottom 20%	Second 20%	Middle 20%	Fourth 20%	Top 20%	Top 5%

Source: Analysis of Census Bureau data by Lawrence Mishel and Jared Bernstein, *The State of Working America* 1994–95 p. 37. Income Ranges in 1979 dollars from March 1996 Census Current Population Survey, Table H-1.

as a whole. For example, the lowest fifth of black income earners saw their incomes fall 9.5 percent between 1979 and 1997. Meanwhile, the wealthiest fifth of black income earners saw their incomes go up 21.4 percent, with the wealthiest 5 percent rising 30.8 percent.[8] As sociologist William Julius Wilson points out, "In 1992, the highest fifth of black families... secured a record 48.8 percent of the total black family income compared to 43.8 percent of the total white income received by the highest fifth of white families, also a record. So, while income inequality has widened generally in America since 1975, the divide is even more dramatic among African Americans."[9]

In the thirty years following World War II, race was a principal barrier to economic advancement for people of color. Research on the economic mobility and advancement of blacks, according to Wilson, "could uncover no evidence of class effects on occupation or income achievements that could rival the effect of race." Beginning in the mid-1960s, however, "class began to affect career and generational mobility for blacks as it had regularly done for whites."[10] In other words, prosperous blacks began to move ahead and low-income blacks began to move backward. Race, while still a major factor, was diminishing as a factor in determining economic security, while class was becoming more significant. This explains why the Reverend Jesse Jackson, when asked to comment on former president Bill Clinton's 1998 proposal to have a national dialogue on race, suggested that we should also have a national dialogue on class.

We've looked at income and race; what about income and gender? The gap between male and female incomes has closed in the last two decades, as efforts to enforce pay equity have succeeded. At the beginning of the 1980s, women earned 62 cents for every dollar of men's earnings. Today, the pay gap has narrowed to 80 cents on the dollar.[11] Unfortunately, only half of this gain comes from an increase in women's wages. The other half is because the wages of working-class men have declined.[12]

The fact that at least two incomes are required to maintain a financially stable household in the last decade means that many more women have entered the workforce, albeit at a lower wage than their male counterparts. The persistent wage gap between men and women means that households headed by single women wage earners make up an enormous percentage of the families in poverty.

THE GAP BETWEEN HIGHEST AND AVERAGE WAGE EARNERS

One measurable facet of inequality is the widening gap between highest and average wage earners, both within individual businesses and within the entire economy. In 1975, the gap between the highest and average paid worker in a firm was 41 to 1. By 1997, the ratio between highest and average worker had risen to 212 to 1. In 2001, the gap catapulted up to 419 to 1 but saw a modest dip to 301 to 1 in 2003.[13]

In its 1997 survey, BusinessWeek called executive compensation "out of control," but they

THE CEO/WORKER PAY GAP*

42 WORKERS	85 WORKERS	141 WORKERS	326 WORKERS	531 WORKERS	301 WORKERS
1980	1990	1995	1997	2000	2003

* In 1980 the average CEO was paid as much as 42 factory workers. In 2003 the average C.E.O. was paid as much as 301 workers
— Business Week

hadn't seen anything yet! In 1998, the average salary and bonus for top executives at the 365 largest U.S. corporations dropped slightly from $2.3 million to $2.1 million. But CEOs weren't concerned, because if you add in the value of long-term stock options, executive pay climbed 36 percent in 1998 to an average of $10.6 million, increasing, in *BusinessWeek*'s words, an astounding 442 percent over the 1990 average of $2 million.[14] After a decline between 1999 and 2001 that tracked the stock market dip, average CEO pay in 2003 was $8.1 million, or about $155,769 a week, or $3,894 an hour. The average produc-

tion worker's annual pay in 2003 was $26,899, or $517 a week, or $12.92 an hour.[15]

Executive or CEO compensation is extremely visible because CEOs sit at the top of publicly traded corporations that report their top salaries in the proxy statements accompanying annual reports to shareholders. But top professional salaries have also risen, especially for bond traders, lawyers, medical specialists, high-tech wizards, sports and entertainment stars, and others who primarily work in the area of corporate finance. Many of these salaries are not subject to public scrutiny or attention.

The More You Downsize and Outsource, the Bigger a CEO's Paycheck

Wall Street corporations have been rewarded for aggressive downsizing and outsourcing (the transfer of jobs from the United States to overseas enterprises). United for a Fair Economy and the Institute for Policy Studies have tracked excessive compensation for over a decade and looked at the correlation between downsizing, outsourcing, and executive compensation.[16]

Today, it is quite likely that when you call for technical support for your computer or read your credit card bill, the work is being done in India or China.

The top outsourcing leader in 2003 was George David, CEO of United Technologies. In 2003, he collected $70.4 million, up 629 percent over his 2002 compensation. In 2001, David set the goal of outsourcing 80 percent of the firm's software development and support to India. They moved rapidly to replace U.S. workers with less expensive Indian workers, opening centers in Pune and Bangalore, as well as outsourcing major contracts with five Indian vendors.

In 2004, Citigroup became sole owner of a company based in Mumbai, India, that employs over 4,500 people. What do they do? E-Serve International provides data management and call center and transaction processing for Citibank. Outgoing CEO Sandford Weill made $54 million in 2003, seven times the average for his CEO peers.

Also getting on the India outsourcing train, software giant Oracle announced plans to double its two research centers in Hyderabad and Bangalore. This would increase the company's Indian workforce to 6,000 employees. Oracle has several hundred employees at research and development facilities in China, the next outsourcing frontier after Indian workers decide they want higher pay. Oracle CEO Larry Ellison is one of the highest paid CEOs in history, earning $700 million in 2001. In 2003, he was still in the top ten, with compensation of $40.6 million. He is the tenth wealthiest man listed on the Forbes 400, with 2004 net worth estimated at $13.7 billion.[17]

Athletes' Salaries in Perspective

People often point to sports stars as having grossly inflated salaries. But do they really add up in comparison to the titans of industry? Retired Chicago Bulls star Michael Jordan had a peak compensation package in 1997 that included a roughly $36-million-a-year contract and about $70 million in advertising promotions. At that salary, he made approximately $51,000 an hour.

$ **If he wants to by a Lexus, he has to save up for two hours.**

$ **While he makes a six-minute egg, he earns $5,096.**

$ **While sitting in a two-hour feature-length movie, he earns $101,924.**

$ **If he continues earning this amount for the next 480 years, he will earn as much as Bill Gates's net worth in 2004.**[18]

CEO Pay: Crony Capitalism—American Style

Apologists for excessive pay indicate that well-paid American CEOs are worth it, that they are valuable in the marketplace because of the skills they bring to the advancement of a corporation. Many CEOs do bring leadership, but their paychecks have little to do with market forces or pay for performance. But as the *Wall Street Journal* observed in one of their annual surveys of executive compensation: "Pay for performance? Forget it. These days, CEOs are assured of getting rich—however the company does."

U.S. free-marketeers criticize Asian countries for "crony capitalism," where government and corporations cut cozy deals and family members scratch each other's backs. But many of the executive pay deals existing in our own country are the American version of "crony capitalism." Even with corporate reforms instituted in the last few years, compensation committees, composed of corporate directors who are CEOs and friends of management, are still found setting CEO pay packages. In the Lake Wobegon world of executive compensation, all the CEOs are above average.

A number of Wall Street analysts, like Robert Monks, now view excessive pay as a red flag indicating that the board might be "cliquish" and not broadly accountable to shareholders. According to the Investor Responsibility Research Center, a coalition of over 100 pension funds, nearly 150 directors serving on the compensation committees of Standard & Poor's 500 companies had affiliations that compromised their independence from the company or the CEO. These conflicts of interest include:

$ **Being on your own compensation committee or having a close relative serve on your behalf.**

$ **Having a friendly CEO serve on your board compensation committee and doing the same for him.**

$ **Doing business deals with members of your compensation committee. George-town University coach John Thompson sits on Nike's board and on their executive compensation committee. In 1998, he voted to give Nike CEO Phil Knight $1.7 million, a salary that is more than 2,000 times the wage of a Nike factory worker in China—a worker who works twelve hours a day, seven days a week.**

Thompson's team, in turn, received more than $400,000 in endorsement money from Nike in 1998.

$ **Putting your lawyer or banker on your compensation committee. The CEO of credit card giant MBNA, Alfred Lerner, got a $10 million pay package in 1998. The chair of his compensation committee was his old college roommate, James Berick, who also acted as Lerner's attorney when he purchased the Cleveland Browns football team. Six months later, the MBNA board of directors approved a ten-year, $30 million marketing agreement with the Cleveland Browns.**

The Inequality of Wealth

WHAT IS WEALTH AND WHY IS IT IMPORTANT?

Income and wages are one index of how prosperity is distributed; the ownership of wealth is another. If income is the stream of money that comes into our lives each year, wealth is our reservoir. From our income stream, we take our bucket and pull out our housing costs, food expenses, and health care costs. At the end of the year, any left over goes into our reservoir, becoming accumulated wealth.

Wealth comprises assets (all the stuff you own) minus liabilities (what you owe). This remainder is called "net worth." If you own a car worth $4,000, but you owe $5,000 in car loans, you are in the red. You might feel wealthy driving that car down the road, but you actually have $1,000 in negative wealth. (WARNING: Do not think about this when you are driving 70 mph on the highway with large trucks next to you).

Wealth for working-class people is usually in the form of savings, consumer goods like cars, and, if they are fortunate, equity in a home. As people move up the economic ladder, wealth takes the form of greater savings and home value—but also includes second homes, recreational equipment

(like boats), shares in corporations (called securities or stocks), bonds, and commercial real estate. It may also include luxury items like high-priced artwork, racehorses, jewelry, and antiques.

Wealth is important because it is what people have to fall back on and pass on to their children. Yet today, about one out of six households in the United States has zero or negative wealth. This means they literally have no financial reserves to fall back on in times of trouble, or, in fact, they owe more than they own. The percentage of households with zero or negative net worth has increased in the last thirty years, from 15.5 percent in 1983 to 17.6 percent in 2001.[19] When factoring in race, the fig-

ures increase significantly. The percentage of African American households with zero or negative net worth is disturbingly high, at 30.9 percent or roughly one in three black households.[20]

Financial planners advise people that they should strive to have at least six months of financial reserves to help them weather a job transition, major illness, or other unexpected change. In reality, 45 percent of the population has only three months or less of financial reserves, even if they were to drop their spending to that of the poverty level: 38 percent of white households, 79 percent of Latino households, and 81 percent of African American households.[21]

Median Net Worth?

MEDIAN NET WORTH: The middle value. Half the households in the country are above the median, and half are below. If you took all the households in the United States and lined them up in order of their net worth, Bill Gates's household would be at one end and the poorest household in the country would be at the other. The household in the middle of that line would have the median net worth.

MEDIAN HOUSEHOLD NET WORTH BY RACE, 2001

The Color of Wealth

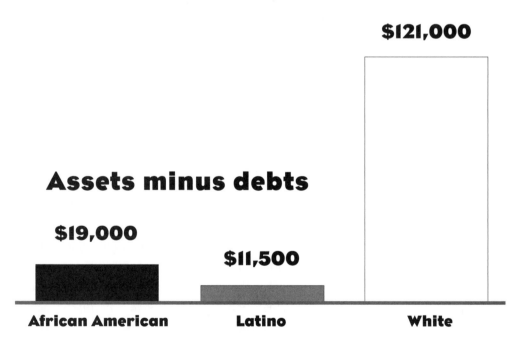

$121,000

Assets minus debts

$19,000

$11,500

African American   **Latino**   **White**

Source: Analysis of 2001 Federal Reserve Bank Survey of Consumer Finances data by Barbara Robles.

It is in the area of wealth and asset accumulation that the legacy of racial discrimination has left its most profound mark. While black and Latino *incomes* have begun to catch up to white earnings, black and Latino *wealth* continues to lag dramatically behind that of white households. Since wealth accumulates over generations, discrimination has taken its toll on wealth accumulation for people of color. Blacks were prohibited from building wealth by slavery and prohibitions against owning property after the Civil War. Bank lending practices have also discriminated against black and Latino households and kept them from home ownership, business development, and other asset-building measures.[22]

In 2001, the median black household had a net worth of just $19,000 (including home equity), compared with $121,000 for whites. Blacks had 16 percent of the median wealth of whites, up from 5 percent in 1989. At this rate, it will take until 2099 to reach parity in median wealth. Blacks were 13 percent of the U.S. population in 2001 but owned 3 percent of the assets.[23] There is obviously a high correlation between income and wealth. Most assetless households are in the bottom fifth of the income ladder. There are people deep in debt all up and down the income spectrum, but in most cases, we can assume that assetlessness correlates with lower income.

THE CONCENTRATION OF WEALTH

In the last twenty years, the overall wealth pie has grown, but virtually all the new growth in wealth has gone to the richest 1 percent of the population.[24]

In 1976, the wealthiest 1 percent of the population owned 20 percent of all the private wealth. The top 10 percent of the population owned about 50 percent of all private wealth.[25] By 2001, the richest 1 percent's share had increased to over 33 percent of all household financial wealth, increasing the top 20 percent's share to 84.4 percent.[26] The top 1 percent of households now has more wealth than the entire bottom 95 percent. As of 2001, to join the top 1 percent club you need at least $5.8 million in net worth.[27]

Financial wealth (net worth minus net equity in owner-occupied housing) is even more concentrated. The top 1 percent of households has nearly half of all stock (44.9 percent) and 39.7 percent of all financial wealth. This is compared to the bottom 90 percent of households, which owns 20.2 percent of all financial wealth.

Between 1962 and 2001, the relative share of wealth owned by the bottom 90 percent of the population declined from 33.1 percent to 28.5 percent.[28] What does this loss of wealth actually mean? It means less savings, growing personal debt, less retirement security, and fewer households having access to home ownership. It means fewer financial reserves to fall back on in the event of a setback or job loss.

TEN MUSICAL CHAIRS

U.S. Private Wealth in Perspective

**Each chair
= 10% of U.S. wealth**

**Each person
= 10% of U.S. population**

Top 10%: Seven Chairs   Bottom 90%: Three Chairs

**2001
10% owns 70%
of all wealth**

**90% owns 30%
of all wealth**

John Lapham

Source: Arthur B. Kennickel, "A Rolling Tide: Changes in the Distribution of Wealth in the U.S. 1989–2001,"
Jerome Levy Economics Institute, November 2003.

WEALTH CONCENTRATION: BACK TO THE FUTURE?

Top 1% Share of Household Wealth, 1922–2001

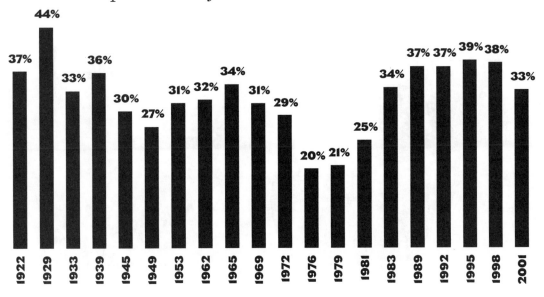

Sources: 1922–81: Edward N. Wolff, *Top Heavy* (The New Press: 1996). 1983–2001: Edward N. Wolff, "Changes in Household Wealth in the 1980s and 1990s in the U.S.," Jerome Levy Economics Institute, May 2004.

What if workers had been paid for productivity gains?

Between 1973 and 1998, productivity increased 33 percent. What if hourly wages grew at the same rate? What if workers shared in the 1990s productivity gains they helped to create? The average hourly wage in 1998 would have been $18.10, rather than $12.77.[29] That's the difference of $5.33 an hour—more than $11,000 for a full-time, year-round worker. The 30 cents workers gained in their hourly wages between 1997 and 1998 pales by comparison. The cumulative wages lost since 1973 will never be recovered—much less their lost investment potential. This is money working families could have saved, invested, or spent on consumer items rather than going into debt. This is money that could have stimulated markets in low- and moderate-income communities rather than benefiting absentee shareholders who take their investments anywhere on the planet in search of the highest return.

OWNERSHIP OF HOUSEHOLD WEALTH IN THE UNITED STATES

In the last 25 years, the top 1% increased their share to 1/3 of the entire wealth pie.

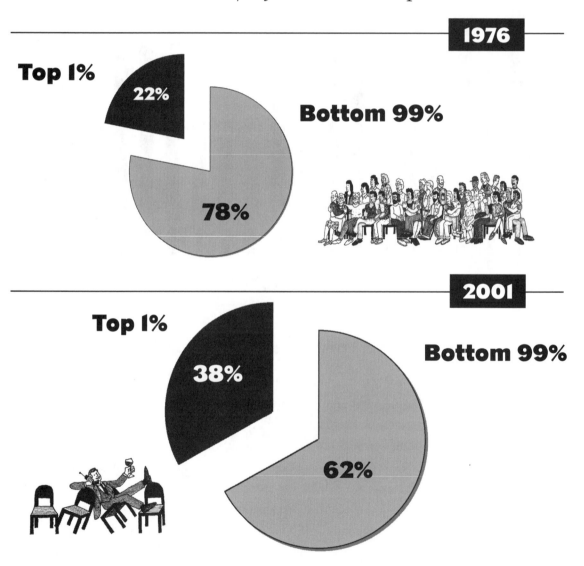

1976

Top 1%

22%

Bottom 99%

78%

2001

Top 1%

38%

Bottom 99%

62%

Sources: For 1976: Edward N. Wolff, unpublished data. For 2001: Arthur B. Kennickel, "A Rolling Tide: Changes in the Distribution of Wealth in the U.S. 1989–2001," Jerome Levy Economics Institute, November 2003.

THE MYTH OF WHO OWNS ASSETS

Reading the newspapers these days, you would think that everyone has money invested in the stock market. According to several surveys, the percentage of households with investments in the stock market has dramatically increased from 32 percent in 1989 to over 51 percent in 2001. Many of these households moved funds from their savings accounts into mutual funds.[30]

The business press likes to trumpet the "democratization" of the market, but when stocks stumble, as they did in the late 1990s, these same publications tell us not to worry—a sinking tide won't lower all boats—because most Americans are not exposed.[31] A growing number of Americans do own stock, but most do not own very much. Less than 40 percent of households owned stock worth $5,000 or more in 2001.[32] This may have appreciated in the last few years, but stock ownership still completely eludes well over half the U.S. population.[33]

And people with substantial stock ownership did lose money in the late-nineties market plunge. Some people nearing retirement age saw the value of their nest eggs plummet to the point where they had to postpone their retirement. All this underscores the fact that the overall distribution of

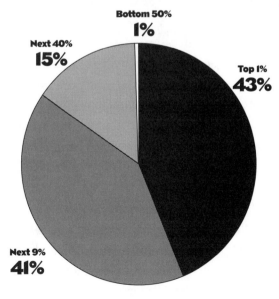

WHO OWNS STOCK IN AMERICA?

Bottom 50%
1%

Next 40%
15%

Top 1%
43%

Next 9%
41%

Ownership of Stocks and Mutual Funds, 2001

Source: Author's analysis of Arthuir B. Kennickel, "A Rolling Tide: Changes in the Distribution of Wealth in the U.S., 1989–2001," Levy Economics Institute, November 2003, Table 10.

ownership of financial assets remains very concentrated. The wealthiest 10 percent of the population owns 84 percent of stocks, excluding pensions, and 43 percent of home equity. The wealthiest 1 percent of households own 43 percent of stocks and 11.1 percent of home equity.[34]

Unlike the top 1 percent, most Americans could not quit their jobs and live solely off their investments. The notion that we should not worry about stagnant wages but rather enjoy the fruits of our stock portfolios does not really wash. Besides, the market could drop without warning at any time, wiping out whatever savings working Americans had managed to invest in the stock market.

THE WEALTH-HOLDERS

I made my money the old-fashioned way. I inherited it.
—JOSEPH KENNEDY JR.

How do people get wealth? The oil billionaire J.P. Getty was once asked how he became wealthy. He replied: "The key to great wealth is threefold: One, rise early each day. Two, work hard all day. Three, find oil." There are three ways in which the very wealthy accumulate money: through slow accumulation over their lifetimes by starting a business and saving; through cornering a critical element of the market and controlling it; or through inheritance.

Most press coverage goes to describing the self-made millionaires, the Horatio Algers of the modern day. In Thomas Stanley and William Danko's best-selling book, *The Millionaire Next Door*, the profile of America's 3.5 million million-

aires is not the stereotype of the high-roller with five fancy sports cars and several mansions in desirable zip codes. According to Stanley and Danko, the typical millionaire is white, over fifty-five years old, has a net worth of between $1 and 10 million, and lives in the same house he bought thirty years ago. The most common sources of wealth: small-business ownership and steadily rising home value. In other words, a majority of millionaires with less than $10 million are thrifty and focused on owning and growing one business.[35]

Like many small business owners, their economic security is based on a lifetime of hard work, financial risk, sacrifice, and commitment. This work ethic, combined with a commitment to saving money, has made many people comfortable in their senior years. But there are many other factors, including timing, luck, and white privilege that are less acknowledged in America's mythology of success. Starting a business in the rapidly expanding economy of the 1950s and 1960s was a very different story than starting a business in today's more competitive global economy. Prior to the 1970s, many domestic small businesses were protected from the full brunt of competition from international producers and national conglomerates. Imagine trying to start a locally owned hardware store or pharmacy today in the same marketplace with Home Depot, Costco, and CVS. Access to credit for the purchase of assets, whether a home in an appreciating neighborhood or a start-up small business, remains a function of education, skill, personal connections, and—despite government antidiscrimination policies—race.

Many of the largest fortunes—those in excess of $10 million—are tied to cornering a part of the market that everyone needs. Indeed, many of the great robber barons of the late 1800s (the Rockefellers, the Carnegies, etc.) dominated some market (usually in natural resources like timber, oil, coal, and steel), or developed a monopoly on a much-needed public service like railroads.

Today, fortunes are made in information-age technology. Bill Gates and Paul Allen, the founders of Microsoft, are good examples. A growing number of the new fortunes on the Forbes 400 annual listing of the richest Americans are built on computers and information technology.[36] Like the railroad barons of the late 1800s, Gates and Allen developed advances in products—computer operating systems and software—that have become central to our lives. Between 1996 and 1999, Bill Gates's personal wealth went from $18 billion to over $85 billion dollars. Thanks to changes in the market and his aggressive charitable giving ($28 billion donated to the Gates Foundation and other charities), Gates's net worth in 2004 was $48 billion, but his personal wealth still exceeds the combined wealth of the bottom 45 percent of the U.S. population.[37]

In spite of the success stories of small entrepreneurs and "dot-com millionaires," the most sure-fire way to get rich remains to be born into a wealthy family. A substantial amount of wealth is passed on from one generation to the next through inheritance. Economist Lester Thurow estimates that between 50 and 70 percent of all wealth is inherited.[38] A 1997 study found that of the 400 individuals and families on the 1997 Forbes 400 list, 42 percent inherited their way onto the list, another 6 percent inherited wealth in excess of $50 million, and another 7 percent started life with at least $1 million. Overall, more than 50 percent started life with at least $1 million.[39] Not a bad start in life. (See the box Born on Third Base on pages 61–64).

While it still is possible for a few to make the "rags to riches" transition, it is important to question the underlying belief and value system that dangles this fantasy before our eyes. This national obsession is so compelling that we are willing to accept large-scale poverty in exchange for the prospect of a few lucky folks hitting the big time. We can't possibly *all* invent the next mousetrap or computer operating system. We can't *all* win the lottery. A few folks cornering the market (or hitting the daily number) depends on many others failing. Unfortunately, the classist belief systems we are indoctrinated by are powerful. We are trained to identify up the class spectrum and fantasize about getting there.

Google Wealth Built on Uncle Sam's Shoulders

When the search engine Google became a public corporation in 2004, founders Larry Page and Sergey Brin joined the billionaires club just nine years after meeting as Stanford University graduate students. They are now each worth an estimated $4 billion.[40]

If anyone fits the bill as a "self-made" man, they do. Or do they? While our society applauds their hard work and ingenuity—and that of their Google colleagues—we should remember this: Google was built on the Internet, which was created by the U.S. Government's Advanced Research Project Agency with public tax dollars and nurtured through a continuing partnership of government, universities, and industry.

The world's greatest venture capitalist isn't one of those demigods who live on Sand Hill Road in Silicon Valley. It's Uncle Sam, whose taxpayer investments and innovations produced the Internet, the Human Genome Project, and much more. Nick Szabo, a retired executive of semiconductor equipment manufacturer KLA and the former mayor of Cupertino, California, calls Silicon Valley "a creation of the taxpayer."

Since 1958, an estimated 75 percent of all engineers and scientists engaged in scientific research have gone into federally subsidized ventures in both the public and private sectors. Google emerged from the synergy of government, Stanford and other universities, and Silicon Valley.

Google's founders and employees come from the nation's top schools, and the top schools—public and private—depend on federal research dollars funded by taxpayers. *Fortune* magazine reports, "For the most part, it takes a degree from an Ivy League school, or MIT, Stanford, Cal-Tech, or Carnegie Mellon—America's top engineering schools—even to get invited to an interview" at Google.

The presidents of MIT and Harvard wrote recently that federal research funding "is the lifeblood of our institutions. The return on this federal investment is enormous. More than 50 percent of U.S. economic growth during the past 60 years has been due to technological innovation, much of it stemming from university research."

American taxpayers have helped Google in other ways. How many of the investors, employees, and customers of Google benefited from public education? How many contracts did Google make that are enforced by a publicly financed judicial system? How many patents protect Google from someone else using its intellectual property thanks to our federally funded patent system?

Google investors are seeing their investments appreciate as Google becomes a publicly traded company and their stock becomes liquid in the worldwide market. This global liquidity is worth some 30 to 50 percent of the value of newly public enterprises, according to informed sources.

A regulated marketplace, with rules governing disclosure and accounting practices, gives investors the confidence they need to part with their money. When confidence is broken by accounting scandals such as Enron and WorldCom, investors have to believe the rules and institutions have been strengthened enough to risk new investment. The wealth possibilities are only as good as the societal institutions that maintain the trust.

In short, Google is a dramatic example of the way in which societal investment creates fertile ground for private wealth creation.[41]

GLOBAL INEQUALITY

The focus of this book is on the growing inequalities in the U.S. economy. It is important to underscore, however, that many of these trends are part of a global trend toward greater inequality. The inequities within the United States pale in comparison to the disparities between the world's super-rich and the billions of people who live without sanitary water or adequate food.

$ **The United Nations Development Program reported in 1999 that the world's 225 richest people now have a combined wealth of $1 trillion. That's equal to the combined annual income of the world's 2.5 billion poorest people.**

$ **The wealth of the world's three most well-to-do individuals now exceeds the combined GDP (gross domestic product) of the forty-eight least-developed countries.**

$ **Although 200 million people saw their incomes fall between 1965 and 1980, more than 1 billion people experienced an additional drop from 1980 to 1993.**

$ **Half the world's population of 6 billion live on less than $2 per day while 1.3 billion get by on less than $1 per day.[42]**

THE CHAMPAGNE-GLASS GLOBAL DISTRIBUTION OF INCOME

What is the global distribution of income? According to the United Nations Development Programme, the distribution resembles a champagne glass.

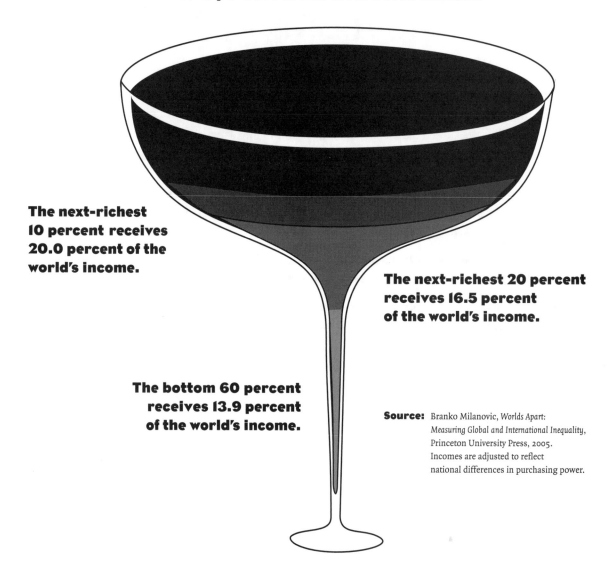

The richest 10 percent of the world's population receives 49.6 percent of the total world income.

The next-richest 10 percent receives 20.0 percent of the world's income.

The next-richest 20 percent receives 16.5 percent of the world's income.

The bottom 60 percent receives 13.9 percent of the world's income.

Source: Branko Milanovic, *Worlds Apart: Measuring Global and International Inequality*, Princeton University Press, 2005. Incomes are adjusted to reflect national differences in purchasing power.

Born on Third Base—Claimed They Hit Triples

Each October, *Forbes* magazine releases the Forbes 400, its list of the wealthiest people in America. The combined net worth of the Forbes 400 has grown dramatically in the last fifteen years. Forbes usually celebrates the bootstrappers, the self-made fortunes. In one survey, they began: "Forget old wealth. Forget silver spoons. There are fortunes being made today by people who didn't have a dime when we started this list in 1980."

Forbes gives the false impression that everyone on the *Forbes* list got there because of their entrepreneurial acumen. In 2004, *Forbes* magazine pronounced as fact: "244 members of the Forbes 400 are entirely self-made. Their average net worth is $2.5 billion."[43] It is true that there are many new billionaires whose wealth has come from technology, and their ranks will grow. *Forbes* does not talk much about those who inherited their way onto the list or who had a wealthy head start. The reality is that the key to great wealth for the majority of the richest Americans is to choose wealthy parents or grandparents. A United for a Fair Economy study, "Born on Third Base: The Sources of Wealth of the Forbes 400," disputes the notion that the

Nick Thorkelson

61

majority of America's wealthiest people have self-made fortunes.[44] The 1997 study found that 55 percent of those individuals and families on the Forbes 400 were there because they either inherited their way directly onto the list, inherited already substantial and profitable companies, or received substantial start-up capital from a family member.

This study grouped Forbes's 400 individuals and fifty families into five categories borrowed from our national pastime, baseball. Those "born on home plate" inherited their way onto the *Forbes* 400 outright. Keeping with the baseball rule that "the tie goes to the runner," the study team gave Forbes 400 members the benefit of the doubt. For example, if researchers could not be sure whether a member belonged on second or third base, they assigned him or her to second base. Initial analysis of the 1997 Forbes 400 shows:

$ **BORN ON HOME PLATE. Forty-two percent of those listed inherited sufficient wealth to rank among the Forbes 400. This percentage is actually higher than that listed by *Forbes* for inheritors. The reason is that *Forbes* considered people as self-made if they inherited substantial sums or property and then later built that stake into a greater fortune. One example is Philip Anschutz ($5.2 billion), who is listed as "self-made" even though he inherited a $500-million oil and gas field. A wee boost!**

$ **BORN ON THIRD BASE. Six percent of those listed inherited substantial wealth, in excess of $50 million or a large and prosperous company, and grew this initial fortune into membership in the Forbes 400.**

$ **BORN ON SECOND BASE. Seven percent of those on the Forbes list inherited a medium-sized business or wealth of more than $1 million or received substantial start-up capital for a business from a family member.**

$ **BORN ON FIRST BASE. Fourteen percent of those listed have a personal biography that indicates a wealthy or upper-class background: one that, to our knowledge, provided them with less than a $1 million inheritance or with a more modest amount of start-up capital from a family member. Due to the study team's conservative coding rule of erring on the side of a lower base when information is inadequate, it is likely that some of those listed as born on first base actually belong on second or third base.**

$ **STARTED IN THE BATTER'S BOX. Thirty-one percent of those listed did not have great wealth or own a business with more than a few employees.**

While the wages of average Americans continue to stagnate, in 2004 the number of billionaires in the United States increased to 312. In 2004, the combined net worth of the wealthiest 400 individuals in the United States was $1 trillion, up $45 billion from 2003.

Forbes 400 Examples[45]

BORN ON HOME PLATE

J. PAUL GETTY JR. inherited the oil fortune from his father.

DAVID ROCKEFELLER SR. ($2.5 billion) is the grandson of Standard Oil founder John D. Rockefeller.

S.I. AND DONALD NEWHOUSE ($7 billion each) inherited the nation's largest private newspaper chain, plus Condé Nast Publications, from their father in 1979.

SAMUEL CURTIS JOHNSON ($1.5 billion) is the great-grandson of the flooring salesman who founded the floor-wax giant S.C. Johnson and Sons.

BORN ON THIRD BASE

KENNETH FELD inherited Ringling Brothers Circus in 1982 when it was worth tens of millions.

EDWARD CROSBY JOHNSON III ($6 billion) inherited Fidelity Investments from his father and was involved in growing it into the "pace car" of the mutual-fund industry.

WALTER ANNENBERG, who died in 2002, took over his father's publishing business and took TV *Guide* national.

MICHEL FRIBOURG inherited his family's Continental Grain Co. in 1944 and has reaped a bountiful harvest.

BORN ON SECOND BASE

FOREST MARS SR. ($10 billion) took over a small European candy business founded by his grandparents.

DONALD TYSON ($925 million) inherited a small company, Tyson Foods, from his father in 1967, but then built it up into a substantial business.

Poultry magnate **FRANK PERDUE** ($925 million), who died in 2005, inherited his father's egg farm and hatched millions in chickens.

BORN ON FIRST BASE

BILL GATES's ($48 billion) parents were comfortable professionals; he went to private school and then to Harvard University, but quit for better prospects. He and Paul Allen transformed their childhood fascination with computers into a global empire.

TED WAITT ($1.4 billion) got financial help from his grandmother to secure a $10,000 loan and start the computer mail-order business that blossomed into Gateway 2000.

AMOS HOSTETTER JR. ($2.1 billion) got a $4,000 boost from his stockbroker father to start Continental Cablevision.

STARTED IN THE BATTER'S BOX

H. ROSS PEROT ($4.2 billion) was the son of a horse trader and was born into a comfortable but not affluent family.

WAYNE HUIZENGA ($1.8 billion) got his start by buying a garbage truck and starting a waste-hauling company. He took over the nineteen-store Blockbuster video-rental chain and built it into an industry leader.

JOHN WERNER KLUGE ($11 billion) immigrated from Germany to Detroit with his mother at age eight and was raised in a tenement. He started his $11 billion Metromedia empire after World War II by buying a single radio station.

Chapter 3

THE CAUSES OF INEQUALITY

Why Has Inequality Grown?

While the 1950s and 1960s were still times of economic inequality, prosperity was shared significantly more equitably than during the last couple of decades. Why was inequality declining in the 1950s and '60s? Why has inequality grown so dramatically in the last two decades? There is no simple answer. What is clear is that economic inequality is not the result of some natural phenomenon like sun spots or shifting winds. It is the result of the rules that govern the economy—over three decades of public policies and private corporate practices—that have benefited asset-owners at the expense of wage-earners. Tax policy, global trade policy, government spending, and regulation have all been tilted in favor of asset owners and large corporations.

For most economists, politicians, and media outlets, growing inequality is not even newsworthy. For those who acknowledge this phenomenon, most attribute it to unnamed "market forces." Most orthodox economists

point to three primary reasons for growing inequality: changing technology, lack of education (resulting from technological change), and globalization.[1] As James K. Galbraith writes in *Created Unequal: The Crisis in American Pay*, "To a predominant faction within the economics profession, the 'why' of rising inequality has been answered by a single, all-encompassing phrase: *skill-based technological change*."[2] The basic theory is that workers in our economy have not kept up with the dramatic changes in technology, creating a shortage of highly skilled people who have made the leap into the new technological arena and whose services, by virtue of supply and demand, command high salaries. The labor of underskilled workers, on the other hand, is less valued, so their wages plummet. The policy implications of this are, if anything, to invest in worker training and education and sit back and wait for the supply of skilled workers to catch up to demand.

Galbraith challenges this theory, arguing that rising wage inequality is neither "mysterious nor necessary nor the dark side of a good thing." Rather, it is the result of recession, unemployment, slow economic growth, inflation, and a stagnant minimum wage. The growth of inequality is the result of political forces, the result of changes in the rules and decisions governing the economy. Technological change and global competition *do* contribute to inequality. Yet even in these areas, there are political decisions and rules that govern how we choose to evolve technologically and how we integrate into the global economy. Other nations have experienced technological change and global integration without dramatic increases in inequality.[3] Inequality will be reduced through policies such as those that increase full employment, control the negative effects of globalization, and raise the minimum wage.

There have always been great inequalities of wealth and power, but the imbalance of power has accelerated in the last two decades as result of a power shift. The owners of capital have triumphed over those who work for a living. As a result, the rules have been changed to help asset-owners at the expense of wage-earners. It's as if we were playing a game of Monopoly, and the first one who passed "Go" not only collected $200 but also got the ability to rewrite the rules for the rest of the game. "We the people" can and should decide the rules that govern our economy. "We the people"—not just the few large asset-owners who got there first.

This chapter looks at the causes of growing inequality. The first section, The Power Shift, examines the ways in which corporations and large asset-owners have gained influence in our democracy. The second section examines a number of specific rule changes in the economy that have worsened inequality.

The Power Shift

During the last twenty-five years, the United States has witnessed the concentration of money and power in the hands of fewer and fewer individuals and corporations. Supreme Court Justice Louis Brandeis once observed that "You can have wealth concentrated in the hands of a few, or democracy. But you cannot have both." Brandeis understood that money is power and that concentrated economic power would ultimately subvert democratic institutions.

There has been a fundamental shift in power. On one hand, the power of large corporations and the wealthy has dramatically increased. On the other, the institutions providing a countervailing power to corporations—including unions, political parties, and other civic institutions—have declined. In the first part of this chapter, we will look at several power shifts:

$ **money power in our democracy,**

$ **the rise in corporate power,**

$ **the declining power of workers,**

$ **the declining influence of the civic sector, and**

$ **the declining independence of politics.**

Q: WHY HAS THIS HAPPENED?
A: A POWER SHIFT LED TO RULE CHANGES

The Power Shift since the 1970s

Who sets the agenda for economic policies?

On the Rise:

Big Campaign Contributors

Corporate Lobbyists

Corporations

Big Asset-Owners

CEOs

Wall Street

In Decline:

Popular Political Movements

Voters

Labor Unions

Wage-Earners

Employees

Main Street

Q: WHY HAS THIS HAPPENED? A: A <u>POWER</u> <u>SHIFT</u> LED TO <u>RULE</u> <u>CHANGES</u>

Rule changes since the 1970s

What policy changes reflect and reinforce the power shift?

Unions: **Anti-union climate** weakens the power and voice of workers.

Trade: **Global treaties** benefit corporations, not workers or communities.

Taxes: **Big tax cuts** for the wealthy.
No tax relief for working families.

Budget: **Corporate welfare** expands. Human services cut.

Minimum Wage: **Not raised** to keep up with inflation.

Fed Policy: **"Whip inflation" policy** helps investors, hurts wage growth.

Privatization: **Government dismantling** helps investors, hurts consumers and workers.

MONEY POWER IN OUR DEMOCRACY

Large corporations and the wealthy have always exercised disproportionate power and influence in our democratic process. In 1757, George Washington, one of the wealthiest men in America, was charged with purchasing and distributing liquor for voters in his district in an attempt to buy their votes.[4]

As wealth has become more concentrated in the last few decades, so has the quantitative influence of big-money donations in our democracy. The campaign-finance abuses of the last few years are an example of the growing importance of the large donations required to run for political office. In order to secure and maintain political office, candidates must court wealthy donors. Once elected, they become accountable to serve the political agendas of their benefactors. In the words of columnist Molly Ivins, "They dance with the ones who brung them."

While in office, most politicians argue that money is not a factor in shaping their decisions. Yet many former politicians, once released from the shackles of having to raise money, have harsh words for our nation's system of campaign-finance contributions. As retired U.S. representative Romano Mazzoli from Kentucky said, "People who contribute get the ear of the member and the ear of the staff. They have the access—and access is it. Access is power. Access is clout. That's how this thing works."[5]

Many qualified and strong potential leaders are completely excluded from participation in the democratic process because of their inability to raise the money to compete. This effectively creates a "wealth primary" where wealthy donors decide which candidates will appear as choices for the general electorate. This explains why the general public does not get to consider candidates who might challenge policies tilted in favor of the affluent and corporate domination.

Some of the trends in recent years include:

$ **Prior to 2004, 94 to 96 percent of the U.S. population did not make political contributions. This did change during the 2004 presidential election, with the explosion of small Internet contributions. We shall see if it becomes a long-term trend.[6]**

$ **Less than 1 percent of the population contributes more than 80 percent of all money in federal elections in amounts of $200 or more.**

$ **In 1994, the total contributions from just one zip code—10021, on New York City's Upper East Side—were larger than the combined contributions made in twenty-four states.**

$ **Ninety-five percent of contributors to Congressional campaigns who give $200 or more are white, and 81 percent have annual incomes of $100,000 or more, with the top 20 percent in the $500,000-or-more category.[7]**

Why Vote When You've Got Cash?

The corrupting influence of money in politics is sometimes exposed in humorous ways. During a Senate hearing on campaign-finance abuses chaired by then senator Fred Thompson (R–Tenn.), one witness, Roger E. Tamraz from Oil Capital, Ltd., confessed that he was not registered to vote. Rather, he donates $300,000 in contributions to candidates.

SENATOR JOSEPH LIEBERMAN: You have not registered to vote?

MR. TAMRAZ: No.

SEN. LIEBERMAN: So that your participation in the political process has been limited to contributing to campaigns?

MR. TAMRAZ: Well, I think this is a bit more than a vote.

SEN. LIEBERMAN: That's the problem. (laughter)…And part of what discourages people from voting…I think our voter turnout is as low as it is because a lot of people out there have decided that people with money have more access….

MR. TAMRAZ: Maybe that's why I didn't register.[8]

Unfortunately, there are numerous examples of politicians paying more attention to the needs of corporations and wealthy contributors than to the concerns of the broader public. The agenda in the U.S. Congress is almost entirely dictated by who is funding politicians, leaving issues important to working families off the radar screen. For a decade, the majority of Americans have wanted a universal health care system that wasn't dominated by for-profit health insurance companies. Yet big-money insurance companies have blocked reform.

The over-influence of concentrated wealth in our democracy creates a vicious cycle. As the rich get richer and more powerful and the clout of corporations grows stronger, their voice in the democratic system gets louder and louder. Inevitably, they write the rules that govern our economy in their own interests, advocating for tax cuts for the wealthy, deregulation, unfettered global trade and investment, privatization, and more. Once implemented, these policies further concentrate wealth and power and the cycle continues. Breaking the connection between money power and our democracy is essential to building an economy that works for everyone.

THE RISE IN CONCENTRATED CORPORATE POWER

A key factor in the imbalance of power in the United States has been the increasing clout of global corporations and their ability to write the rules in our economy.

Two hundred large transnational corporations now dominate the United States and global economy. Of the world's one hundred largest economies in 2001, comparing the gross domestic products of nation states with the annual sales of corporations, fifty-three are corporations and forty-seven are countries.[9]

The sales figures for some of America's largest corporations exceed the gross domestic product of countries such as Denmark, Thailand, Hong Kong, Turkey, and South Africa.[10] With $256 billion in 2003 sales, Wal-Mart is the twentieth-largest economy in the world. It is larger than the economies of 188 countries, including Sweden ($230 billion), Austria ($222 billion), and Norway ($189 billion).[11]

In the last five years, there has been an acceleration of corporate concentration, with the dollar volume of corporate mergers exceeding any other period in modern history. In 1999, over $1.75 trillion in mergers were announced, up from $195 billion in 1990. These massive mergers and consolidations have taken place in every sector of the economy, but they are occurring most rapidly in technology, financial services, and communications.[12]

In many cases, the only real winners are top managers, while the losers include long-term shareholders, employees, consumers, and the communities where these plants are located.

The MCI-WorldCom Merger

One example of "merger mania" and its negative effects on workers, consumers, and communities was the MCI-WorldCom merger.

The Telecommunications Act of 1996 was supposed to give consumers more competition, better service, and lower prices. Instead it unleashed a corporate scramble to merge, acquire, and restructure that has done a lot more for the pocketbooks of a few executives and investment bankers than for the public.

The story of the 1998 merger between MCI Communications and WorldCom, Inc., and the subsequent 2002 scandals represents corporate gluttony on a grand scale. MCI's top executives reaped tens of millions from the merger, but things didn't turn out so well for their employees, shareholders, or customers.[13]

Even before the merger deal was approved by shareholders and regulators, wheeling and dealing around the merger had already generated millions for MCI chairman Bert Roberts and for the Wall Street investment banks helping to drive the merger through. Merger announcements usually bounce stock prices, and Roberts personally made $6.1 million from stock options he cashed in after the deal was made public and MCI stock climbed 17 percent.[14]

MCI's top five executives made tens of millions more in retention bonuses, severance packages, and more, in addition to the millions they

TRANSNATIONAL CORPORATIONS: LARGE, AND GETTING LARGER

Of the world's 100 largest economies…

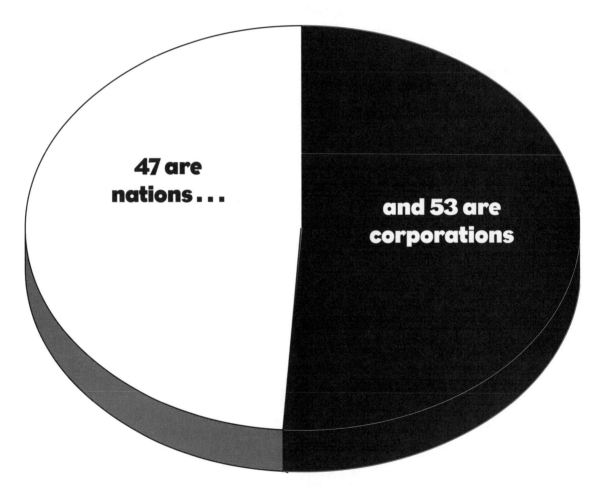

47 are nations…

and 53 are corporations

Source: Institute for Policy Studies

were paid in salaries, bonuses, stock awards, and luxury perks.[15]

The merged company, WorldCom, was to focus on high-revenue business customers, abandoning MCI's plans to extend local networks and compete for residential customers. This hurt consumers, as MCI had been an aggressive competitor for residential and small-business customers in local phone service. As Merrill Lynch analysts pointed out, "reduced intra-industry competition" resulting from the merger raised phone prices, further delayed the benefits of competition promised by the 1996 Telecommunications Act.[16]

The workforce effects of the merger were devastating to working families and the communities where MCI facilities were located. An estimated 5,000 jobs were immediately lost after the merger.[17] In backing away from serving residential customers, MCI scrapped plans to invest $2 billion in building local facilities in over 100 cities. According to the Communication Workers of America, the combination of immediate cuts and scrapped plans for future jobs eliminated 75,000 job opportunities in the telecommunications industry.[18]

In 1999, WorldCom announced a $115 billion plan to merge with long-distance provider Sprint. But the U.S. government refused, on antitrust grounds, to allow the merger to proceed. In 2001, WorldCom did acquire a smaller company, Intermedia Communications, for $6 billion. But then the scandals started to emerge that have now become legendary.

The first sign of trouble was in February 2002, when the high-flying WorldCom told analysts that

their revenue would fall short of expectations. In April 2002, CEO Bernie Ebbers was forced to step down when it was revealed that he had illegally borrowed $408 million from the company to cover his own personal stock losses. In June 2002, WorldCom revealed $3.9 billion in bogus accounting, leading to a halt in its trading on the stock exchange. Eventually the company would report over $11 billion in improper accounting. The Securities and Exchange Commission charged WorldCom with defrauding investors.

Some of those investors were the approximately 50,000 workers at WorldCom who lost billions in their 401(k) pension program. These employees sued to recover their losses, and in July 2004 the company settled by agreeing to pay about $51 million. Under the deal, former CEO Ebbers would personally have to pay at least $400,000 and as much as $4 million—a small price to pay after bilking shareholders and workers for hundreds of millions to pay for a once-lavish lifestyle.[19]

In June 2002, WorldCom filed for Chapter 11 bankruptcy to protect itself from its creditors. A year later, WorldCom emerged from bankruptcy with a reorganized company and a new name: MCI! But the new MCI was banned in 2004 from taking on additional federal contracts because it lacks ethical standards. MCI didn't appeal the decision.[20]

THE CORPORATE ASCENDANCY. Charles Derber, in his important book on the concentration of corporate power, *Corporation Nation*, describes the enormous cultural power of corporations.

Like the "feminine mystique" Betty Friedan identified in the 1950s as the invisible power relationships between men and women, the corporate mystique is a belief system that for decades has effectively disguised the rising power of corporations in our lives.

We take for granted the "corporate ascendancy," the way in which corporations now shape our reality. In Derber's words,

"The corporate mystique has helped to obscure not only the very question of corporate power, but how deeply personal the subject is. The personal identity of today's worker, consumer, and citizen is becoming a corporate construction. Corporations help create our growing obsession with money and success, molding both our morality and material lives."[21]

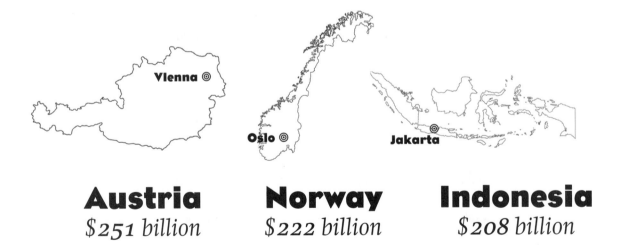

THE REPUBLIC OF WAL-MART?

With $256 billion in 2003 sales, **Wal-Mart** is the 20th-largest economy in the world. It is larger than the economies of 188 countries, including ...

Austria
$251 billion

Norway
$222 billion

Indonesia
$208 billion

Source: Hoover's online, World Bank Development Indicators.

Corporations shape our sense of reality through the ownership concentration of the media.

CORPORATIONS IN THE SCHOOLS. Since 1989, thousands of schools have subscribed to the network called Channel One, which provides "free educational programming" in the classroom. In exchange, students must sit through commercials from companies eager to market their products to young people. Constance L. Hays writes in the *New York Times*, "School districts are seen as prime targets by computer software publishers, fast-food chains, soft-drink bottlers and other corporations, which believe that brand loyalty begins at an early age. Some offer schools lucrative contracts intended to promote their products and keep their competitors out."[22]

Corporation Education: Brand-Name Math Book

Joe Stein got a big surprise one afternoon when he went to help his eleven-year-old son, Noah, with his math homework. Noah's math textbook, published by McGraw-Hill, in Stein's words "looked like an ad for a chain electronic store." It was full of references to brand-name consumer products, including Nike, Gatorade, Disney, McDonald's, Nabisco, Mattel Barbie dolls, Sony PlayStations, Kellogg's Frosted Flakes, Spalding basketballs, and Topps baseball cards.

Math problems in the book included questions such as "Will is saving his allowance to buy a pair of Nike shoes that cost $68.25. If Will earns $3.25 per week, how many weeks will Will need to save?" Next to the text is a full-color picture of a pair of Nikes.

Another word problem states: "The best-selling packaged cookie in the world is the Oreo cookie. The diameter of an Oreo cookie is 1.75 inches. Express the diameter of an Oreo cookie as a fraction in the simplest form."

McGraw-Hill doesn't get any money from corporations for these product placements. They justify salting the textbook with brand names as a way to make the math problems more relevant and real to students.

"This is the first time we've seen advertising in state-subsidized textbooks," said Andrew Hagelshaw, senior program director at the Center for Commercial-Free Public Education, in Oakland, California. "It crosses a line that hasn't been crossed before."[23]

Corporations and Your Health Care

In the last two decades, large corporations have taken over the health care industry in the United States. Health care is a $1 trillion–a-year industry and makes up about one-seventh of the U.S. economy. Health Maintenance Organizations (HMOs) are becoming the biggest and most profitable corporations in the country as they take control of more and more hospitals, doctors, local clinics, and patients. Megadrug companies and the manufacturers of medical equipment are the other big winners. Drug companies often get large government subsidies to research drugs, but then get exclusive patent protections lasting decades to ensure that all the publicly funded benefits flow into private pockets.[24]

The goal of these corporations is to make a profitable industry into a superprofitable industry. What does all this mean for the quality of health care? One effect is that money that could be allocated for providing health care instead funds enormous profits and excessive salaries. Health care CEOs are among the highest paid in the country. According to a *Time* magazine

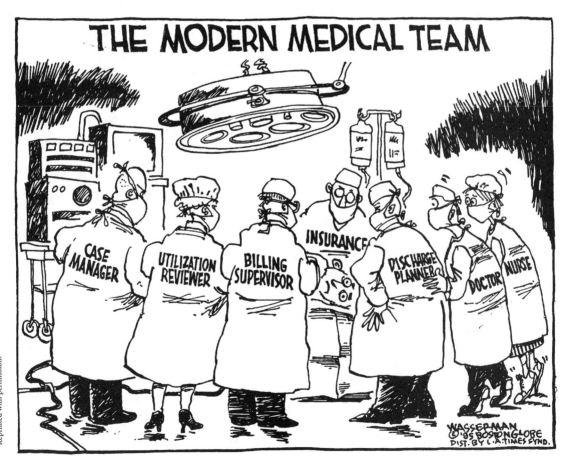

THE MODERN MEDICAL TEAM

CASE MANAGER · UTILIZATION REVIEWER · BILLING SUPERVISOR · INSURANCE · DISCHARGE PLANNER · DOCTOR · NURSE

WASSERMAN © '85 BOSTON GLOBE DIST. BY L.A. TIMES SYND.

report, U.S. Healthcare only used 75 cents of every health care premium dollar for health care in 1996; 14.5 cents went to administration, including millions for CEO Leonard Abramson; 10.5 cents went to profits.[25] In 1996, Aetna acquired U.S. Healthcare, giving CEO Abramson a "golden parachute" pay package that added up to over $1 billion, including a corporate jet with annual operating expenses of $2 million.[26]

The impact on the quality of care is clear. HMOs are squeezing dollars to make profits. During 1997, Congress passed legislation to limit "drive-through baby deliveries" as insurance companies were discharging mothers and newborns out of the hospital after one night. This dramatically increased the cases of readmission of babies with jaundice, dehydration, or infection. One Illinois obstetrician gained national media attention because he insisted that new mothers sleep in the hospital lounge so they would continue to be monitored and get nursing care after their insurance companies had "officially discharged" them.[27]

Copayments and other out-of-pocket expenses for patients continue to climb. Copayments have increased in the last fifteen years for all patients covered by virtually every health insurance plan. This has a particularly harsh impact on senior citizens, whose medical expenses are generally higher. In 1999, 19 percent of senior citizen incomes went to out-of-pocket health care costs, particularly for prescription drugs.[28] Senior citizens with low incomes spent a higher percentage of their income on health care. In 2000, senior citizens with incomes between $10,000 and $19,000 spent 21.6 percent of their income on health care. Those with incomes of $10,000 and under spent 29.2 percent on health care.[29]

The corporate takeover of health care has caused a restructuring of the workplace similar to other industries—including downsizing, subcontracting and outsourcing, work speed-ups, and mandatory overtime. This has led to increased workloads for current health providers and a push for more part-time and temporary workers who receive no benefits. Even doctors are now forming unions because of the squeeze giant corporations are putting on them. The 290,000 members of the American Medical Association voted at its June 1999 annual meeting to form a "national negotiating organization" to bargain on behalf of physicians.[30] The effect on the human bottom line in health care is the erosion of quality care for patients and increased stress on providers.

Who Gave Them This Power?

How did corporations gain the power to commit these harms in the first place? Who gave corporations the power to pollute, to influence elections, or to take away the constitutional rights of employees in the workplace? Why do we widely accept that a corporation like Union Carbide can, through negligence, kill and maim for life thousands of people in Bhopal, India, and still be allowed to exist and produce profits for their shareholders?

These questions about corporations are, fundamentally, questions about our attitudes about democracy. We need to reexamine our attitudes about corporations and our predilection to respond to their individual harms without looking at the larger questions of their power. We must rethink how we as citizens surrender our power to corporations that are supposedly subordinate legal entities. After all, we the people, the sovereign, allow these corporations to exist.

At the time of the American Revolution, corporations were granted limited charters by state governments to serve specific purposes for limited periods of time. Failure to perform their stated purposes would be considered a violation of the law and result in the revocation of their charter. Corporations were restricted from owning other corporations, and owners were personally liable for the debts and misdeeds of their corporations. Today, of course, a corporation's owners are protected by the "corporate veil" and are not held accountable or personally liable for harm caused by their companies.

Over the eighteenth century, corporations worked through the nation's legal system and legislatures to expand their rights and induce states to compete against one another to lower their standards. By the late 1800s, corporations legally gained the rights and powers of personhood. In 1886, the Supreme Court ruled in the landmark Santa Clara case that corporations should be considered natural persons entitled to the due-process rights guaranteed to all persons by the Fourteenth Amendment. In a perverse twist of law, corporations were using the antislavery provision in the constitution to expand their rights and protections. Between 1886 and 1910, federal courts, citing the Fourteenth Amendment, struck down hundreds of federal, state, and local laws enacted to protect people from the excesses of corporations. The high court ruled that governments had been taking corporate property without "due process of law."[31]

One of the personhood rights granted to corporations under this logic was the right of free speech, which gave them the power to influence elections and lobby on legislation and policy. State charters became indefinite and the actions of corporations were protected by the right to privacy, undermining the ability of the government to hold them accountable.[32] As Charles Derber writes, "For the first time, individuals were being unambiguously instructed by the Court that their own liberties were intertwined with those of corporations—and that taking away corporate rights was equivalent to challenging their own constitutionally guaranteed rights."[33]

Chapter 5 not only examines how to respond to individual corporate harms and hold corporations accountable, but also discusses how to reverse the ways in which corporations have gained the power and protections of personhood status. Reclaiming our power from corporations is key to unlocking the solution to growing economic inequality.

THE ATTACK ON WORKERS' RIGHTS

As corporate power has increased, the power of workers, communities, consumers, and others has decreased. In the 1950s, when prosperity was shared relatively more equitably, 35 percent of the U.S. workforce were represented by a labor union.

By 1983, that number had dropped to 20.1 percent. In 2003, less than 12.9 percent of the workforce was unionized[34] and fewer than one in ten workers in the private workforce were members of a union. In the last several years, more than 100,000 people have joined unions each year, but the number of new jobs in the economy grew even faster, so the percentage of workers in unions declined overall.[35] This represents a tremendous loss in clout for the institutional voice of wage workers, a voice that continually asked, "Hey, what about the workers?" whenever national economic policies were debated.

During the years after World War II, unions were a countervailing force to the power of domestic and transnational corporations. These unions enforced a "social contract," ensuring that the fruits of economic growth were shared. This sharing was not entirely equitable, as many unions excluded people of color and women from their ranks, but evidence is clear that unions raised the standard of living for most low- and moderate-income people, whether they joined unions or not.

In the last two decades, public attitudes about unions have grown more negative. Some corporations have mounted sustained propaganda battles to tarnish unions and "union bosses." Unions haven't helped their cause by sometimes failing to invest in organizing new members or failing to be accountable to their rank and file. Stories about corrupt unions seem to make a more lasting impression than stories about corrupt corporations. Yet people who haven't considered unions relevant to the modern economy are now rethinking the essential role unions can play in protecting the interests of workers and their communities.

The Teamsters' successful strike at United Parcel Service during the summer of 1997 received overwhelming public support because of its focus on part-time workers. The Teamsters' slogan "Part-time America Won't Work" resonated because the public understood that companies like UPS, which made $1 billion in profits in the year before the strike, were profiting by replacing full-time workers with full benefits with temporary and part-time workers at much lower wages and no benefits.

In 2003, Safeway and other California grocery companies led a push to demand deep cuts in workers' health care coverage as well as low wages for new hires. These grocers, whose 2003 profits were 91 percent higher than in 1999 and whose health care contributions are far below the national average, claim they must slash health care benefits in order to compete with nonunion, low-wage Wal-Mart, which plans to open forty superstores over the next four years in California. But United Food and Commercial Workers have led a strike and other workplace actions to defend basic health care coverage.[36]

Unions today make tremendous improvements in the lives of workers and protect entire communities from irresponsible employers who, in the new global economy, have no loyalty to nation-states, let alone to communities and employees. In Chapter 1, we discussed many of the trends facing lower- and middle-income individuals and families, including declining wages, longer work hours, insufficient health

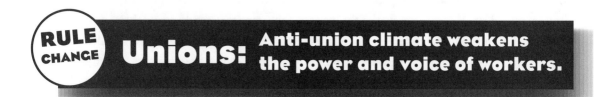

RULE CHANGE

Unions: Anti-union climate weakens the power and voice of workers.

Percentage of the workforce represented by a labor union, 1930–2003

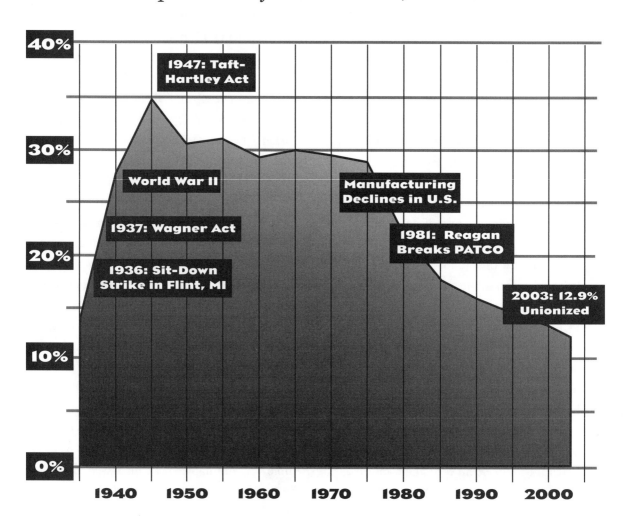

1947: Taft-Hartley Act

World War II

1937: Wagner Act

1936: Sit-Down Strike in Flint, MI

Manufacturing Declines in U.S.

1981: Reagan Breaks PATCO

2003: 12.9% Unionized

Source: Bureau of Labor Statistics.

insurance, increased education and child-care costs, declining retirement security, and other forms of economic insecurity. While people in unions face insecurities brought on by the restructuring and globalization of the economy, they have much greater protection than nonunionized workers. Their wages are higher. Workers who join unions earn an average of 26 percent more than workers who don't. Joining a union raises earnings by 31 percent for working women, 29 percent for black workers, and 53 percent for Latino workers.[37]

Unionized workers also have much better benefits than nonunionized workers. Eighty-four percent of union members receive health benefits on the job, compared to only 62 percent of nonunion workers.[38] Seventy-two percent of union members are covered by guaranteed (defined-benefit) pensions, compared with only 44 percent of nonunion workers.[39] Union members have more secure jobs and make longer commitments to employers. Six in ten union members have been with the same employer for ten years or more, compared with three in ten nonunion workers.[40]

There are a number of theories about why there has been a decline in union power in the United States. Some argue that the decline is the result of our shift from a manufacturing to a service economy. Still others say public policies made union organizing difficult. Others point to the internal failure of unions to invest in organizing more workers rather than servicing their existing memberships. Technological change is another explanation. But Canada and most European countries, while also experiencing techno-

logical changes, maintained high rates of unionization. In Sweden, 82 percent of all workers are represented by unions. In Germany, about 40 percent of all workers are union members, while 90 percent are covered by collectively bargained agreements.[41] Worker representation on governing boards in both Germany and Sweden has allowed workers to participate in planning and control of technological change.

From our perspective, the primary explanation for declining unionization lies with the legal barriers to organizing unions in the United States. Canadian workers, who have stronger

legal protections, have more effective unions.[42] Many obstacles exist in the United States for people wanting to organize a union. Corporations are hiring sophisticated union-busting law firms, intimidating workers who want to organize and using the bureaucratic maze of the National Labor Relations Board to stall organizing drives. In case after case, workers who dare to lead workplace organizing drives are illegally fired, only to be reinstated three years later when the wind has gone out of an organizing effort.[43]

Most industrialized countries, including Japan and European nations, would not tolerate the employer practices that occur every day in the United States. The process of union recognition in these other nations is virtually automatic and voluntary, much the same as the formation of a voluntary association. Meanwhile, the process in the United States is complex and bureaucratic. Workers wishing to organize a union must play by a long list of rules that give employers not only control over who is eligible to join a union and the timing of elections, but also the time to wage an antiunion campaign.

An estimated 50 million people in the United States would like to join a union but are afraid to do so. When workers consider joining a union, businesses fight back with aggressive tactics.[44]

So You Want to Join a Union?

$ Seventy-five percent of companies hire a consultant to stop employees from forming a union. Employers spend an estimated $300 million a year employing such consultants, not including litigation and legal expenses used to fight or delay a unionization effort.

$ Ninety-two percent of companies force employees to attend antiunion information meetings, 77 percent distribute antiunion leaflets, and 58 percent show antiunion videos.

$ Twenty-five percent of employers illegally fire at least one activist during a union campaign.

$ Fifty-one percent of companies threaten to close the office or plant when people try to unionize.

$ In one-third of cases where workers vote for a union, employers never agree to a first contract.[45]

AVONDALE SHIPYARDS. What can workers do when a company resists their desire to form a union? Under existing U.S. labor law, not much. Avondale Shipyards was one of the nation's largest defense contractors and the largest private employer in Louisiana. Since 1993, Avondale has received over $3.1 billion in contracts from the U.S. Navy. The company has a history of serious employee health and safety problems, resulting in a death rate over three times higher than any other shipyard with major navy contracts. These conditions and substandard wages prompted the 4,000 Avondale workers to vote for a union in 1993. The company, however, refused to recognize the union and used endless appeals and illegal tactics to deny them the right to negotiate a contract. Union supporters faced threats and firings, and the company was charged with over 400 labor law violations. Clearly, Avondale's dependence on taxpayer-funded contracts has not lessened the company's hostility to union efforts to gain recognition.

One main issue of contention for Avondale employees has been the company's failure to cooperate with the Occupational Safety and Health Administration (OSHA). In January 1998, federal courts ordered Avondale to turn over thirteen different kinds of records pertaining to health and safety issues. "Workers are getting hurt and killed at that yard at an alarming rate, and it's been Avondale's dirty little secret for too long," said Jim Evans of the Justice for Avondale campaign. "It's astonishing that it took a court case for Avondale to stop hiding its safety records."[46]

In 1999, six years after workers voted to establish a union, Litton Industries purchased the shipyard and agreed to recognize the union. Subsequently, the Northrop Grumman Corporation purchased Litton Industries, including the shipyard. In a July 2001 ruling, the National Labor Relations Board found Avondale guilty of an additional 141 federal labor law violations. The judge required Avondale to rehire, with back pay, twenty-two workers who were illegally fired for union activities, and restore lost wages to more than two dozen other workers who were suspended illegally. Avondale was also required to reimburse the U.S. Navy for $5.4 million in legal fees it billed them to pay for antiunion law firms.[47]

But Avondale is a stunning example of how the wheels of labor law justice turn slowly. Eight years later, where are the workers who were fired for wanting to join a union? How many other injuries could have been prevented? What about the lost livelihoods of other workers and local businesses affected by aggressive antiunion practices? Under existing labor laws, unfortunately, there will continue to be many more Avondales.

Avondale is a particularly bad actor, breaking the law to avoid unionization. But its behavior is reinforced by the structural and legal barriers that workers face attempting to organize and the ways in which the National Labor Relations Board allows companies like Avondale to lawyer a union-organizing drive to death. Avondale is one of thousands of examples of companies that refuse to recognize unions, even though a majority of workers have voted in a supervised election to have union representation. This simply wouldn't happen in any other industrialized country, where mutual recognition is the accepted custom of the land. Protecting the right to organize a union is central in rebuilding the power of workers and creating a countervailing power to organized corporations.

DECLINE IN THE INFLUENCE OF THE CIVIC SECTOR

Our democracy depends on the ability of people to participate in the institutions and decisions that govern their lives. In addition to formal participation through voting, people also take part in what social scientists call "civil society," the part of society that is neither in the private for-profit market nor the government. A strong civil society depends on a dynamic fabric of voluntary organizations, including political clubs, fraternal organizations, women's organizations, religious congregations, mutual-aid associations, cooperatives, and nonprofit community development organizations.

In addition to the decline in union power, there has also been a decline in the vitality of other community institutions that defend the interests of workers and communities against the unbridled power of private capital. As we have seen, when people work longer hours they have less time for caregiving in their families and communities. They also have less time to participate in the civic organizations that not only enrich their lives but protect their interests.

In the last two decades, civic institutions have become weaker, for reasons that are widely debated, ranging from overwork to the influence of television.[48] The result is that many communities are "disorganized," lacking the basic community institutions and infrastructure to support a vital civic life. Many disinvested urban neighborhoods have lost the ethnic fraternal and political clubs and stable religious congregations that existed as recently as a generation ago. Many new suburban commuter communities never had them to start with.

Community organizer Ernesto Cortes posits that there are two kinds of power: the power of organized people and the power of organized money. When communities are disorganized and fragmented, they lack the power to protect and advance their interests. The power vacuum is filled with the power of "organized money," whose interests include privatizing public institutions, commercializing the private and sacred spheres, and promoting consumption as the purpose of human existence. In recent decades, the power of organized money has come to dominate our lives and fuel economic inequality.

As organized money gains the upper hand, it feeds a "wheel of misfortune" (see graphic on page 85). The breakdown of organized community leads to a decline in civic and political participation. The political center of gravity shifts to a "corporate power elite" advocating for public policies and rule changes that advance their narrow economic interests. As a result, inequality grows. This further fragments and disorganizes communities, and as people work longer hours, they have even less time to participate in civic life and to build "organized people power." As

THE WHEEL OF MISFORTUNE

Power shifts to corpora-tions & big investors

Decline in political participation

- Scapegoating
- Divided communities
- Individualism
- Escapism

Rule changes that favor the top 1%

- Big money in politics
- Longer work hours
- Rising personal debt

Greater economic inequality

inequality grows, so does the insecurity that leads to increased scapegoating and division within communities. The cycle continues. As there is less mutuality and community, as people both see and depend on their neighbors less and less, they gradually withdraw from the public sphere, believing their survival depends only on their individual action and effort.

The civic sphere is not without hope. Americans have a resilient tradition of civic action and grassroots organizations. Organized people come together through grassroots environmental justice organizations, neighborhood block associations, self-help associations, children's play groups, and interfaith organizations. Reorganizing a community, in the words of Father Leo J. Penta, a priest who works with a congregation-based organizing project in East Brooklyn, is the process of "weaving a network of new or renewed relationships" among unorganized peoples. The process begins with "the wounded and struggling institutions which mediate relationships: families, congregations, churches, workers' organizations, civic and cultural associations."[49] Rebuilding civic institutions to wield people power is another key to reducing economic inequality.

DECLINE IN INDEPENDENT POLITICS

The decline of independent politics and all political parties is another example of the weakening of an institution that used to mediate between the interests of ordinary people and their elected leaders.[50] Historically, the urban political machines, ward committees, and their equivalents across the country were racially exclusionary and corrupt. But they gave rise to a generation of political leaders accountable to some working-class people and urban communities, not just financiers.

Their decline has contributed to a "hollowing out" of democracy. William Greider, author of many books on American politics and democracy, writes in *Who Will Tell the People: The Betrayal of American Democracy*:

> For all their flaws, the parties once provided a viable connection for citizens, even quite humble citizens, to the upper realms of politics. People who would never be present themselves in the debate, who lacked the resources or the sophistication to participate directly, had a place to go—a permanent organization where their views would be taken into account and perhaps mobilized to influence the government.[51]

Political parties and clubs incubated and tested candidates and ideas, educated and mobilized the electorate, and held elected officials accountable to a base of organized, largely white voters with the power to withdraw their support if a candidate broke his or her promises.

As the two major political parties erode into nothing more than donor lists, they become beholden to the moneyed class. They depend on the power of organized money rather than the power of organized people. Neither Democrats nor Republicans have the people-power networks of previous generations that reached down to local poll-workers and precinct captains to mobilize voters. Instead, they have bank accounts, pollsters, spin-doctors, and television "ad buys." The only difference now between the two parties at the national level is that the Republicans always do what corporations want while the Democrats *almost* always do what corporations want. In the words of Texas populist Jim Hightower: "We don't need a third party in the U.S.—we need a second party."

Public debate shaped by organized money and the concentrated corporate ownership of the media has become extremely narrow. A whole universe of important issues and concerns are rarely on the radar screen: child-care policy, rising trade deficits, declining free time, the percentage of people without health insurance, and many other economic security and quality-of-life issues facing most Americans.

With the voices of workers, consumers, community members, and environmentalists shut out of important debates about the economic priorities of our nation, the "mainstream" economic agenda becomes the agenda of big corporations and large owners of capital. This agenda includes cutting capital gains taxes, privatization of public services, deregulating corporations, loosening environmental restrictions, and opening up international markets for trade with no consideration for human rights or environmental standards. Unfortunately, these narrow concerns squelch other voices and needs in our society.

The Rules Governing the Economy

Markets are obviously very important in the economy, but they are surrounded by a lot of rules—rules about how easy it is to organize unions and how free trade is—and those rules are determined by the political process and those rules right now are shaped by money.
—FRANK LEVY, *THE NEW DOLLARS AND DREAMS*

Inequality has grown because the rules that govern our economy have been changed to benefit corporations and the large owners of wealth to the detriment of people who depend on work for a living or on a social safety net. In the words of *BusinessWeek* reporters William Wolman and Anne Colamosca, there has been a "triumph of capital and a betrayal of work."[52] The winners are those who own substantial assets—much more than just a home, a car, and some savings. The losers are people whose security is linked to a paycheck or who rely on a government check like Social Security.

In this section, we will examine the patchwork

of rules that have fueled the growth of income and wealth inequality and jeopardized the security of most working people in this country. These include rules regarding taxation, global trade and investment policy, federal monetary policy, governmental regulation, and spending. A detailed discussion of how to address these rule changes will come in Chapter 5.

Types of Rule Changes That Have Worsened Inequality

$ **Global trade and investment practices**

$ **Taxation**

$ **The restructuring of work and the breakdown of the social contract**

$ **Regulation and deregulation**

$ **Federal Reserve and monetary policies**

$ **Government spending and the safety net**

$ **Corporate welfare**

GLOBAL TRADE AND INVESTMENT POLICY

Global trade and investment policies increasingly contribute to economic inequality in the United States and abroad, as the rules of the new global economy are written to serve the interests of investors and transnational corporations. This section will briefly discuss how this type of globalization contributes to economic inequality in the United States and how it threatens democracy, the environment, and global fairness.

A great deal of attention has been paid recently to globalization and what it means for the United States. For our purposes, globalization refers to the corporate-driven internationalization of the economy through "liberalized" or "free" trade in goods and services and the removal of barriers to the flow of capital. It refers to the system of rules and global financial institutions set up after World War II to expand "free market capitalism" around the planet. The institutions central to this expansion were the World Bank (to stimulate production), the International Monetary Fund (to oversee finance), and the General Agreement on Tariffs and Trade (to reduce barriers to trade). Unfortunately, by the early 1980s, the agenda of these institutions had been further twisted by corporations and banks to promote "neoliberalism," a system of beliefs that virtually all government intervention in the economy is bad and that unfettered or free markets are good.

Global trade is centuries old. Since the 1600s there have been different forms of global capitalism. Well before the formation of the United States, there was a trade triangle among Europe, Africa, and the Western hemisphere that dealt mainly in rum, sugar, and enslaved humans. What's new is that technology has made it possible to accelerate the pace of global capital investment and the movement of raw materials, manufacturing capacity, and consumer goods. In

1980, over $296 billion a day (in 1999 dollars) circulated around the planet through the Clearing House Interbank Payments System (CHIPS), the single largest processor of U.S. dollar transactions. By 2004, the amount of funds transferred through the CHIPS system quadrupled to $1.3 trillion a day.[53] This is five times the amount that national central banks have on hand. What's also new is the relative size and power of transnational corporations and their influence on an infrastructure of institutions designed to facilitate and regulate global trade and investment. We

should also be concerned about globalization and its link to U.S. inequality out of concern for economic security, environmental protection, democracy, and global justice.

ECONOMIC SECURITY. Global trade and investment policies, as they are currently written and practiced, undermine the wage, workplace safety, environmental, and other standards that people in our country and elsewhere have fought so hard for. They undermine the economic security of people in this country by encouraging a "race to the bottom," pitting U.S. workers and communities against workers and communities around the world in competition to lower their labor and environmental standards to attract global investment.

DEMOCRACY. The current rules and institutions governing the global economy undermine democracy and erode people's power to determine their own standards and destiny at the local level. These super global institutions, like the World Trade Organization (which replaced GATT in 1995), largely serve the interests of transnational corporations. They are writing new rules that supersede laws and protections forged at the local and national level. They are not democratically elected or accountable.

ENVIRONMENT. The policies of globalization that favor economic interests in isolation and without regard to environmental interests have brought us to a real crisis in our natural world. The destruction and contamination of water, forests, soil, air, and biodiversity have been well documented, as have the climate changes brought on by global warming. The globalization of the world's economy and the adoption of a worldwide unsustainable consumption model, coupled with the absence and uneven application of worldwide standards, has led to threats to our atmosphere and oceans.

GLOBAL JUSTICE. The tremendous debt burdens placed on our brothers and sisters in the global south—Asia, Africa, and Latin America—have caused massive suffering. Instead of developing their nations by reinvesting in their own economies and societies, these countries have been paying interest to northern banks and multilateral lending institutions like the International Monetary Fund. The last thirty years have been "lost decades" in the global south as literacy rates have dropped, disease and infant mortality rates have risen, infrastructure has crumbled, and the quality of life has deteriorated.

THE RACE TO THE BOTTOM. For centuries, governments around the world concerned about protecting national interests and industries have erected barriers against free trade. For generations, the United States imposed tariffs on imports of textiles, steel, and agricultural products to protect their domestic industries and their workers from global competition. Nations also develop their own environmental, labor, and commercial standards. Part of the new global trade regime is to "harmonize" these standards downward by adopting uniform standards above which countries can't go.

The problem with removing barriers to trade with countries like Mexico, China, and Malaysia is that these countries have weaker health and safety laws, lower wages for workers, and lax environmental standards. U.S. workers cannot and should not compete against workers in countries like China, where wages are very low, reports of forced prison labor abound, and workers are not allowed to form unions. Nor should U.S. workers compete with countries with high rates of child labor. Corporations operating in Kenya and Nepal benefit from the fact that over 40 percent of children between the ages of 10 and 14 in those nations are full-time workers.[54] This places strong pressure on workers in the United States, where there are strong restrictions against child labor (although violations of labor laws are growing in the U.S. apparel and agricultural sectors).

Free trade agreements as they are currently written create a climate in the United States where employers are more emboldened to threaten to move plants overseas to extract wage concessions or discourage unionization efforts. A study of 500 union-organizing drives after the North American Free Trade Agreement (NAFTA) was signed found that over 50 percent of employers made threats to close all or parts of plants if a union was elected. The figure was 62 percent in mobile industries such as manufacturing, transportation, and warehouse distribution. Some companies intimidated workers by placing shipping labels on equipment in the workplace with a Mexican address or posting maps of North America with an arrow pointing from the current plant site to Mexico.[55]

Global trade agreements could be written to stop the race to the bottom by establishing a uniformly decent floor for labor rights, wages, and environmental standards. However, the global standards and rules currently being written tend to lower the bar rather than raise it. Environmental activists in many communities around the planet have worked hard to protect the natural environment and pass stricter environmental laws prohibiting the dumping of toxic wastes and the fouling of the air, land, and water. In the

past, manufacturing companies could "externalize" the pollution costs of production by dumping waste in a stream and letting society live with the degraded environment or foot the bill for cleaning it up. But thanks to stricter rules, companies in some countries often have to bear the real costs of production.

In order to avoid these costs and to increase profits, companies have moved thousands of manufacturing operations to countries with lower environmental standards, no unions, or lax enforcement of existing environmental and labor laws. For plants remaining in the United States, companies often use the threat of moving to prevent communities from imposing stricter environmental regulations. When international treaties codify low environmental standards, this puts tremendous pressure on U.S. communities to lower their standards.

Race-to-the-bottom competition has meant that the United States imports more products from countries with reduced production costs and lower environmental and labor standards. The American consumer market is flush with inexpensive consumer goods manufactured in low-standard nations in Asia and Latin America. Meanwhile, domestic manufacturing firms, bound by higher standards, find it increasingly hard to compete. This swells our national trade deficit, the difference between what we, as a nation, import (buy) and what we export (sell). In 2003, the annual trade deficit was a record-breaking $489.4 billion. This is 280 percent higher than the record-breaking trade deficit in 1998 of $170 billion.[56]

The solution is to raise global standards by

expanding the right to organize, establishing a bottom-line core set of labor standards, eliminating child labor, and raising human rights and environmental standards. Instead of being pitted against one another, workers, consumers, and communities should be allied in raising standards and improving the quality of life for everyone on the planet. This is the opposite of a race to the bottom. (These action strategies are discussed further in Chapter 5.)

UNFAIR TRADE AND INVESTMENT AGREE-MENTS. Global trade and investment agreements are the primary mechanisms through which U.S. workers are forced to compete in the race to the bottom.[57] In the last fifteen years, free-trade and investment agreements such as NAFTA and the expansion of GATT into a World Trade Organization (WTO) have reflected the biased and narrow interests of the worldwide governing corporate elite.

These agreements spell out in careful terms the rights for global corporations and investment capital—while remaining shockingly silent on the concerns of workers, communities, and the environment. The WTO, for instance, has intricate legal protections for "intellectual property rights," which are the rights of ownership related to patents, inventions, research, and artistic materials. WTO rules carefully spell out how a corporation like AOL/Time Warner could sue the government of India if they allow an "underground market" in compact discs by Michael Jackson. Yet the WTO says virtually nothing about human rights, conditions for

workers, the right to organize labor unions, minimum wage standards, worker safety conditions, or protections for the environment.

Because of agreements like NAFTA and the WTO, owners of capital can quickly move their investments and operations offshore with minimal constraints. Meanwhile, U.S. workers have little bargaining power against countries that allow slave labor, outlaw unions, or have minimal environmental standards. Despite promises of job growth, the U.S. Department of Labor certified that, between 1994 and the end of 2002, 525,094 workers lost their jobs directly as a result of NAFTA.[58] And this number includes only those who qualified for NAFTA Transitional Adjustment Assistance (NAFTA-TAA), special job-training benefits for production workers who lose their jobs because their employer shifts production to Canada or Mexico. In actuality, these job losses are just a small fraction of the total number of jobs lost under NAFTA. In fact, Robert Scott of the Economic Policy Institute argues that between 1993 and 2003, 879,280 jobs were lost due to NAFTA.[59] Service workers are ineligible for NAFTA-TAA, and many eligible workers do not even apply for the program because they do not know it exists or choose to seek other forms of assistance. Proponents of NAFTA claim that over 200,000 jobs have been created by the agreement, yet they are unable to produce evidence. A survey of companies that pledged to expand jobs after the passage of NAFTA found that 89 percent admitted that they had failed to do so. Many had relocated jobs to Mexico.[60]

MOCKING DEMOCRACY. Recent global trade and investment treaties have created governing bodies that float above the democratic institutions of nation-states while setting the rules for how the global economy will work. For example, the WTO is working to set uniform standards and shared regulatory systems across borders in an effort to remove barriers to free trade. As a result, the rules of dozens of individual nations on such vital issues as auto emissions and food safety standards are viewed as impediments to open markets.

WTO officials, elected by no one, meet behind closed doors and create rules that can supersede the laws of local jurisdictions. "The Geneva negotiators do not have to adhere to many of the rules requiring openness to the public and interest groups that govern similar proceedings in the United States," observed Jeff Gerth in the *New York Times*. Former U.S. Trade Representative Mickey Kantor remarked: "This is about sovereignty, multinational corporations, the new post–Cold War world, global standards, and international harmonization. These are important issues. But it is like they are being dealt with in a closet somewhere and no one's watching."[61]

Reprinted with permission.

Because there is no democratic accountability, large transnational corporations have constant and ample access to influence the agenda of the WTO while community, labor, environmental, and consumer groups have limited access. For instance, the WTO committee charged with developing automobile standards for the planet had sixty-two government regulators, twenty-six industry representatives, and two consumer representatives. Needless to say, the forthcoming global auto-safety regulations will put the interests of industry before those of the environment or consumers.

With corporations in the driver's seat, the new rules governing the global economy are leading a race to the bottom in global environmental, labor, and safety standards. When a country like the United States tries to maintain higher standards and regulations, these rules are subject to legal challenge before international panels because they represent a barrier to imports and trade.

New treaties are being proposed to extend NAFTA-style free trade to other parts of the planet including Africa, other Latin American countries, and Asia. The Central America Free Trade Agreement (CAFTA), if it is approved by Congress, will include most Central American countries and several Caribbean nations in a new free-trade regime.

In the late 1990s, the Organization for Economic Cooperation and Development, the association of the twenty-nine wealthiest countries in the world, proposed a new treaty, the Multilateral Agreement on Investment (MAI), to take global corporate dominance to new heights. The MAI would enable corporations to sue local government jurisdictions directly over restraints in trade, bypassing sovereign governments and elected bodies. The city of Peoria, for instance, might have a living-wage ordinance or a law requiring businesses receiving city subsidies to hire local workers or use locally produced materials. Under the terms of the MAI, however, such laws would be considered a restraint on trade. A foreign corporation denied access to local markets could sue the city of Peoria in the WTO, seeking monetary damages or changes in their laws.

Thanks to grassroots activists from around the world, especially those from Canada, the MAI treaty was posted on the Internet and came under enormous attack. Opponents sought to expose the provisions of the MAI, pointing out that though none of the representatives of these trade bodies have been elected by citizens in any country, their agreements will have worldwide impact on local communities everywhere if adopted.[62] MAI treaty negotiations at the Organization for Economic Cooperation and Development have temporarily come to a stop. But we must be vigilant. The components of the MAI are the long-sought aims of transnational corporations, which will not easily be discouraged. They will resurface in other trade and investment treaties, including the "millennium round" being negotiated through the WTO.

Trade negotiators at the World Trade Organization and in other multilateral bodies thrive on secrecy. Their worst nightmare, observes one trade commentator, is that citizen organizations around the world, an "NGO specter"—referring to non-government organizations—will start to hold them accountable. As journalist Reginald Dale observed, this is an "uncomfortable new reality for the exclusive club of high-powered negotiators used to settling the future of the world trading system in inaccessible conference chambers, or the backrooms of fine restaurants, in Geneva."[63]

NAFTA Forces a Canadian Environmental Retreat

Canada maintains tougher environmental standards than the United States, but NAFTA is gradually chipping away at the differences. In 1997 the government of Prime Minister Jean Chretien introduced legislation in the Canadian parliament to ban methlycyclopentadienyl manganes tricarbonyl (MMT), because it is suspected of causing nerve damage. In response, the manufacturer of MMT, the U.S.–based Ethyl Corporation, sued the Canadian government for $250 million for violating NAFTA provisions guaranteeing free trade. In July 1998, the Canadian government lifted the ban and agreed to pay the Ethyl Corporation $13 million in compensation for legal costs and lost sales.[64]

This was a dramatic reversal of policy. Canadian environmental activists were appalled, pointing to the Canadian government's cave-in as evidence that Canada will not be able to maintain its sovereignty around environmental regulations. "It is outrageous that a U.S.–based multinational has more weight with the Chretien government than our Parliament, public health and our own environment," said Elizabeth May, director of the Sierra Club–Canada.[65]

These conditions of the new global capitalism can make citizens feel hopeless about the prospects for change and powerless to make a difference. After all, we are up against powerful transnational corporations with deep pockets. The good news is that across the planet, people's movements are in motion to counter the new rules of the neoliberal global order.

Since 1997, labor and community organizations in the United States have mobilized to slow the granting of "fast track" authority to Presidents Bill Clinton and George W. Bush. With fast track, a president could put a treaty before Congress for an up or down vote with no possibility for amendment, as was the case with NAFTA and the WTO. Stopping fast track was a significant victory for those who want to put the brakes on the pace of global trade agreements. A form of fast track was reinstated in 2002, but the prospects for future trade agreements have changed since the Seattle WTO meeting.

Activists from around the world converged on Seattle for the first round of new WTO trade talks at the end of November 1999. Twelve thousand religious activists linked hands and formed a human chain to call on northern nations to cancel the international debt. Over 50,000 labor and environmental activists marched in protest of WTO policies, pressing for adoption of higher labor and environmental standards. And thousands of people engaged in nonviolent direct action to surround the Seattle Convention Center and delay the beginning ceremony of the WTO meeting.

Most media attention from Seattle focused on a small band of self-proclaimed anarchists who broke windows, and on the police's decision to use tear gas and rubber bullets on demonstrators. But the long-term impact of the "Battle of Seattle" is that the global trade and investment debate will never be the same in the United States. The concerns of farmers, workers, environmentalists, and food safety activists will no longer be left off the table.

Transnational corporations are still the dominant voice in many of the new global trade treaties and institutions managing the global economy. The biased rules they write only worsen the growing economic divide in the United States and abroad. In Chapter 5 we will examine strategies for stopping future unfair trade and investment agreements, expanding democracy in the global economy, and increasing economic justice in the southern half of the world.

TAXATION

Tax policy is one of the areas in which we can easily understand how the rules have been tilted in favor of asset-owners, corporations, and the wealthy, against the interests of wage earners, small businesses, and working families.

With the negative image taxes now have, it may be surprising to learn that the income tax and the estate tax were initially the result of a nationwide, popular movement to amend the constitution. Populists in the 1880s advocated for an inheritance tax and a progressive income tax system—not just to raise revenue for public services, but to break up overconcentrations of wealth and power that were threatening to a truly democratic, self-governing society. Given the grotesque inequalities that exist as we enter the twenty-first century, we need tax policies that prevent inequities from worsening and ensure equality of opportunity.

The first income tax, levied after the Sixteenth Amendment was ratified in 1913, was extremely progressive and taxed only the richest 5 percent of households.[66] Subsequent tax "reforms" have steadily broadened the tax base to include lower- and middle-income households. Starting during World War II, taxes have increasingly been levied on a majority of the population. The Victory Tax of 1942 expanded taxation to low-income households to cover the costs of war. In 1942, composer Irving Berlin wrote a patriotic song called "I Paid My Income Tax Today" to mark the unprecedented tax collections on workers. One verse went: "You see those bombers in the sky, Rockefeller helped to build them, so did I." After the war, the Victory Tax was not repealed and federal income taxes continued to be assessed on low- and middle-income working households.

The top tax rate paid by the richest taxpayers in the years following World War II was extremely progressive, reaching a 91 percent rate in 1954 on household income that exceeded $400,000. However, the effective rate, the rate at which the rich actually paid taxes, was lower thanks to myriad loopholes that chipped away at progressivity in the 1950s and 1960s. Automaker Henry Ford used to say that if he had to pay any taxes, he would fire his accountant because they obviously had not been working hard enough to find all the loopholes he could use.

In the last two decades, the U.S. tax system has become a two-tier, two-class tax system. Investiga-tive journalists Donald L. Barlett and James B. Steele argue that there is one system for the wealthy, what they call "the Privileged Person's Tax Law," and another for everyone else, the "Common Person's Tax Law." When Congress pushes for progressive tax changes that ask the wealthy to pay more, it is labeled "class warfare." However, when the tax burden is shifted onto middle-class and poor people, it is packaged as "tax reform." In their analysis, when corporate-funded politicians start talking about tax reform, working people better hold onto their purses and wallets.[67]

Never before in U.S. history has our government passed tax cuts for the wealthy during a time of war.
The inequality of sacrifice is unprecedented.

The pace of tax cutting has picked up in recent years. Each year between 2001 and 2004, Congress passed a federal tax cut. These tax cuts have not been "cuts" for everyone. While the lion's share of the tax breaks have gone to the richest 1 percent of taxpayers, most taxpayers are experiencing a tax *shift* in the form of fee increases for services, property-tax hikes, and cuts in local services. These tax cuts have fueled massive deficits and blocked possibilities for spending on human needs. These tax cuts have "trickled down" to worsen state and local budget deficits, forcing deep and immoral cuts in social spending on poverty, health care, and education.

What Do I Get for My Tax Dollars?

Many of us feel ambivalent about taxation and government, particularly at the federal level, where it has been hijacked by militarists and large corporations. But our federal tax dollars have also advanced social justice, created economic opportunity, and reduced economic inequalities. Consider student loans, low-income housing assistance, Title IX funding that has opened up sports to girls, fair housing and employment laws, the post–World War II GI Bill for education, environmental protections, and national parks.

Over the last century, successful social movements have pressured the government (which belongs to all of us) and engaged political leaders to create Social Security, almost abolishing elderly poverty. These movements are pushing for greater federal involvement to end child poverty, widen access to education, create affordable housing, establish universal health care, and legislate basic worker rights.

THE RIGHT-WING ANTI-TAX MOVEMENT

How did we get to a situation in which raising taxes is the ultimate political sin? Why are state tax systems allowed to remain so regressive, with undue burdens on low-income taxpayers? Part of the explanation is that there is a well-funded anti-tax, limited-government movement that includes national organizations such as Americans for Tax Reform and Citizens for a Sound Economy. It includes a network of state and local limited government policy and grassroots groups, which have a long-term strategy and program.[68]

Over several decades, this movement has succeeded in changing the terms of the debate and political climate on state and federal fiscal issues. As a result, most state legislators are afraid to raise taxes to face their budget deficits. Nor will the federal government provide meaningful aid to the states to enable them to overcome the budget shortfalls. And according to some of the architects of the right-wing "shrink government" program, the state budget crisis is right on schedule. Their agenda could be characterized as "shrink, shift, and shaft."

SHRINK. Right-wing politicians have long had a goal of greatly shrinking or limiting government, essentially rolling back central elements of the New Deal and Great Society reforms, such as college loans, home-ownership programs, public health insurance and pension programs, and programs that help the poor. Budget deficits force budget cuts and thwart new spending initiatives. Underlying this program is a vision about the role of government that is deeply out of step with the needs and desires of a majority of Americans. How else can we explain the rationale for further federal tax cuts while our annual deficit exceeds $400 billion?

In truth, they don't want to shrink all parts of government. These tax cutters want to dismantle the "Opportunity State," the government programs that foster social justice and broaden wealth and opportunity for all Americans. They also aim to weaken the elements of government that regulate corporations to protect workers, the environment, and community interests.

Their vision of limited government could be characterized as a "Watchtower State"—with our tax dollars paying only for military, police, fire, and property-rights protection.

SHIFT. Central to the right-wing tax and budget program is shifting tax responsibility and dismantling the progressive tax system. For three decades, the basic thrust of this agenda has been to cut taxes on wealth and capital gains—and shift the burden of paying for government onto wage and consumption taxes. Hence the focus on tax cuts that primarily benefit the rich, such as repealing the federal estate tax and cutting dividend and capital gains taxes.

A second shift is to move tax and spending from federal government to states and towns. Local tax systems, as we'll discuss below, are much more regressive because of their dependence on broad-based consumption taxes. The irony of this was dramatized in 2003 when some parents received checks from the IRS for the expanded Child Tax Credit. But as some families got a $400 check per child, they simultaneously witnessed their local services deteriorate, while local and state fees, sales taxes, and property taxes were increased to make up for the federal tax cuts.

Shifting Burden

In the last thirty years, the tax burden has been transferred from:

$ **large corporations to individuals.**

$ **the wealthy owners of assets to low- and middle- income wage earners.**

$ **foreign corporations to domestic corporations.**

$ **foreign investors to U.S. workers.**

$ **multinational corporations to medium-sized and small businesses.**

$ **the federal government to state and local governments whose taxes are the most regressive.**

$ **today's taxpayers to the next generation of taxpayers.[69]**

The *Shaft* part of the program comes in the form of budget cuts and shifts eroding the quality of life for working people. But these tax cutters are counting on the American public not to connect the dots between local service cuts and federal budget policies.

We can now look forward to a "permanent tax cut offensive," with a long list of additional tax cuts on the agenda for years to come, including new corporate giveaways and tax-free savings accounts. "You'll have a tax cut each year," said Grover Norquist of the Americans for Tax Reform, one of the architects of the "shrink, shift, and shaft strategy. "Our goal is to shrink government to the size where we can drown it in a bathtub."

CORPORATE TAXES. Since the 1950s, corporations have paid a smaller and smaller share of overall federal tax revenue. After World War II, corporate taxes accounted for 28 percent of federal revenue. By 2003, their share had fallen to 7.4 percent.[70] In fact, 60 percent of large U.S. corporations avoided paying any taxes in at least one year between 1996 and 2000.[71] While corporate tax rates have remained constant on paper, the expansion of corporate welfare—loopholes and special exemptions—has dramatically chipped away at their real tax bill.[72] As corporate taxes slipped, the burden shifted onto the individual taxpayer. After World War II, individual taxpayers paid about 43 percent of the total Federal tax pie; by 2003, they paid almost 90 percent.

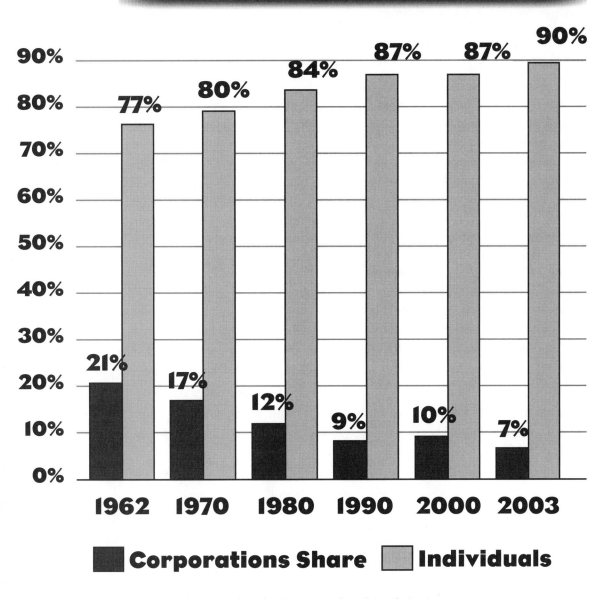

PERCENT OF FEDERAL TAX COLLECTIONS FROM INDIVIDUALS AND CORPORATIONS

RULE CHANGE

Corporations Share   **Individuals**

Source: Barlett and Steele, *America: Who Really Pays the Taxes?*, 140.

Big Business: Avoiding Corporate Taxes

Under the federal tax code, corporations are required to pay 35 percent of their profits in income taxes. But a 2004 analysis of 275 large corporations by the Institute of Taxation and Economic Policy found some startling facts:

$ **The average effective rate these companies paid was 18.4 percent.**

$ **Eighty-two of the 275 companies paid zero federal income taxes in at least one year between 2001 to 2003. During this period, these same 82 companies earned $102 billion in pre-tax profits.**

$ **Twenty-eight companies enjoyed negative federal income taxes over the entire 2001–2003 period, generating so many excess tax breaks that in some cases they got outright rebate checks.**

$ **General Electric led the list in receiving corporate tax breaks, with $9.5 billion over three years.[73]**

THE RISING BURDEN ON WORKING FAMILIES. One way to measure the burden of the tax code is to look at the effect of tax policies on the median-income household. Here we find two trends that have contributed to the tax burden on the middle class. First, personal exemptions in the 1950s were much higher—over half the income of working families was exempted from income taxes. By the 1990s, the value of the personal exemption had eroded to less than 25 percent of the median family's income. Second, the bite that payroll taxes took out of the median family's paycheck was about 1.5 percent in the 1950s. By the 1990s, payroll taxes, including Social Security withholding and Medicare, claimed over 7.0 percent.

STATE AND LOCAL TAXES. Even with the changes that shifted the tax burden from the wealthy onto the middle class, the federal tax code maintains certain progressive elements. Wealthy people still pay more based on their ability to pay. On the other hand, state and local taxes tend to be highly regressive, with lower-income people paying a higher percentage of their income than wealthier people from state income taxes, sales taxes, and local property taxes. This is because local taxes tend to be "flat taxes," where individuals pay at the same rate regardless of income or ability. When we add together federal, state, and local taxes, low- and moderate-income people actually pay about the same effective rate as high-income people.

Between 2001 and 2004, almost every state in the union was plunged into its worst budget crisis since World War II. According to the Center on Budget and Policy Priorities, states faced over $200 billion in cumulative budget shortfalls during these three years. This forced localities to lay off teachers, firefighters, police officers, and social workers; close libraries and health clinics; cut child care, mental health services, public transit, and pollution control; raise public college tuition and reduce financial aid; and let schools, playgrounds, roads, and bridges go unrepaired. Oregon shortened its school year by three weeks. Thirty-four states cut spending on Medicaid and the State Children's Health Insurance Program over the past two years, removing between 1.2 million and 1.6 million low-income people from health coverage, including an estimated 490,000 to 650,000 children. The list goes on.

Most of these state tax systems are highly regressive, imposing a higher burden on the poor than on the wealthy. According to the Citizens for Tax Justice, the average state and local tax rate for the bottom fifth of income earners is 11.4 percent, more than twice the effective rate of 5.2 percent paid by the richest 1 percent of taxpayers. In some states, such as Washington and Florida, the lowest-income fifth of taxpayers pay as much as 14 percent of their income in state and local taxes; whereas the wealthiest 1 percent of income earners pay less than 3.5 percent.[74] Some states—such as Alabama, Tennessee, and Virginia—tax food and basic needs at a higher rate than income from investments. State and local sales taxes on items like food take a larger percentage of the income from the pockets of the poor, making the state systems more highly regressive.

At the state and local level, most communities are facing their fiscal disasters as if they were parochial problems. Local homeowners see their property tax bills go up and voice their rage at local politicians. In Portland, Maine, twenty-six firefighters were laid off and the focus of anger is the local city council. It is not easy to dramatize the chain of decisions connecting local budget cuts and seemingly remote federal tax policies.

These dire budget straits are not natural disasters nor accidents, but largely the result of politi-

"Welcome to budget cut middle school. Our first lesson is on...no money resourcefulness."

cal and moral choices. In addition to factors such as recession, war, and increased prescription-drug spending, many states during the 1990s gave away massive tax breaks to corporations and the wealthy. Some states are reversing these tax giveaways, but most politicians are afraid to reverse the tax breaks made in fat times. Rather than set aside adequate funds for the lean times, states have irrevocably returned these revenues to the political donor class. Legislators throw up their arms and ask "but what can we do?"

Most significantly, every state has been clobbered by federal tax policies. Each of the four federal tax cuts since 2001 has directly and indirectly chipped away at state revenue. At the same time, federal devolution policies and mandates have shifted responsibilities and costs to states for such big-ticket items as education testing, security, health care, and social welfare.

RECENT REFORMS AND COMING DISTRAC-TIONS. In the coming years, there will be a push to abolish the progressive federal income tax and replace it with either a flat tax or a national sales tax. This will be packaged as a "tax reform" aimed at simplifying the tax code. But its stealth agenda will be to continue to shift responsibility for who pays the bills.

Instead of simplifying the system, the tax cuts of the last decade have added additional complex loopholes written for the well-to-do and corporate special interests. Even *BusinessWeek* complained that politicians had "complicated" instead of "simplifying" the tax code. The first tax code in 1916 was much simpler, twenty pages in length with none of the fine-print loopholes of the present tax code. Conservatives and progressives alike lament the complexity of the current U.S. tax code. Yet much of the complexity comes from loopholes and shelters created by and for wealthy individuals and corporate special interests. Complexity for tax filers comes in defining what constitutes taxable income, not in looking up one's rate in the tax table.

In Chapter 5, we will discuss how to respond to some of the coming tax proposals—and suggest what a fairer tax system might look like.

THE RESTRUCTURING OF WORK AND THE BREAKDOWN IN THE SOCIAL CONTRACT

One factor contributing to wage stagnation and growing inequality is the restructuring of work. The move toward "lean and mean" workplaces has helped corporations cut labor costs, but it has also depressed wages. Due to downsizing, outsourcing, and the expansion of temporary and contingent work, workers have considerably less clout and bargaining power.

Distribution of 2001–2003 Bush Tax Cuts

Between 2001 and 2003, Congress passed tax cuts worth $455 billion. The richest 20 percent of households got almost 70 percent of these tax cuts.[75]

What Share of Tax Cut Did Different Income Groups Get in 2003?

Top 1%	Incomes over $337,000	28.3%
Next 4%	Incomes $145,000–337,000	15.0%
Next 15%	Incomes $73,000–145,000	25.8%
Fourth 20%	Incomes $45,000–73,000	16.1%
Middle 20%	Incomes $28,000–45,000	9.1%
Second 20%	Incomes $16,000–28,000	4.8%
Lowest 20%	Incomes below $16,000	1.0%

During the industrial revolution of the late 1800s, this country operated with a lean and mean system that included inhumane and dangerous working conditions, no job security, and child labor. Fabulous profits and fortunes were created as a result of this labor system. Inequality reached its modern peak, with the "robber baron" industrialists owning over half of the nation's wealth.[76] As the result of a number of social movements, new rules began to govern work, including improved health and sanitation conditions, the implementation of the eight-hour workday, and prohibitions against child labor.

In the years after World War I, the nature of work changed as many employers recognized that productivity would increase with new personnel policies that made work more humane, thus reducing turnover and employee disloyalty. Prior to the historic wage increase at Ford Motor Company in 1913, the annual employee turnover rate was 400 percent. Once Ford adopted its $5-a-day policy, absenteeism plummeted and productivity soared.[77] Other companies, such as Goodyear, General Electric, and Bethlehem Steel adopted elements of the modern job including expectation of long-term employment, a regular work schedule, company-based benefit plans, and formal personnel policies. Some went further, as Robert Pollin and Stephanie Luce describe in The Living Wage (1998), including

> profit-sharing arrangements, pension plans, health insurance, and educational subsidies for employees and their children. A careful

analysis of these and related efforts demonstrates that they also produced significant changes in turnover and morale, which in turn brought gains in efficiency.[78]

With the expansion of unionization after World War II, some worker protections were codified in collective bargaining agreements. This enforced a social compact between corporations and employees that contributed to job stability and shared prosperity for the majority of working Americans.

In the 1970s, these advancements came to a grinding halt. With U.S. corporations encountering competition from European and Asian firms, and a slowdown in corporate profits and economic growth rates at home, they turned to harsh forms of economic restructuring to reduce labor costs. As Bennett Harrison wrote in Lean and Mean, corporations dropped their commitment to the elements of the modern job, substituting a core of salaried workers surrounded by a large contingent workforce of disposable workers, temps, on-call workers, and independent contractors.[79]

Industry by industry, this move toward economic restructuring has swept the nation. In unionized sectors, this has occurred with some negotiation and protections for workers, but in most cases the restructuring has continued. As companies shed workers, Wall Street roared in approval, boosting the share value of the new "lean" companies. All indications are that more and more firms will continue these labor-cost-cutting trends.

Temporary Work and Outsourcing

A central part of the corporate restructuring of work is the elimination of full-time, regular workers who have benefits, replacing them with temporary, part-time, and leased workers without benefits. Today, one of largest employers in the United States is Manpower, Inc., a temporary employment agency with 4,300 offices in sixty-seven countries employing over 2.3 million people per year and over 431,000 workers in the United States.[80] In 2001, U.S. temp agencies employed over 9.6 million people.[81]

The restructuring of work has taken a number of forms, some of which are not bad. Many workers enjoy greater flexibility in the temporary or contingent workforce, which may accommodate the flexible needs of workers with children and other caregiving responsibilities in ways traditional full-time jobs often cannot. But for most contingent workers, their work arrangements are linked to lower wages, no benefits, and uncertain futures.

For the purposes of this discussion and the solutions discussed in Chapter 5, we use the words "contingent" or "nonstandard" to describe a number of different types of work arrangements. These include people who work for temp agencies, on-call workers, day laborers, part-time employees, and contract workers. These are sometimes referred to as "flexible

workers," "nonstandard work arrangements," and "temps." (See the box, Types of Nonstandard Work Arrangements, page 108.) If we mention temporary workers, we are referring specifically to the segment of contingent workers who work for temporary employment agencies.

According to a 2001 survey, at the peak of the business cycle, one in four workers were in the contingent workforce.[82] One private-sector study of 550 employers nationwide with five or more employees found that 78 percent used some form of contingent work arrangements. The principal motivation was reduced labor and benefit costs. At about 40 percent of the companies, wages and benefits were substantially lower for contingent workers. Two-thirds of the companies indicated that they would expand their use of contingent workers in the next five years.[83]

. Based on several studies examining the entire workforce, we have the beginning of a picture of the nonstandard workforce and the problems associated with it.[84] The following are a few trends associated with the rise of nonstandard work:

LOWER WAGES. Nonstandard workers, on average, receive lower wages than do regular full-time workers with similar personal characteristics and educational qualifications. The median wage for temp-agency workers is 75 percent of that of full-time workers.

WORKING BELOW THE POVERTY LEVEL. Contingent workers are more likely to be in the ranks of the working poor in this country: 52.3 percent of female and 33.4 percent of male non-standard workers do not earn enough to lift a family of four out of poverty, as compared to 35.4 percent of all female and 21.5 percent of male workers in the labor force as a whole.[85]

WOMEN AND PEOPLE OF COLOR ARE THE MAJORITY OF CONTINGENT WORKERS. Women and people of color are overrepresented in the contingent workforce. In 2001, 31.0 percent of women worked in nonstandard employment, compared to 22.8 percent of men.[86] Black workers comprise 10.8 percent of the total workforce, but 24.5 percent of the temp-agency workforce.[87]

FEWER BENEFITS. Health insurance coverage for contingent workers is well below that of regular full-time workers. Only 14.8 percent of women and 12.4 percent of men in nonstandard employment receive health insurance through their own employer, compared to 66.8 percent of women and 70.8 percent of men employed in regular full-time jobs. In terms of pension coverage, only 20.1 percent of women and 11.1 percent of men in contingent jobs receive a pension through their own employer, compared to 66.5 percent of women and 66.0 percent of men employed in regular full-time jobs.[88]

JOB INSECURITY. Nonstandard workers have greater job insecurity than standard workers. One study conservatively estimates that nonstandard workers are three times more likely to have jobs of uncertain duration than regular workers.[89]

MOST WANT TRADITIONAL PERMANENT JOBS. According to the Bureau of Labor Statistics, two-thirds of contingent workers desire traditional permanent jobs.

Types of Nonstandard Work Arrangements

REGULAR PART-TIME. Wage and salary workers who work less than thirty-five hours each week.

TEMPORARY HELP AGENCY OR "TEMPS." Workers paid by a temporary help agency to work for other firms on an as-needed basis.

ON CALL. Workers called to work only as needed. Examples are substitute teachers and workers supplied through a union hiring hall.

DAY LABOR. Workers who wait in a place where employers pick people up for day work, such as small paint jobs or clearing brush.

INDEPENDENT CONTRACT. People who work on a consultant, contract, or freelance basis to provide a service.

Privatization

Job restructuring and outsourcing are not limited to the private sector. A growing number of public and governmental functions have been restructured and "privatized" along the same model. While in some cases this has led to greater efficiency, it has also eroded public services and subjected public employees to the same race-to-the-bottom lowering of wages and standards that private-sector employees are experiencing.

Public agencies now outsource a number of functions, including cleaning services, data systems, garbage collection, and other public services, to low-paying vendors. Nonunionized minimum-wage workers with no benefits are now performing jobs that were once union jobs with benefits.

As worker insecurity in the private sector has increased, private workers and the public have been encouraged to resent the largely unionized public-sector employees with their greater job security, benefits, and salaries. Right-wing politicians and their think tanks attack government for its waste, inefficiencies, and lack of business principles. This has helped fuel antigovernment sentiments that have been used to justify both the dismantling of regulations unfavorable to corporations and undermining the security of public-sector workers.

But privatization has been no panacea. There are numerous examples of private contractors failing to balance both the public interest and the cost-cutting goals they were hired to accomplish. Examples of four of the largest corporations that benefit from privatization indicate that there is no monopoly on cost overruns, fraud, delays, mismanagement, or inefficiency.[90]

$ In 2002, the state of Pennsylvania took over Philadelphia's public schools, the sixth largest system in the country. They hired the for-profit Edison Schools, Inc., to manage twenty of the schools. Edison operates 150 schools in twenty-three states, but Philadelphia is its largest market. But soon after taking over, Edison failed to comply with the basic requirement to deliver financial reporting to the school board, putting them in default on their contracts. Then Edison saw its stock crash, falling from $21 to less than a dollar a share. Edison had to resort to desperate measures to remain solvent. Trucks showed up at Edison schools to take away most of the textbooks, computers, lab supplies, and musical instruments. Edison needed to sell them for cash.[91]

$ Lockheed Martin Company, known for its fighter jets, is now administering government contracts in a number of states. Its checkered track record includes $8 million in errors while administering Connecticut's foster-care program, and in New York City, it has twice been barred from contracts to collect parking fines because of practices such as bribes and kickbacks.

$ Unisys Company was fined $525,000 for failure to meet performance standards in its Florida contract to process state employee health insurance claims, including high error rates, slow turn-around, poor services, and security problems. Florida put Unisys under criminal investigation after evidence surfaced that the company was automatically denying employee health insurance claims and shifting benefit start dates to avoid late fees. Unisys bungled Medicaid claims processing contracts in a number of states, prompting cancellations and lawsuits in Iowa, Kentucky, and Wisconsin.

$ The now-defunct Andersen Consulting experienced a $24-million cost overrun and a one-year delay in automating Nebraska's welfare, food stamp, and Medicaid programs. In Fairfax, Virginia, its contract to redesign computer systems for the county's social-service programs came in 150 percent above original contract costs. In Texas, its contract for an automated child-support tracking system had a cost overrun of $63.7 million and is four years behind schedule.

Downsizing and Fear of Losing One's Job

Growing economic insecurity is now a fact of life for many American workers. The growth of outsourcing and temporary work means there are more workers who know they are disposable.

Workers in large and small companies know that they are at risk of being replaced by automation, outsourcing, and other corporate restructuring practices aimed at reducing labor costs. The downsizing of the 1990s means that no workers are safe. Even top managers get fired when short-term profits drop. In 1998, the worst year of the 1990s for job cuts, U.S. corporations axed 677,795 jobs, 56 percent more cuts than in 1997. In the fourth quarter of 1998, 245,339 lost their jobs, the highest since 1989, when such cuts began being tracked.[92] Between March of 2001 and January of 2004, 2.3 million people lost their jobs.[93]

Employee fears of job loss have risen steadily over the last two decades. In 1980, only 12 percent of the workforce reported they were anxious about losing their jobs. By 1990, the percentage of anxious workers rose to 20 percent, and by 1996 the figure had reached 46 percent.[94] This anxiety has held constant for the last decade.

The restructuring of work is having a dramatic effect on the quality of life for millions of working families, as well as contributing to larger economic trends such as stagnant wages. Fewer and fewer workers have access to health care and pensions through their employers. The social safety net, meanwhile, is currently inadequate to cover the growing number of workers without health insurance, savings, and retirement plans.

Education is an important element of workforce productivity and living standards for most workers. Since many companies tend not to invest in training and education resources for temporary workers, the whole issue of workforce education needs to be rethought.

A growing percentage of workers have no job security and, given their temporary status, are likely to experience longer spells of unemployment, especially in the face of an economic downturn. Yet many of these workers are ineligible for unemployment insurance or protections against discrimination and sexual harassment. Labor laws written when most of the workforce was employed in standard work arrangements need to be updated to incorporate the experience of this growing share of the population.

REGULATION AND DEREGULATION

Historically, restraints on the unbridled excesses of capitalism have been key in the making of an economy that works for everyone. The shared growth the United States enjoyed in the post–World War II years was rooted in the regulations and protections instituted by the government during the New Deal of the 1930s. Dozens of new regulations put the brakes on runaway corporate behavior and reduced the exploitation of working people and the environment. This ensured that the prosperity and productivity gains of the economy were better shared. These regulations included health and safety laws, environmental protections, and ordinances discouraging capital flight and businesses relocating, or what's called "runaway shops."

In the last three decades, however, there has been a full-scale attack on the power of government to regulate corporations. Under the guise of "eliminating red tape" and "getting big government out of our lives," corporations have worked to dismantle many of the regulations protecting communities and workers. These include cutting the number of labor inspectors and the budget for the Occupational Health and Safety Administration.

One example of a regulation that significantly affects inequality is the minimum wage, the federal wage floor. The federal minimum wage was instituted in 1938 to set a standard for all nonfarm workers. When first instituted, the minimum wage slowed a race-to-the-bottom

The Minimum Wage and the "Living Wage," 1968–2004

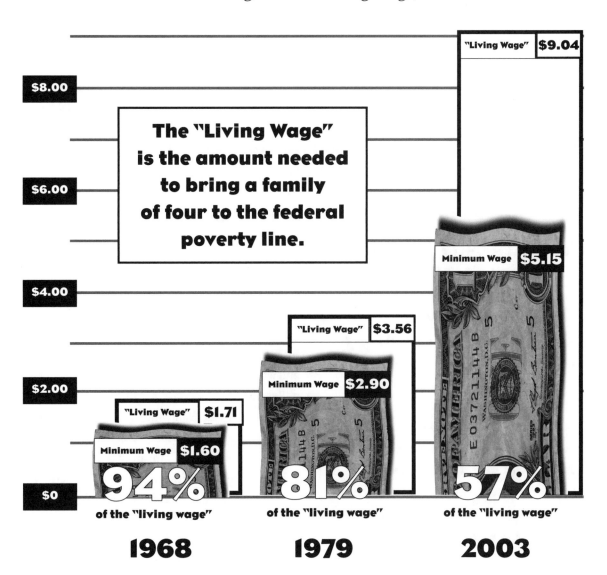

The "Living Wage" is the amount needed to bring a family of four to the federal poverty line.

"Living Wage" $9.04

$8.00

$6.00

Minimum Wage $5.15

$4.00

"Living Wage" $3.56

Minimum Wage $2.90

$2.00

"Living Wage" $1.71

Minimum Wage $1.60

$0

94% of the "living wage"

81% of the "living wage"

57% of the "living wage"

1968

1979

2003

Source: Living wages calculated by dividing that year's poverty threshold for a family of four by 2,080 hours (52 weeks x 40 hours). Poverty thresholds from U.S. Census Bureau, Historical Poverty Tables, Table 1.

war between higher-wage Northern states and lower-wage Southern states. Companies pitted workers against each other and moved businesses from the North to the South to cut labor costs. During the 1950s, the minimum wage was quite close to the amount required to lift a family of four out of poverty.

Today, the minimum wage is way below the poverty line. A full-time worker earning the federal minimum wage of $5.15 per hour has an annual paycheck of $10,712 a year, hardly enough to escape poverty. A *survival wage*, enough money to lift a family out of poverty, would average $9.04

an hour in the United States.[95] In San Francisco; Boston; Washington, D.C.; Seattle; and other cities with expensive housing markets, the living wage would need to be much higher.

The minimum wage created a wage floor, a level below which wages could not legally fall. This wage floor has the positive effect of lifting wages all along the pay scale. When the minimum wage goes up, so do the bargaining power and the paychecks of workers farther up the economic ladder. When the minimum wage lags behind, it keeps other wages depressed, as workers essentially compete with those one rung down the ladder.

FEDERAL RESERVE AND MONETARY POLICY

There has been, as we know and discussed over the years, a significant opening up of income spreads, largely as a function of technology and of education, with the increased premium of college education over high school, and high school over high school dropouts becoming stronger. The whole spread goes right through the basic system. It is a development which I feel uncomfortable with. There is nothing monetary policy can do to address that, and it is outside the scope, so far as I am concerned, of the issues with which we deal.

—FEDERAL RESERVE CHAIRMAN ALAN GREENSPAN, TESTIMONY TO CONGRESS, MARCH 5, 1997

Contrary to the statement by Chairman Greenspan, the Federal Reserve, through its monetary policy, does write some of the rules that affect the distribution of income in the United States. The Federal Reserve's policy of preventing inflation above all other goals depresses wages and worsens inequality. The policies of the Federal Reserve (the Fed) have a direct impact on our jobs, our retirement income, tax burdens, mortgage payments, and credit card balances.

Higher interest rates mean higher consumer debt in terms of mortgage payments and credit card interest rates. In recent years, a large percentage of the population have borrowed money to maintain their standard of living in the face of stagnant or falling wages. The next round of monetary tightening will reveal serious stress fractures in the personal finances of many Americans.

LINT TRAP

*Almost 90% of the increase in the stock market went to the top 10% of households (42% going to the top 1%). At the same time, real wages are now less than they were when Nixon was president

— United for a Fair Economy — www.stw.org

Higher borrowing costs for business mean cuts in investment, causing some workers to lose their jobs. According to the independent Financial Markets Center, less-skilled, lower-income workers are always the first to feel the pinch during a monetary tightening. If there is a wave of downsizing, underemployment, or greater job insecurity, most workers lose leverage in bargaining for a fair share of economic gains and control over working conditions.

Born out of the populist protests and banker anxieties about the instability of the economy at the turn of the century, the Federal Reserve was founded in 1913 to modernize and rationalize the nation's financial sector and stabilize the economy during boom and bust cycles, financial panics, and deflationary pressures.

The Fed encompasses the Washington-based Board of Governors, twelve regional Federal Reserve Banks, and the Federal Open Market Committee that sets interest rates. It has largely served the interests of Wall Street and conservative economic policy makers and, in the words of William Greider, has functioned as a "fourth branch of the U.S. government." It is the central bank for the United States, but the effects of its policies ripple around the world.[96]

Fed critics and conspiracy theorists often portray the Fed as protecting the privileged since its inception, but it is important to understand the Fed's history, accountability structure, and potential for democratic influence. The Federal Reserve is a public-private hybrid organization. It is technically an agency of the federal government, with the chairman and governors appointed by the

president and confirmed by the Senate. The law governing the Fed requires that there be public representation on the Reserve Bank boards of directors, including consumer and labor interests.

The Board of Governors selects some of those public representatives, oversees the activities of the Reserve Banks, and wields veto power over the selection of Reserve Bank presidents. In practice, these governing boards are controlled by corporate CEOs and high-finance leaders. Board terms are fourteen years. This, in economist Doug Henwood's words, is "supposed to insulate the governors from political pressures; in reality, it insulates them almost completely from anything like democratic accountability."[97] The Fed is self-financing, since virtually all its income comes from a portfolio of $400 billion in U.S. Treasury securities. It maintains secrecy about its deliberations, shielding the public from the discussions at its Federal Open Market Committee meetings, where interest-rate policies are determined.

Chairman Alan Greenspan's tenure, now in its fourth term, has been a period entirely attuned to the desires of Wall Street. The Fed's dual legal mandate is to stabilize prices and attain full employment. The Fed is also obligated to address the kind of deflationary pressures that have been devastating to rural America and that remain a powerful force in the global economy. But because of its subservience to conservative economic doctrine, the Fed has been almost entirely concerned with reducing inflation and maintaining higher levels of unemployment, ensuring a large surplus of labor that minimizes the pressure to raise wages. Low inflation and stability are good but should be balanced with policies that promote fuller employment, which also have positive macroeconomic effects. Debates within the Fed have focused on what is the "natural rate of unemployment," the point at which joblessness would be low enough to trigger price increases and inflation.[98]

During the last several years, the Fed has played an unusual role in attempting to stabilize the economy. When the speculative hedge fund Long Term Capital Management was teetering on the brink of collapse in 1998, the Fed convened a consortium of banks and other lending institutions to bail Long Term Capital out. The Fed should play a role in supplying liquidity in genuine crises and serve as a lender of last resort. But here was a case of the Fed intervening to protect a private-placement, high-risk speculation pool for multimillionaires.

Though Chairman Greenspan warned about "irrational exuberance" and stock prices being "overvalued," the Fed moved to cut interest rates in the fall of 1998, after massive stock-market

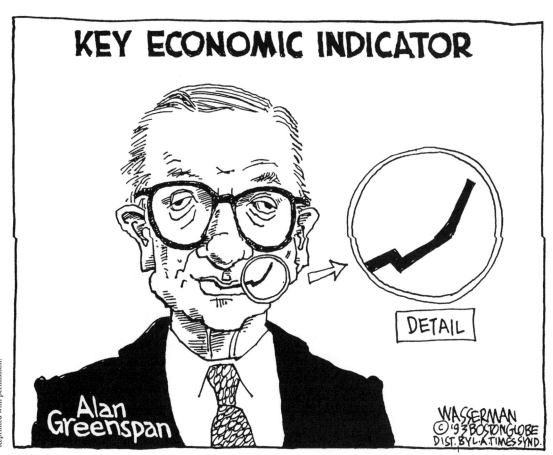

KEY ECONOMIC INDICATOR

DETAIL

Alan Greenspan

WASSERMAN
©'93 BOSTON GLOBE
DIST. BY L.A. TIMES SYND.

losses attributed to global financial instability. This sent the Dow Jones Industrial Average soaring over the 11,000 mark by the beginning of May 1999. As the market bottomed out, the Fed cut interest rates and then began to raise them again during the first term of George W. Bush.

While the Fed was kind enough to lower interest rates to protect investors, what does it do to support wage earners? At the first hint of inflation, the Fed will usually go back to its role of throwing a blanket on economic growth by raising interest rates. This is when the conflict-ing missions of the Fed will come into sharp relief, as such policies have a greater effect on the living standards of working people in this country than anything our elected officials do.

Contrary to Chairman Greenspan's quotation at the beginning of this section, there is a lot the Fed can do to reduce inequality. The answer is to make the Fed more accountable to ordinary citizens and to restore its legal mandate to balance the concern for full employment with its obsession about inflation.

GOVERNMENT SOCIAL SPENDING, THE SAFETY NET, AND CORPORATE WELFARE

One of the reasons that the incomes of all Americans grew at the same rate during the postwar years was that social spending initiated during the New Deal continued into the postwar years. Direct and indirect federal spending helped build this country's middle class.

Returning war veterans received the benefits of the GI Bill, including free higher education and subsidized low-interest home-ownership loans, through the Veterans Administration. These programs worked remarkably well, although white men benefited disproportionately to people of color.

In the area of home-ownership, massive feder-al spending lifted one-fifth of the population from tenancy into home ownership. This rapid increase was accomplished through federally subsidized mortgages, mortgage insurance, tax breaks for home owners, and indirect infrastructure improvements such as the interstate highway system that spurred the growth of the suburbs. This put millions of working-class families on the road to building assets, as home ownership is generally the first—and only—substantial asset for most people. But because the housing supports were targeted to whites, the racial wealth divide actually deepened during these years, preventing people of color from joining the ranks of asset-builders.

Last Century's Wealth-Broadening Program

Half a century ago, the United States made a substantial investment in broadening wealth. The government invested in subsidized mortgages so that millions of Americans could purchase a home. Many more got debt-free college educations that vaulted them into the middle class.

Thanks to federal programs, in the two decades after World War II, millions of families stepped onto the multigenerational wealth-building train. Between 1945 and 1968, the percentage of American families living in owner-occupied dwellings rose from 44 percent to 63 percent, due in large part to a massive public commitment to subsidized and insured mortgages from the Federal Housing Authority (FHA), the Veterans Administration (VA), and Farmers Home Administration (FmHA).

Prior to the 1940s' FHA programs, mortgages averaged 58 percent of property value, excluding all but those with substantial savings from home ownership. FHA and other mortgage subsidies enabled lenders to lengthen the term of the mortgage and dramatically lower the down payment to less than 10 percent. Government guarantees alone enabled interest rates to fall two or three points.

Between World War II and 1972, 11 million families bought homes, and another 22 million improved their properties, according to Kenneth T. Jackson in his history of the FHA, *Crabgrass Frontier*. The FHA also insured 1.8 million dwellings in multifamily projects. The biggest beneficiary was white suburbia, where half of all housing could claim FHA or VA financing in the 1950s and 1960s. All these housing-subsidy programs provided a wealth stake for 35 million families between 1933 and 1978. The home-mortgage interest deduction also benefited suburban homeowners, and interstate highway construction served as an indirect subsidy, as it opened up inexpensive land for suburban commuters.

Unfortunately, for a host of reasons—including racial discrimination in mortgage lending practices, housing settlement patterns, income inequality, and unequal educational opportunities—many nonwhite and Hispanic families were left standing at the wealth-building train station.

Today, racial wealth disparities persist and are far more extreme even than disparities in income. Home-ownership rates for blacks and Latinos are currently stalled at the level where whites were at the end of World War II. While over 70 percent of non-Hispanic whites own homes today, home-ownership rates for blacks and Hispanics combined average just 48 percent.

The post–World War II investment in middle-class wealth expansion was paid for by a system of progressive taxation. The top income-tax rate coming out of the war was 91 percent—and the estate tax included a provision that taxed fortunes over $50 million at a 70 percent rate. (Today the top income-tax rate is 38.6 percent.) In sum, many of the widely shared benefits of postwar spending meant that the progressivity of the tax system enjoyed widespread political support.[99]

The social safety net of welfare, food stamps, and housing assistance also established an economic floor below which, it was hoped, people would not fall. Everyone in society, especially women, had a stake in establishing a basic security platform in the event that they lost their jobs, got sick, got divorced from a wage-earning spouse, or fell on other hard times.

Welfare bashing has not only deflected people's attention from the dangers of growing economic insecurity, inequality, and the growing concentration of wealth, but it has also justified the dismantling of the bottom rungs of the social safety net and ladder. In 1996, President Clinton and a Republican Congress ended "welfare as we know it" by abolishing Aid to Families with Dependent Children (AFDC) and replacing it with Temporary Assistance to Needy Families (TANF). Unlike AFDC, a federal entitlement which provided a guaranteed minimum benefit, TANF includes strict work requirements, a five-year lifetime limit on assistance, and sanctions that can push people off the rolls. TANF is administered by the states, with little federal oversight, allowing for inequities in benefit provisions. Women, children, and people of color were disproportionately hurt by these changes. In the 1960s we waged a "War on Poverty," while in the 1990s we waged a "War on the Poor."

These cuts have had an enormous impact on the ability of low-income families to afford housing or provide opportunities for their children to attend college. Federal Pell grants, created in 1972 to provide aid to working-class college students, are much less generous than they used to be. Whereas the maximum Pell grant in 1975–76 covered 84 percent of the average cost of attending a four-year public institution, today it covers just 39 percent of that cost. The Bush administration's 2005 budget included $1 billion in cuts to Section 8 housing vouchers. These vouchers help 2 million poor, elderly, and disabled Americans pay their rent. A $1 billion cut is 5.5 percent of the program's total funding.

Corporate Welfare

Corporate welfare is emblematic of the imbalance of power in this country and its effect on government policy. Corporate welfare refers to the tens of billions of unproductive subsidies and tax breaks that flow to America's wealthiest corporations and individuals. By one estimate, taxpayers spend the first two weeks of the year devoting their paychecks to paying for federal corporate welfare.[100] There are several forms of corporate welfare that exist both at the federal level and at the state and local level.

The scope of corporate welfare is hard to measure because no government agency monitors the various forms of direct payouts and indirect subsidies received by corporations. In 2003, Citizens for Tax Justice estimated federal corporate welfare to be $175.2 billion.[101] But if you include a wider definition of "corporate subsidy," such as interest on the Savings and Loan bailout ($32 billion a year), the amount of "aid to dependent corporations" exceeds $800 billion a year.[102] In contrast, using the widest definition of "welfare for very low income people" including TANF, food stamps, housing subsidies, Head Start, Low-Income Energy Assistance, legal services, and child nutrition, costs totaled $193 billion a year in 2004.[103]

At the federal level, there are several different types of corporate welfare. These include:

$ DIRECT PAYMENTS FROM THE FEDERAL TREASURY TO CORPORATIONS. The U.S.

Department of Agriculture currently spends nearly $637 million a year helping U.S. corporations market their products overseas.[104] Assistance has flowed to needy corporations like McDonald's, American Legend Fur Coat Company, Dole, and Sunkist Oranges to help with advertising, trade shows, and financing. According to the Government Accounting Office, there is little evidence that the program is actually promoting additional advertising; it is most likely replacing private funds.[105] Because of paid lobbyists, the bigger the corporation, the greater its slice of corporate welfare. Though agricultural subsidies are politically sold as "saving the family farm," the vast bulk of the money goes to corporate agribusiness. Over 74 percent of agribusiness subsidies go to the wealthiest 10 percent of enterprises. Meanwhile, two-thirds of total U.S. farm production remains unsubsidized.[106] Of the $1.4 billion in annual sugar price supports, 40 percent of the money goes to the largest 1 percent of firms, with the largest ones receiving more than $1 million each. Another government giveaway, the Export Enhancement Program, showered Cargill, Inc., with $1.29 billion in bonuses between 1985 and 1996, over a third of the company's net worth at the time, of $3.6 billion.

$ SPECIAL TAX BREAKS AND LOOPHOLES.

These include a provision that allows U.S. companies with foreign operations to indefinitely defer foreign earnings from taxation in the U.S. David Cay Johnston, a *New York Times* reporter who won the Pulitzer Prize for his reporting on tax issues, estimates that the U.S. Treasury loses at least $200 billion a year as the result of wealthy individuals and corporations gaming the tax system.[107] Some corporations use a loophole called Accelerated Cost Recovery System to depreciate capital or equipment purchases faster than equipment wears out. A reasonable reform of this law would save the Federal Treasury $32 billion a year.

$ THE PROVISION OF PUBLIC SERVICES, GOODS, OR RESOURCES WITHOUT ADEQUATE COMPENSATION FROM COMPANIES. Corporations get subsidized access to timber, oil, and minerals on federal lands, grazing rights, and other use of our commonwealth at greatly subsidized rates. This subsidized access is not only a looting of the public's wealth but is environmentally destructive as well.[108] The federal government spent $3.3 billion between 1992 and 1997 building forest roads for private companies like Weyerhaeuser

and Georgia-Pacific, who pay a mere fraction back for the benefit of hauling timber from our national forests. President Clinton tried to slow the rate of forest road construction, but by 2001, the annual cost of forest-road construction had risen back to $173 million.[109]

$ SUBSIDIZED RESEARCH ASSISTANCE WITHOUT ANY FUTURE CLAIM ON PROFITS. The federal government pays for scientific research and development, then allows the benefits to be reaped by private

firms. Bristol-Myers Squibb got $32 million in federal subsidizes to develop the anti-cancer drug Taxol but now keeps all the substantial profits, charging cancer patients $1,000 for a three-week supply.[110] Researchers and policy makers argue that this is the only way to stimulate investment in drug research in the public interest. Research grants, however, could be structured as forgivable loans or investments so that in the event research becomes profitable, the public would share in the success of its investment.

$ FEDERAL PURCHASES FROM COMPANIES OF GOODS AND SERVICES AT MORE THAN MARKET VALUE.

Defense contractors continue to overcharge the federal government and taxpayers for military products. The $700 screwdriver and $1,200 toilet seat are the tip of the iceberg when huge defense corporation monopolies, whose only client is the federal government, receive contracts for trillion-dollar projects.

STATE AND LOCAL CORPORATE WELFARE.

The amount of corporate welfare at the state and local levels is also enormous, but difficult to calculate because it takes many forms. Researcher Greg LeRoy from Good Jobs First estimates that states and cities spend an estimated $50 billion a year in the name of economic development, most of which fails to deliver as promised.[111] These localities compete with one another to attract businesses and retain existing companies with a wide range of property tax abatements, low- or no-interest loans, research and development tax credits, corporate income-tax loopholes, and outright direct subsidies. This creates a "war between the states," as they compete to give away the local treasury and steal businesses away from one another—all in the often mistaken hope of creating more jobs.

In the 1990s, there was a proliferation of costly state and local giveaways. The number of states offering tax credits for research and development, construction loans, tax-exempt revenue bond financing, and corporate income-tax exemptions has at least doubled since 1977.[112] In 1998, the *Wall Street Journal* published a special supplement called "Grabbing the Goodies: Government Incentives Aren't Just for Big Firms Anymore. Here's how to snare yours."[113]

Some municipal leaders go to extreme lengths to attract businesses. In their effort to entice companies to relocate, city officials from Amarillo, Texas, have stooped to appearing in photo ads in the *Wall Street Journal* holding $8 million subsidy checks.

$ **In 1993,** the State of Alabama gave $253 million in incentives to Mercedes-Benz to build an assembly plant in Tuscaloosa that would employ 1,500 workers. Subsidy cost: $169,000 per job. Subsidies included $77.5 million for infrastructure; $92.1 million to build the plant; and $83.6 million in training funds, tax rebates, and other incentives. Meanwhile, elementary school classrooms in Vance, Alabama, are so overcrowded that trailers have been set up as portable classrooms.

$ In 1997, the State of Pennsylvania gave $307 million in economic incentives to Kvaerner ASA, a Norwegian global engineering and construction company that promised to reopen a shipyard at the site of the former Philadelphia Naval Shipyard. The subsidy per each of the 950 employees was $323,000.

$ In 1997, the Commonwealth of Massachusetts shared a bit of its commonwealth with the Raytheon Company and the multi-billion-dollar Fidelity Investments Company, which threatened to move jobs to Rhode Island and other states unless it received $40 million in tax breaks.[114]

$ In 1999, the State of Maryland gave Marriott $42 million in tax breaks to remain in the state.

STADIUM BLACKMAIL. Professional sports teams routinely extort state and local officials into building them taxpayer-subsidized new stadiums. In many cases, current stadiums are adequate but lack the profitable corporate "skyboxes"—which happen to be tax-deductible for these corporations. In city after city, new baseball, football, and basketball facilities are being built to placate wealthy owners and keep the local team in town.[115] Between 1990 and 1998, over seventy-seven new professional sports stadiums were constructed or significantly expanded at a total cost of over $12 billion. In twenty-five of the largest U.S. cities, municipal governments have chipped in amounts in excess of $100 million each to pay for facilities.[116] A report by the Brookings Institution estimates that the total cost of stadium construc-tion since the early 1980s is expected to rise to $7 billion by 2006, most of which will be publicly financed.[117] At a time when our nation's urban communities are suffering from disinvestment, this is an irresponsible use of the public's wealth.

Communities are fighting back against stadium corporate welfare. In the fall of 1997, voters in Southwestern Pennsylvania voted against a tax increase that would have raised $700 million to build new stadiums for the Pittsburgh Steelers and the Pirates. One Steelers fan, Patty Schmidt, remarked that "it's the fans who made the Pittsburgh Steelers and the taxpayers who built the first stadium. You can't just keep gouging the public. If the NFL is embarrassed by our stadium, they have billions of dollars. They can kick in half the money if they want to see the luxury boxes and all these things put in the stadium. We're not just taxpayers. We're also fans who buy the tickets and the merchandise. Enough is enough."[118]

Even President George W. Bush has been a beneficiary of stadium blackmail. Bush's main "value added" as the lead owner of the Texas Rangers baseball franchise was to threaten to relocate the team unless the city of Arlington, Texas, built a taxpayer-funded new stadium. The city increased local sales taxes to raise the $191 million required to build the stadium. As Molly Ivins wryly notes, Bush can thank "the taxpayers of Arlington, where every cab driver, burger flipper, lawyer, schoolteacher, and bank teller has paid for a few bricks in the pretty Ballpark at Arlington." This public investment boosted the book value of the team from $83 million to $138 million. In 1998, while serving as Texas governor,

Bush sold his 11 percent interest in the team for $15.4 million, bolstering his claim that he was a "successful businessman."[119]

In 2004, the city of Washington, D.C., in its zeal to lure a professional baseball team back to the city, proposed a plan to use $440 million in taxpayer money to build a new stadium. But a robust opposition to the park emerged, led by a coalition called No DC Taxes for Baseball.[120] "Bringing a major league baseball team back to Washington would be great for the District, but not if the price is a huge public subsidy," declared Adrian Fenty and David Catania, two D.C. city councilors. "It's far more important for D.C. residents and for the future of the District to focus on issues such as schools, health care, public safety, employment, affordable housing, opportunities for youth, neighborhood development, libraries and environmental protection."[121]

THE CULTURE OF GREED VS. THE COMMON GOOD

The economic inequality of the last two decades is rooted in rule changes, but it is also rooted in cultural changes that reinforce and legitimate rule changes in economic policy. As a result of the breakdown of civil society and the mobility of capital, unrestrained greed in our culture has been allowed to grow unchecked. As Charles Derber writes in *The Wilding of America*, there are now two cultures: civic culture and wilding culture. The traditional American civic culture is concerned with democracy, participation, the common good, and balancing individual and community responsibility. "Wilding" often refers to the violent breakdown in the streets, but also in the suites. The wilding culture is marked by a selfish individualism that acts with no regard to consequences for community and others. There is now a competing struggle between these values for the heart and soul of America.[122]

A 1993 cover of *BusinessWeek* features the ten biggest paycheck recipients of 1992 and reveals a lot of what is wrong in America today: excessive wage inequality, the influence of big money in politics, and the explosion in health care costs. The ten highest-paid executives depicted on the cover are all white men, four of whom work for large health providers or insurers. Thomas Frist, the CEO of Columbia/HCA, a hospital conglomerate, was the top wage earner with a salary of $127 million dollars. In the early nineties, Columbia/HCA was convicted of committing massive Medicare fraud and bilking taxpayers out of megamillions.[123]

Frist's 1992 salary of $127 million was approximately $61,000 per hour, or $15 dollars per second. He is paid about 9,000 times more than an entry-level worker at Columbia/HCA and about 3,000 times more than a nurse with ten years' experience. In terms of his contribution to Social Security, he was done paying into the Social Security "trust fund" after his first hour and five minutes of work that year, at 10:05 A.M.[124] Meanwhile, most Columbia/HCA workers have payroll taxes taken out all year long until December 31.

All those years in the health care business have been good to Thomas Frist. His 2004 net worth was $960 million according to the Forbes 400.[125]

The story gets even seedier. Thomas Frist has a brother, Senator Bill Frist, from Tennessee. He was first elected with help from $1.5 million in family money (less than a week's wages for brother Thomas) and insurance industry political action committees. When President Clinton proposed his national health insurance plan in 1994, Senator Frist chaired the Senate's health care committee and blocked proposals for universal health coverage and regulation of the health care industry. In 1999, he was criticized in his home state for not abstaining from a vote on the HMO Patient's Bill of Rights even though he owns a multimillion-dollar stake in Columbia/HCA. In 2002, he became the Senate Majority Leader in the U.S. Congress.

Thus, all in one little picture, we've got the seamy world of money and politics, nepotism, grotesque overcompensation, illegal price gouging, and political conflicts of interest.

Fortunately, not everyone is like Thomas or Bill Frist. In December 1995, a manufacturing division of the textile company Malden Mills, based in Lawrence, Massachusetts, burned to the ground. Even before the last flames were extinguished, the owner of Malden Mills, Aaron Feuerstein, pledged to rebuild the plant in Lawrence and to continue paying all of the employees during construction, even though the plant would be idle.

By September 1997, the plant was completely rebuilt in Lawrence with state-of-the art equipment, and all of the workers were rehired. Feuerstein was lauded by the public and honored for his actions in the president's State of the Union address. When he was asked why he did not just take the insurance money from the burned-down facility and cash out, he replied: "What would I do with all that money? Go to some Caribbean Island and overeat the rest of my life? It's unthinkable."

Unthinkable. That is a voice we do not hear much these days. It is a voice of civic responsibility in contrast to the "wilding" culture of individual greed. Certain types of behavior such as abandoning one's children or putting an elderly parent out on the sidewalk are *unthinkable*. It's not that the unthinkable doesn't happen. We are confronted with daily doses of unthinkable acts. But it is not culturally sanctioned behavior. It elicits outrage and criticism.

In Japan, the idea of paying a top manager a thousand times as much as another worker would be *unthinkable*. There is no Japanese law outlawing excessive compensation, but there is a cultural compact against such individualistic behavior. Japanese CEOs believe that such a disparity in pay would undermine the teamwork culture that they place a higher value upon. Ultimately, it would undermine productivity. They would feel ashamed to have their pictures and salaries listed on the cover of *BusinessWeek*.

In European countries, a reasonable wage ratio is enforced by a strong trade union movement which has resulted in unions having a direct role in corporate governance through seats on boards of directors. In the United States, there are vestiges of a civic culture and a social compact in what we call Main Street capitalism. Distinct from Wall Street capitalism, Main Street capitalism includes smaller locally owned and family-owned private firms that are accountable to other interests besides absentee shareholders. Unfortunately, this compact is fast disappearing as smaller businesses are forced out by large corporations.

The growing salary gap contributes to the erosion of trust within corporations. Peter Drucker, the respected dean of corporate organizational management, believes that excessive pay ratios are toxic. "The resentment against the big salaries of top executives," writes Drucker, "poisons the political and social relations within the plant, aggravates the difficulty of communication between management and employees, and reduces management's chance to be accepted as the government of the plant."[126]

Some U.S. companies do maintain a much smaller gap between workers and top executives. Since 1984, Herman Miller, Inc., a Michigan-based office-furniture maker, has limited top management salaries and bonuses to twenty times the average paycheck in the firm. The company's retired CEO Richard Rueh told the *Wall Street Journal* that "the way the CEO gets more compensation is if he can raise the average workers up. From a fairness standpoint, it seems like a good idea."

Herman Miller adopted a narrow pay ratio policy, says former board chairman Max DePree, after consulting with Peter Drucker, who advised that a small compensation differential would strengthen the company team culture and productivity. "People have to think about the common good," notes DePree. "Our CEO and senior officers make good competitive salaries when the performance is there."[127] Herman Miller is a

publicly traded Fortune 500 company, but many other privately held and public companies have adopted similar internal policies.

Indeed, some firms are trying to buffer themselves from the "wilding" appetites of Wall Street. Three hundred key employees joined together in the late 1990s to purchase the public stock of the Dynatech Corp., a Massachusetts-based maker of communications test equipment. Their motivation in moving the company's ownership into employee hands was "to get away from the short-term pressures of Wall Street so that management can make the kinds of long-term strategic investments it thinks are prudent." Dynatech's chief executive, John Reno, said going private would buffer them from "short-term stock speculators," with their desire for immediate short-term profits, so they could do the right thing strategically for their customers and employees.[128]

For a system of inequality to endure and be stable, those who have more must convince the majority who have less that the unequal distribution is just, fair, proper, the natural order of things, or inevitable. In the United States, inequality is justified by an ideology of meritocracy. Reducing inequality means challenging the tenets of meritocracy, which is so pervasive in our consciousness.

Reducing inequality requires changing not only the rules of the economy, but the values that permit and encourage high levels of inequality and the culture that glorifies it. It requires the strengthening and expansion of an ethical business sector concerned not only with the profit bottom line, but with the social bottom line as well.

Chapter 4

BUILDING A FAIR ECONOMY MOVEMENT

The alarming development and aggressiveness of great capitalists and corporations, unless checked, will inevitably lead to the pauperization and hopeless degradation of the toiling masses. It is imperative, if we desire to enjoy the full blessings of life, that a check be placed upon unjust accumulation and the power for evil of aggregated wealth.

—CONSTITUTION OF THE KNIGHTS OF LABOR, 1869[1]

The first step in taking action to reduce income and wealth inequality is to remind ourselves that there is an alternative to the current way the economy is organized. The second step is to remember that people can bring about change. After several years of organizing around these issues, we have found that many people feel discouraged and hopeless about our collective ability to build a fairer economy.

One way we maintain our hope is to remember our history. There have been cycles of great economic inequality in the history of the United States. On several significant occasions in the last 120 years, broad-based social movements have arisen to correct the excesses of economic inequality.

The Tradition of Taking Action to Reduce Inequality

Fill our souls with thy beauty, our hearts with thy inspiration, till every man of us shall deeply resolve that our laws shall be so framed, our Government so administered that every citizen however rich shall bear an equal share of its burdens and every laborer however poor, an equal share of its blessings.
—Tom Watson, 1888[2]

Industrialization in the late nineteenth century led to great wealth accumulation in the hands of the robber barons as a result of their ownership and control of the nation's infrastructure and natural resource base. It is estimated that over one-half of the nation's private wealth was in the hands of the richest 1 percent of families, compared to almost 40 percent today.

As the big trusts rose in power, they aggressively changed the rules of the economy—including monetary policy, corporate governance, and trade tariffs—to suit their own interests. Railroad land, accompanied by massive subsidies, was given to large corporations as they "opened up" the West to settlement for whites. Government giveaways of land and money were a form of eighteenth-century corporate welfare. "In industry after industry," writes historian Howard Zinn, "shrewd, efficient businessmen were building empires, choking out competition, maintaining high prices, keeping wages low and using govern-

ment subsidies."[3] Large monopolies grew as the trusts merged and expanded.

The trusts advocated keeping the money supply constant, even as the population grew, making it harder for farmers and smaller businesses to get credit. In rural communities, the brutal crop-lien system, where merchants would take usurious liens on future crops in exchange for supplies, forced farmers deeper into debt and eventually took their farms.

In the years after the Civil War, there was a major power struggle over how the country would industrialize and what the role of corporations would be. On the one hand, both the Democratic Party and the Republican Party served the interests of the large trusts and banking interests. Laws were changed to give corporations more power and the legal rights of personhood. On the other hand, populist challengers attempted to rein in the power of these trusts. Unfortunately, in 1886 alone, the Supreme Court overturned over 230 state laws that had been passed by populist-oriented political coalitions to regulate corporations.

These conditions gave rise to the Populist movement, the largest social movement in our nation's history. The Populist movement was composed of rural farmers and urban workers. It cut across racial and geographical divisions to build a movement that was specifically concerned with the overconcentration of wealth and power. The movement's base came from the Knights of Labor's efforts to organize urban wage workers and the Farmer's Alliance's organizing in rural areas.

The Populist movement had over a thousand newspapers and journals. The Farmer's Alliance Lecture Bureau had a network of 35,000 lecturers who traveled the nation's highways and byways, speaking at grange halls and railroad stations, spreading the Populist program. Historian C. Vann Woodward, who closely studied the Populists' "yellowed pamphlets," found that the "agrarian ideologists undertook to re-educate their countrymen from the ground up," through an ambitious program of grassroots education.4 By 1892, the farm lecturers had reached into forty-three states and to over two million farm families in what historian Lawrence Goodwyn, author of *The Populist Moment*, called "the most massive organizing drive by any citizen institution of nineteenth century America."5

The Populists built the People's Party, an independent political party that either ran its own candidates for local, state, and federal offices or, in some cases, fused with progressive Democrats and Republicans. Fusion allowed the same candidate to run for office on two different ballot lines. Populists used fusion voting as a way to support progressive major-party candidates without giving up their own party identity. They had an economic program through their producer cooperatives that helped farmers jointly purchase supplies and market products like cotton. In addition, the Populists had all the dimensions of modern movements—media,

political education, and electoral machines. With limited money and large numbers, they challenged the fundamental power of the robber barons.

The Populists talked explicitly about the dangers of concentrated wealth and power. Because their movement preceded the Russian Revolution, populists could talk about social class in America without being dismissed as "foreign imports" or "socialists," as later efforts to discuss inequality were. They pushed for the first income tax as a means to break up overconcentrations of wealth. They won passage of an income tax in 1896, only to have it struck down by the Supreme Court as unconstitutional. It was not until 1916, a generation later, that the Populist vision of a progressive income tax came into law with the passage of the Sixteenth Amendment to the Constitution.6

The main threads of the Populist movement came apart as a result of a number of internal and external forces. Racism and anti-Semitism poisoned some elements of the Populists, breaking apart their coalitions and high-road approach to democracy. A number of states began to outlaw fusion elections, making it difficult to mount third-party candidacies. Both the Republicans and the Democrats absorbed Populist issues into their platforms. President Theodore Roosevelt, a Republican, became a boisterous spokesperson for progressive taxation and antitrust legislation. In some regions of the country, particularly in the northern Midwestern states, a strong populist influence in politics still exists to this day.

The last time the wealthiest 1 percent of the American population owned 40 percent of the country's wealth was in 1929, on the eve of the Great Depression.[7] The 1920s, a decade of anti-labor repression and unrestricted market activity, allowed for a rapid concentration of wealth. Some economists have argued that growing inequality contributed to the Depression because the falling incomes of working people led to massive defaults on debts. At the same time, wealthy people had so much money that they were speculating wildly, destabilizing the economy with unsound business deals, mergers, and risky lending.

The Depression and the great inequality of that era inspired a variety of social movements that advocated for a fundamental redistribution of wealth and power. The industrial labor movement came of age, pushing for the right to organize, as codified in the National Labor Relations Act (Wagner Act) of 1935 and the Fair Labor Standards Act in 1938. The founding of the Congress of Industrial Organizations (CIO) in 1935 was a landmark event, since before this workers were organized by craft, like carpenters and butchers, rather than by industry. The CIO launched militant organizing drives that expanded the ranks of unionized workers by millions of industrial workers, ensuring that over 35 percent of the workforce was unionized by 1950.

The End Poverty in California (EPIC) movement had over one million members and almost succeeded in electing Upton Sinclair (author of *The Jungle*, a muckraking novel about the meat-packing industry) as governor in 1934. Sinclair believed that the Depression was part of a long-term cycle of unemployment. He called for massive public-works projects, cooperatives, and a progressive tax on property assessed at over $250,000 in order to "advance sufficient capital to give the unemployed access to good land and machinery, so that they may work and support themselves."[8]

Another mid-1930s movement, Share Our Wealth, led by the colorful and tainted Louisiana Populist Huey Long, claimed seven million members in 27,000 local chapters. The Share Our Wealth program called for a cap on excessive income and wealth, with the maximum amount of wealth allowed for any one person capped at $8 million in 1935, the equivalent of $96 million in 1999 dollars.[9] The program also called for a shorter work week, free higher education, a guaranteed minimum income, and retirement security. That last plank eventually came into being as Social Security.[10]

Evidence shows that these social movements pushed President Franklin Roosevelt to advocate progressive taxation and stronger social and economic reforms during his second term in office, beginning in 1936. Roosevelt, feeling threatened by labor power and from Huey Long's challenge to his presidency, sought to steal some of Long's thunder with rhetoric that spoke against the "economic royalists" in control of America. Reforms established after 1936 included expansion of federal relief and Social Security, regulation of stock exchanges, legislation establishing the right to organize unions and bargain collectively, initiatives to eliminate rural poverty, massive public works programs, and progressive taxation.[11]

Although social and economic conditions are different today, the challenges we face one hundred years after the Populist movement are similar. The concentration of media and its ability to shape our collective consciousness is much greater. The network of face-to-face institutions that existed in the 1880s and the 1930s is weaker today. Nonetheless, the seeds of the next economic fairness movement have been planted and are beginning to sprout.

Movement-Building

Organizations like United for a Fair Economy and Class Action, founded by the authors of this book, conduct educational programs on the changing global and national economy and what people can do to respond to growing inequality. During these programs, we often ask people to "close their eyes and imagine they had a magic wand that would allow them to enact one public policy to reduce inequality." In thirty seconds, participants cite policies including progressive income taxes, universal health coverage, a living wage, publicly funded elections, money for education and job training, a tax on wealth, and eliminating corporate welfare. It is apparent that change has not been hindered by lack of good ideas about how to address inequality. We know what to do, but right now we don't have the power to make it happen.

But we *can* build a fairer economy. The key is building a broad-based social movement that has the vision and power to change the rules governing the economy. We must organize to address both the democracy issue and the power imbalance that has contributed to inequality. We must change the rules that worsen inequality. We must change the consciousness that allows such extreme inequality. We must also address the cultural conditions that reinforce inequality.

What is a social movement? It is people coming together to change the cultural norms and the rules, build new institutions, and organize for power. Being in a movement doesn't always feel coherent. It is not neat, clean, or linear. Movements go through different stages and life cycles, starting on the margins of our public awareness and moving toward finally being accepted. Within social movements, there are competing organizations and leaders with egos. There are proponents of different tactics and strategies. Some factions hold tight to certain tactics or viewpoints on direction and attack others as too radical or not radical enough. But the operative word is "movement." People come together around some unifying analyses, values, and reforms. Movement participants are sometimes discouraged and frustrated even as a social movement is being built because they fail to recognize the early stages of movement growth.

In a quote often attributed to philosopher Arthur Schopenhauer, "All truth passes through three stages. First, it is ridiculed. Second, it is violently opposed. Third, it is accepted as being self-evident." Social movements develop in a similar fashion. In order to keep working toward the day when there is wide acceptance of the values underlying economic justice and fairness, it is useful to have a framework. To appreciate the dynamics of social change movements, it helps to understand the various stages and cycles they go through.

Today all the preconditions exist for a powerful and broad-based economic fairness movement to address economic inequities. We see evidence in growing grassroots organizations around the country. However, we are at an early stage of movement building, so it may be difficult to perceive growing momentum. A rumbling within existing constituency institutions and identity groups indicates that many people are eager to address the fundamental causes of economic insecurity and the scapegoating bred by inequality.

Stages of Social Movements

It is our belief that social movements create change. We are all indebted to the social movements that preceded us. The Civil Rights movement, women's movement, labor movement, environmental movement—all have brought concrete improvements to our society and our lives. One of our favorite bumper stickers is: "The Labor Movement: The Folks Who Brought You the Weekend." Social movements have defined who can vote, eliminated child labor, ended slavery and racial segregation, ensured that we can drink clean water, and improved our lives in many other ways. So many of the things we take for granted today were struggled for and won by those who came before us.

It is important to understand how movements work for several reasons. First, it helps us be strategic about where and when we should direct our energies in order to have maximum impact. And it helps us maintain perspective and hope. Movements often experience multiple setbacks and moments when efforts appear to be losing—when in fact, a movement may actually be succeeding.

Social movements go through many different stages and cycles. However, when most people think of movements, they think of people marching in the streets, mass participation, and nightly news reports. This release of energy and action places a concern before the public and builds broad-based support. Movements are usually symbolized and publicized by their trigger events. Trigger events are watershed moments, incidents, and actions that serve as turning points in a movement's progress.

They are characterized by broad public participation and action. Trigger events can be planned or serendipitous.

The conventional view of history is that some incident or event acts as a trigger and the next thing you know, people are marching in the streets. Rosa Parks, as the story goes, was tired and sat down on a bus, causing the Montgomery Bus Boycott to spontaneously erupt and the Civil Rights movement to attract major attention and support. A near meltdown at the Three Mile Island nuclear power plant near Harrisburg, Pennsylvania, magically triggered an anti–nuclear power movement that changed the future of the nuclear-energy industry.

This simplified history is inaccurate and misleading. Years of training, education, and organizing preceded the Montgomery Bus Boycott and the anti-nuclear movement. Without preparation, these historical opportunities may have been missed. Rosa Parks, for example, attended citizenship schools at the Highlander Center in Tennessee. She studied nonviolent direct action and was a secretary of her local NAACP. She was chosen to be the visible person to trigger the Bus Boycott because of her unassailable personal character. Weeks of strategy meetings and planning went into setting the stage for the boycott. Activists from an unsuccessful bus boycott in Baton Rouge visited Montgomery to offer their lessons and their model for an alternative transportation system to replace the buses during the boycott.[12]

Stages of Social Movements

MOVEMENT PHASE	Preparation	Agitation	Consolidation
	Business as usual Failure of established channels Ripening conditions	Takeoff Perception of failure Winning over majority	Achieving alternatives Consolidating and moving on
Power-holders	Promoting the status quo Organizing countermovements	Organizing backlash to movement Discredit/repress leaders and organizations Allies and whistle-blowers support movement goals	Accommodation of movement demands Cooptation of leaders Acceptance and integration
Public	Moves from dormancy to high levels of sympathy over preparation phase	Moves to near-majority support for movement/issue Wide public involvement	Cultural changes Broad acceptance Public falls back into dormancy
Social change organizations	A few infrastructure groups exist to research and prepare Catalyst groups form	Formation of mass organizations and coalitions Splits in tactics	Long-haul compliance organizations form
Activities	Cultural work Research Grassroots education Independent media Leaders developed Small actions	"Trigger Events" Mass protest Electoral work Initial legislation Mainstream media	Implementing/watchdog policy gains
Funders	Shoestring operations Very visionary entrepreneurial social change funders Social change foundations	Public dues More centrist foundations Individual contributions	Sustainer dues and memberships Mainstream foundations and institutional funders Individual bequests

Source: United for a Fair Economy (2004), adapted from Bill Moyer

Often, trigger events are lost due to a lack of movement preparation. In October 1966, the Enrico Fermi nuclear power station near Detroit had a serious fuel melting accident (similar to the one at Three Mile Island), inspiring Gil Scott-Heron's song "We Almost Lost Detroit." But because there was no organized antinuclear movement, this potential trigger event passed without response.[13] In 1978, twelve years later, an accident at the Three Mile Island nuclear power plant near Harrisburg, Pennsylvania, spawned a movement that prevented the construction of any new nuclear power plants in the Unied States. The difference between Enrico Fermi and Three Mile Island was years of public education about the economic and safety problems of nuclear power and a decade of organizing antinuclear coalitions, direct action training, and media work.

To consider only the visible trigger moment as the movement undervalues all the preparation work that goes into building any movement, not to mention all the follow-through and sustained organizing it takes to win real victories once the TV cameras are gone.

The late writer and social movement historian Bill Moyer identified eight stages of social movements.[14] Moyer studied direct action social change movements that aimed to build broad popular support. Movements are all different and by no means linear in their progression. Many are met with organized countermovements. A model has its limits; you certainly wouldn't want to fly in a model airplane. Nonetheless, a model is a useful tool in helping us gain perspective and think strategically about some of the movements that exist today and what stage they are in.[15] For simplicity's sake, we will focus on the three overarching phases of social-movement development.

Phase One: Cultural Preparation and Organization

The first phase in the development of a social movement could be summarized as cultural preparation and organizing. In the beginning of this phase, the general public is oblivious to the issue at stake and the power-holders are promoting the status quo. We need to develop messages that counter the dominant ideology. We need to hear the movement's message again and again in order to counteract the daily miseducation that bombards us and is advanced by proponents of the status quo. Those who are alerted to the issue are involved in researching and documenting the problem, educating one another (a step sometimes denigrated as "preaching to the choir"), developing language and materials, and communicating through independent media, such as radio and publications not dominated by large corporations. Actions tend to be small and unsuccessful. Politicians shy away from the issue because it will not win them votes. Advocates at this phase are often portrayed as extreme, paranoid, idealistic, or members of a radical fringe.

As they reach more people, grassroots social change organizations form and begin actively educating, organizing, and trying to get their point of view into the mainstream media. Strategy work is done to anticipate or proactively catalyze potential trigger events to catapult the issue into the public eye. Legislation for policy changes may be introduced, but usually fails; its value at this stage is largely educational. At the late part of this phase, visionary people begin running for office, advocating the movement's issues.

Movement organizations tend to be shoestring operations, with lots of "sweat equity," donated time, and precariously low budgets. Yet they accomplish a great deal. Social-change funders are essential at this phase of movement development, because traditional funders are not aware of these organizations or consider them outside the mainstream.[16]

Phase Two: Building Public Support

Phase two begins after a trigger event that dramatically brings people together. The trigger event could be unsolicited, responding to some powerful incident like the U.S. invasion of Cambodia in 1972 that brought the anti–Vietnam War movement to an advanced stage. It could also be carefully planned by movement strategists like the 1965 Selma Civil Rights March, which provoked a violent response and swung broad public opinion to support the Voting Rights Act.

Whatever the trigger event, several things happen. First, the majority of public opinion swings in favor of the movement. People begin to participate in mass actions and join organizations. Eventually, media coverage of the key issue increases greatly.

Meanwhile, the power-holders commit massive resources to repressing, discrediting, and co-opting the movement. They attack the leaders and ideas of the movement, giving some the

impression that the movement may be losing ground. At the same time, whistle-blowers and allies among the power-holders step forward and lend legitimacy to the movement's goals.

Politicians, aware of the majority's sentiments, begin to speak out about the issues and introduce legislation if appropriate. Legislation may lose, but not for lack of public support. The public's sentiments are now way out in front of most elected officials, who are still responding to the will of the power-holders.

New organizations emerge, playing different roles and bringing new skills and strategies to the movement. Differences emerge over strategies and tactics. These differences are the inevitable result of success. Some grassroots catalyst organizations will go out of business, their phase in movement-development having passed. Others change to adapt to the evolving movement.

Phase Three: Consolidation

In the consolidation phase, a movement enters a long period of consolidating the gains, institut-

ing policies, monitoring compliance, and engaging in a larger cultural paradigm shift. Submovements may emerge, like the sustainable-energy movement that was spawned by the anti–nuclear power movement. Even after there is broad acceptance of a movement's concern or issue, it may take another generation before the gains are institutionalized into our laws and culture. The National Organization for Women, Friends of the Earth, and the NAACP are all organizations that have kept the flame alive and continue to ensure that their long-term goals are sustained.

Building a Movement Infrastructure

As we have seen, movements do not magically appear; they are the result of hard work. A variety of different groups and organizations are necessary to build social-change movements. It is important to support and strengthen all the components of movement-building, which include:

GRASSROOTS ORGANIZATIONS. Locally based grassroots organizations are a foundation for any social movement.

COALITIONS. No single group or issue can advance alone. Coalitions bring together different organizations and constituencies around shared interests. Movements need an organization and communication infrastructure to connect local activists, get input and feedback, and mobilize people.

PROGRESSIVE RESEARCH ORGANIZATIONS. A movement needs a research or think-tank capacity to test proposals, research ideas, and marshal intellectual arguments, as well as to develop tools for grassroots organizations and coalitions.

MEDIA. Movements need a media and message infrastructure to move ideas and respond rapidly to current events and media opportunities. Independent media organizations as well as progressive media consultants help frame media stories and plan strategies to reach broader publics. A movement also has its own media, a way to communicate directly with its members and allies.

EDUCATION AND TRAINING. Movements need training centers and cadres of trainers to provide opportunities for political education and skill-building. This helps movements to develop a shared understanding and analysis of the problem, to create a clear vision of the alternatives, and to develop effective action strategies. Grassroots activists need a place to learn the necessary skills and an opportunity to practice articulating their message.

CULTURAL WORK. Movements need a cultural component to move people's hearts, to celebrate victories and mourn setbacks, to allow us to experiment with living our visions, and to build the community necessary for long-term movement-building and social change. We need culture that nurtures and sustains us in the work.

All of these components are essential for a successful social movement. The 1880s' Populist movement had such an infrastructure. It had local grassroots chapters and action groups, a thousand local Populist newspapers, and a political party with local and national candidates. The Populists had a practical economic program in the form of cooperatives and an educational apparatus in the form of 35,000 lecturers who traveled the grange-hall and church-supper circuits promoting the Populist program. The Populist movement had a cultural component that included music and large multiday family jamborees that combined food, celebration, dancing, political oratory, and music.[17]

The Civil Rights movement that started in the late 1940s also serves as a model revealing many of the components of movement-building. Grassroots organizing, happening through churches and student movements, was a foundation for the movement. The cultural work— music and arts—was part of its spirited strength.

Creative Action: Billionaires for Steve Forbes?

Dateline: March 17, 1999
Concord, New Hampshire

As Steve Forbes announced his year 2000 candidacy for president in Concord, New Hampshire, a group of well-dressed supporters called Billionaires for Steve Forbes rallied to cheer for a candidate so attuned to their needs.

Dressed in business suits and fur coats, they held signs saying FREE THE FORBES 400, and TAX CUTS FOR ME, NOT MY MAID. They chanted, "Let workers pay the tax, so investors can relax," and "Spare the wealthy pain, no tax on capital gains."

Forbes's real supporters, puzzled at first, quickly came to realize that the "billionaires" were actually criticizing their candidate. A few of them tried to herd the Billionaires for Forbes away, but not before the pranksters had unfurled a banner reading, BILLIONAIRES FOR FORBES—BECAUSE INEQUALITY IS NOT GROWING FAST ENOUGH.

The press corps, expecting a routine campaign kickoff story, jumped with excitement to cover the sarcastic protest. "Steve Forbes is the only potential candidate who has known since birth that the wealthy are the real engines of our economy, and everyone else is just along for the ride," said spokesbillionaire Ted Duncanson as the TV cameras rolled. "That is why we shouldn't pay taxes on our investments. His flat tax would tax only those people foolish enough to depend on wages and salaries for their incomes."

Organized by United for a Fair Economy in Boston, the Billionaires were attempting to draw attention to the harmful effects of Forbes's flat tax, which would tax income from work but not capital gains or other income from investments.

In a leaflet handed to passersby, the Billionaires group explained their support for Forbes for president: "During the 1950s and 1960s, the middle class had the nerve to think that they too could become prosperous and secure. Fortunately, for the last twenty years, inequality has grown and wages of half the population have fallen or stagnated.... But inequality is not growing fast enough. And there are dangerous signs that wages for middle-income people might start to rise again."

The Billionaires for Forbes successfully altered the coverage of Forbes's candidacy. The spoof was featured in broadcast stories on CNN, CNBC, and National Public Radio, and in articles in the *New York Times, Washington Post, Chicago Sun-Times, U.S. News and World Report, Boston Globe*, and the *Manchester Union-Ledger*.

See the evolution of this effort as "Billionaires for Bush" at www.billionairesforbush.com.

One of the challenges at an early stage of movement-building is to find campaigns that are relevant, educational, and not so far afield that people will not seriously work on them. What timely issues and policies could be promoted today that would advance a real debate about the economy, bring people together, and help shift public consciousness?

Since people are focused on scapegoating low-income women and new immigrants, campaigns that get people to focus, instead, on corporations and greed at the top end of the economic ladder may be useful. Because a wedge has been driven between low-income people and other working people, it is important to find issues that unite these divided segments and forge common ground among the bottom 90 percent of the U.S. economic pyramid. Classism, as well as racism and sexism, has made it difficult to experience our common ground. For those on the lower end of the economic spectrum, getting rid of internalized classism is necessary. For those on the other end, unlearning classist attitudes and behaviors and consciously becoming allies around the issues of class are essential.

Most important, we need activities to encourage people to organize communication and action networks. Each neighborhood or small town needs clusters of activists and institutions willing and able to come together to organize, educate, agitate, and hold elected officials accountable. We need to deal with classism within our groups and organizations to build effective and strong cross-class alliances. We also need to deal with racism and other systems of oppression that prevent solidarity and effective action.

These clusters of activists can be existing organizations such as a union local,* a women's group, a neighborhood association, or the social action committee of a local religious congregation. They can also be new groupings that come together around a fair-economy agenda. Each cluster needs to develop the capacity for the following:

$ **GRASSROOTS EDUCATION. The ability to lead and facilitate informative workshops and discussions about issues of class and the current economy, and how they affect us, and the capacity to host study groups to deepen the knowledge base for the truly engaged.**

$ **DIRECT ACTION/CREATIVE ACTION. The willingness and ability to integrate culture, humor, and creativity into actions.**

$ **ACCOUNTABILITY SESSIONS WITH ELECTED LEADERS. Relationships with elected officials and the ability to mobilize people to attend accountability sessions and meetings, and to vote.**

$ **LOCAL MEDIA WORK. The ability to influence local media—to become sources and write letters to the editor and op-eds—is vital to promoting a movement's message. This involves the willingness to call in to locally produced talk radio programs and the capacity to respond rapidly to proposals and policies advanced at the state and federal level.**

What will be the trigger moments for our economic fairness movement? What can we anticipate? We know that some potential trigger moments have passed us by, opportunities lost because our movement-building preparation was inadequate. The radical economic restructuring of the last decade, including welfare reform, downsizing, layoffs, and the changing nature of work could have brought about and still might provoke a trigger event. Perhaps rising interest rates and the massive amount of consumer debt will be the provocation. Most likely, an economic downturn that reveals the precarious house-of-cards nature of our speculative economy will create the conditions necessary for trigger events and mass action. But we must be ready.

Challenging the Mythology Underlying Inequality

Even after learning that the current distribution of income and wealth is the manufactured result of three decades of classist propaganda and public policies tilted toward the rich, many people will view remedies that result in greater equality as an attack on "successful people." The complaint that "I made this money and the government is taking it away" has enormous resonance in an economy in which most working people are overtaxed.

But let's go back to the analogy we used before: Imagine we are playing a game of Monopoly. What if the winning player not only gets $200, but gets to change one of the rules of the game whenever she or he passes "Go"? The winner would likely make rule adjustments to enhance her or his chances of winning.

This underscores a fundamental confusion many Americans have about winners and losers in the economy. Myths abound about merit and "who deserves," and confusions about "what's mine" and "what belongs to the community." In a culture that celebrates the rugged individual and the self-made fortune, people are often reluctant to admit that they got help from family or government—or that their security and prosperity is as much the result of luck and privilege as it is of hard work.

President George W. Bush has spoken about how his family name may have afforded him certain opportunities, but says that his success in business is because of his "results and perform-

ance." How much of his success is the result of Ivy League schools, family connections (like being the son of a president), the summer jobs with family friends, the self-confidence, and the ability to hope that come from a privileged upbringing? How much of his success as owner of the Texas Rangers was the result of his business acumen—and how much was the winnings from a taxpayer-funded stadium and luck in the marketplace? Gwendolyn Parker, a black woman who spent ten years as a Wall Street lawyer, wrote about Bush's statements about his business success.

> How can George W. Bush, born into a family whose wealth and power and privilege far outstrip my own, not simply see the truth about his own life?...I wouldn't think less of Governor Bush if he just admitted that he'd been lucky, certainly very lucky, and left it at that. Few of us have led luckless lives, and there is neither merit nor shame in the truth. But I worry about a presidential candidate who feels compelled to reform luck and privilege into primarily the sweat of his own brow. I worry particularly about how many American lives he'll need to misinterpret so that he can continue to tell the story he likes to tell about himself.[18]

Unfortunately, the myth of individual achievement exists throughout our entire culture. For example, many home owners don't believe that the government helped them to purchase a home, yet their mortgages may be publicly subsidized or they may take advantage of the Home Mortgage Interest Deduction, an $80 billion a year subsidy that primarily goes to middle- and upper-income home owners. Part of the challenge of proposing policies that address inequality is to tackle the myths about meritocracy, individual achievement, and individualism that most Americans have internalized.

Understanding Class in U.S. Society

The United States is a class society, and power relationships exist among groups of people based on economic factors. We can understand power as the ability of an individual or group to carry out their will even over the opposition of others. We can tell who has more power at any given time by seeing whose interests prevail.

© 1998 Lindsay Robertson

What Do We Mean by Class?

In the United States, class is a confusing and elusive thing. We generally prefer not to talk about it. We think of ourselves as a "classless" society, or we believe that everyone except for a few lucky ones at the "top" or unfortunate ones at the "bottom" are "middle-class." Class can evade any attempt at categorization or simplistic definition. One person's definitions may not make sense to another. We present these definitions in the hope of starting a dialogue about class and how it affects us.

Class is relative social rank in terms of income, wealth, status/position, and social power.

A **class** consists of a large group of people who occupy a similar economic position in the wider society based on income, wealth, property ownership, education, skills, or authority in the economic sphere.

Class affects people not only on an economic level, but also on an emotional level.

CLASS IDENTITY: A label for one category of class experience, such as ruling class, owning class, middle class, working class, poor.

CLASS INDICATOR: A factual or experiential factor that helps determine an individual's class or perceived class. The criteria for determining class membership or identity can be easily debated.

CLASS CONTINUUM: There are no hard and fast divisions between class groups. Income, wealth, and occupational status exist as spectrums, and most of us move slightly up or down the spectrums during our lifetimes. Immigrants can change class status from their country of origin to their new country. Some people grow up in one class and live as adults in another. Class operates along a continuum or hierarchy. Lines may be drawn at different points along this continuum, and positions can be labeled differently. Class is a relative thing, both subjectively (how we feel) and objectively (in terms of position or resources). Our felt experience often varies depending on whether we look up or down the continuum. However, it is clear that everyone at the top end is mostly dominant with respect to class and derives substantial benefit and privilege, while everyone at the bottom end is mostly subordinate and has limited access to benefits. The graphic on page 143 visually demonstrates this.

DOMINANTS	RULING CLASS	"HAVE MORES"
	OWNING CLASS	
Mostly DOMINANT	MIDDLE CLASSES	"HAVES"
Mostly SUBORDINATE	WORKING CLASS	
SUBORDINATE	POOR/LOW INCOME	"HAVE NOTS"

Felice Yeskel

What Is Classism?

Classism is the systematic assignment of characteristics of worth and ability based on social class. It includes individual attitudes and behaviors; systems of policies and practices set up to benefit the upper classes at the expense of the lower classes, resulting in drastic income and wealth inequality; and the rationale and the culture that perpetuates these systems and unequal valuing.

Classism is differential treatment based on social class or perceived social class.

Classism is the systematic oppression of subordinated groups (people without endowed or acquired economic power, social influence, or privilege) by the dominant groups (those who have access to control of the necessary resources by which other people make their living).

Classism is the systematic oppression of subordinated class groups to advantage and strengthen the dominant class groups.

Classism is held in place by a system of beliefs and cultural attitudes that ranks people according to economic status, family lineage, job status, level of education, and so on.

It is necessary to think in a visionary manner about the kinds of public policies that will fundamentally correct the inequities of our economy. We believe these proposals should include progressive taxation of income and wealth, democratic controls over corporations, and a guarantee of economic rights comparable to our political rights. Clearly, none of these proposals are part of the political debate today. In fact, things seem to be moving in the opposite direction under Republican and Democratic leadership that worships at the altar of large corporations and wealthy campaign contributors.

This much we know: We are in an early stage of movement-building, in the formative stage of writing a new chapter in U.S. history. A modern economic fairness movement is building steam. Across the country, people are coming together to learn, organize, reflect, and assemble a movement-building infrastructure. We know that unions and organized workers will play a central role in building this movement. It is also likely that young people, religious people, people of color, students, and others will play significant roles in building power and taking mass action to build a fair economy. We know that the movement will advance its goals through a wide range of activities and tactics: consciousness-raising and education, direct action, legislative action, electoral politics, cultural resistance, consumer action, shareholder action, workplace action, media work, educational work, and more.

Our work today is to educate ourselves to understand the roots of these problems and discuss strategy. We need to identify our real needs and allies. We need to do the internal consciousness-raising work and build relationships across class and across race. We need to operate outside of our comfort zones. We need to build our organizations, both at the local level and at the national level, and create a communication infrastructure. We need to identify strategic actions and campaigns to educate the broader public, win real reforms, and build power to tackle more fundamental rule changes.

We are not sure what the different trigger events will be. We don't know what resistance will look like in the age of the Internet. We don't know who the leaders of this movement will be, but we know that people are preparing, perhaps not consciously, for their role in making history. We know that the time will come. We are preparing for that time.

Myths in a Class Society

In order to successfully implement policies that benefit such a small minority, class-based ideological messages must be advanced that try to persuade us that what's good for the top is good for us all. Some of these basic enabling class myths have been around for a while: the U.S. is a classless society; we are a meritocracy; anyone who works hard can achieve the "American Dream"; what's good for business is good for the rest of us; inequality is natural and necessary.

MYTHS	Tax policy	Welfare policy	Labor policy	Global policy	Monetary policy
The U.S. is a classless society	We all share common interests. We should all be taxed the same—class mobility means that we are all roughly middle-class and taxes should reflect this.	People can move up the ladder if they really want to. Lots of class mobility exists in the U.S., and if people are stuck in poverty, it's because they aren't trying hard enough.	We all are in the same boat together—workers and owners have the same interests (with no class divide) because we all need each other for a productive economy from which we all benefit.	Compared to other countries, everyone in the U.S. is doing very well economically.	We're all hurt by inflation, and it benefits no one. Regulating the business cycles helps everyone, even if the Fed slows down the economy.
The U.S. is a meritocracy	People work hard by expending their own effort for what they have, and they should be able to keep it and do with it what they want. Individualism: Freedom to do with your money what you want is key, instead of having the government decide. You will have no need for public resources when you can afford private ones. Fend for yourself. Income earned from capital is a result of one's own intellect and effort, so it should be taxed just like work. Income from capital takes just as much work and effort as income from labor.	We need to enforce a work ethic, so no one should be able to get by without working. No "handouts." There must be something innately wrong with people who receive public benefits. They're choosing their situation. If they only worked harder . . . If you can't find a job that pays enough for you to get by, it's your own fault. You need more education or training. Survival of the fittest reigns.	You can get rich from hard work, you just need to work your way up the ladder. You don't need collective bargaining because you can move up based on individual merit instead. CEOs should be paid so much because they worked hard to get where they are. Stockholders deserve their share of profits because they worked hard for their money too, and obviously made good choices or they wouldn't be wealthy. People need more education and training to get out of low-wage jobs. There are plenty of jobs out there, but there's a skills mismatch.	Workers can get out of their low-wage jobs, or get more training and education to keep up with the changing technology. If people are displaced by globalization (job loss because business goes overseas, etc.), workers need to adapt and figure out how to use their talents to fit into the new system. Competition, not communal efforts, rules the global market. Corporations deserve to expand into poorer nations because they need to work hard to succeed.	People choose to be unemployed—they can always find a job if they really want one. Wealthy people got rich based solely on their own efforts and hard work. They've become even richer since the 1970s because they were smart and had foresight.

MYTHS	Tax policy	Welfare policy	Labor policy	Global policy	Monetary policy
What's good for business is good for the rest of us	If corporations pay less taxes, they have more money for investment and then more jobs are created. There is a trickle-down effect: If rich asset-owners profit, then they'll invest—we all benefit.	Businesses need low-wage labor to keep labor costs down and profits up (which benefits stockhold-ers). If there's a safety net, the bargaining power of workers goes up, which increases inflation and decreases profits.	Whatever increases profits benefits workers too. Keeping labor costs low also benefits consumers because then inflation stays low, and prices don't rise. Economic growth benefits us all. Every-one's standard of liv-ing goes up when productivity increases. Unions are bad for profits, so they must be bad in general. Workers need busi-ness to give them jobs.	A rising tide lifts all boats. Free trade means more develop-ment and therefore increased equality in developing countries. Free trade means more profits for businesses, too. More trade means lower costs to con-sumers because imports will increase. More trade means more jobs at home because demand from new markets will increase, and exports will increase.	Anti-inflationary policies are good for business, so therefore they are good for the economy in general. Recessions are nec-essary in the business cycle, and sometimes the Fed needs to induce recessions to slow economic growth to prevent inflation. Wages can't rise too much because this creates inflation and reduces profits.

Thanks to Jen Matthews

Chapter 5
ACTIONS TO CLOSE THE ECONOMIC DIVIDE

Many people across the political spectrum now agree that rampant materialism and consumerism, unstable families and communities, and the wrong values are problematic. There is agreement that the concentration of corporate power and growing income and wealth inequality are a problem. But there are many different opinions about what course of action should be taken to remedy these problems.

For example, at a symposium on income equality at the Bush Presidential Library in Texas, the invited speakers recognized the problem but had divergent solutions. Calling the wage gap "one of the most serious problems of our time," centrist and conservative thinkers like Charles Murray and Marvin H. Kosters of the American Enterprise Institute discussed the causes and remedies for lagging pay. Many of their proposed interventions focused on job training, access to education, reducing immigration, and "fixing" the people at the bottom of the income ladder.[1]

Leading liberals have also put forward searing proclamations on the dangers of inequality, and like conservatives, advocate for expanded education and job training. They also advocate for stronger social safety nets, programs to boost savings, and increased housing opportunity. They are also likely to oppose new rule changes that will worsen inequality.

The labor movement has focused on opposing "free trade" agreements and advocating that "America needs a raise" through boosting the federal minimum wage. All of these strategies focus on helping those at the bottom of the U.S. economic canyon get a better leg up in the economy. The limitation is, however, that if wealth and power continue to concentrate at the top of the economic ladder, all these remedies will not ultimately address the problem. The solution lies in not only lifting the floor, but also lowering the ceiling. The solution must include addressing the overconcentration of wealth and power to ensure that the economy doesn't continue to create these great inequalities.

At the heart of growing economic inequality lies an imbalance of power. As discussed in Chapter 3, low- and moderate-income people, our communities, and our civic institutions have lost power to large corporations and asset-owners in the top 5 percent of households. In order to build a more equitable economy, we need to shift this power balance. We need organized *people power* to counter the power of megacorporations and their owners.

Government can be either an ally to people power or a servant of the corporate elite. In recent years, because of the shift toward corporate power, it has largely served the corporate elite by altering the rules to their benefit. There is no reason, however, why the power of government couldn't function as a stronger ally to ordinary people and a countervailing power to the corporate elite. Many of our economic problems have political answers through a broadened democracy. The antigovernment rhetoric of conservative forces weakens government as a protector of interests for workers, communities, the poor, and the environment—and strengthens the hand of corporations as they usurp public power.

This chapter examines a range of actions we can take to reduce economic inequality. There are two parts to our solution: reforms of our democratic process to reduce concentrated power, and fair-economy rule changes to increase equity and reduce concentrated wealth.

EXPANDED DEMOCRACY. We suggest a range of reforms and interventions to increase the power of ordinary people and reduce the inordinate power of concentrated wealth and corporations. All of these efforts must be accompanied by educational and consciousness-raising efforts that break the taboo against talking about class, and address the myths and classist beliefs we have internalized. The interventions include

$ **increasing the power of working people,**
$ **reducing the influence of money in our electoral democracy,**
$ **strengthening independent political organizations that are not beholden to big money, and**
$ **reining in corporate power.**

FAIR ECONOMY RULES. The second set of actions is aimed at changing the rules that govern the economy to reduce inequality and ensure shared prosperity. These include

$ **global trade and investment rules,**
$ **rules governing wages,**
$ **rules governing asset-building,**
$ **rules governing taxation,**
$ **rules governing subsidies for corporations,**
$ **rules governing monetary and fiscal policy, and**
$ **rules strengthening the social safety net and reversing privatization.**

When we asked economists and ordinary people about what remedies or rule changes would reduce income and wealth inequality, they offered a long list. Their recommendations fall into three categories: leveling up, playing fair, and addressing concentrated wealth.

LEVELING-UP RULES reduce inequality by lifting the income and wealth floor for people at the bottom of the economic ladder. Proposals like raising the minimum wage, universal health care coverage, and expanding access to home ownership focus on people in the bottom three quintiles. They address current problems of assetlessness, retirement insecurity, and job instability.

PLAYING-FAIR RULES guard against future inequalities by ensuring that shared prosperity is built into the economy. Such approaches are less concerned about redistributing wealth and more focused on creating a level playing field. These rules include expanding worker ownership, eliminating special subsidies, and negotiating trade agreements that aren't biased against wage-earners in favor of investors.

RULE CHANGES TO BREAK UP CONCEN-TRATIONS OF WEALTH include progressive taxation on income and wealth and policies that fundamentally redistribute power and wealth.

The broadest political support exists for "leveling-up" interventions because they are the least controversial and generally do not challenge the power of corporations and large-asset owners. However, we must go beyond these to playing-fair and leveling-down proposals in order to effectively reduce inequality in a way that is both meaningful and sustainable. In the current economy, remedial action must be taken to redress the over-concentration of wealth and power and its corrupting influence on our democracy and economy. Otherwise, reforms will ultimately fail.

Proposals for policies that dare to challenge the ascendancy of concentrated wealth and corporate power face severe attack. The media and our culture encourage all of us to identify with the interests of those at the top. Thus, solutions that level the playing field, reduce corporate power and profits, and break up concentrated wealth and power can expect few allies—at least initially. Even after the Cold War and the fall of Soviet communism, we don't have the space in our collective imaginations to think about what alternatives lie between extreme market capitalism and the state-managed economies of communism. The lines of arguments fall into the familiar ruts of left versus right, equity versus freedom, capitalism versus communism. When the defenders of inequality and unfettered corporate power attack pro-fairness proposals as socialist, they expect the wider public to begin frothing at the mouth and reject them out of hand. Part of our job is to carve open the space to have a democratic discussion about these matters. We must make the case that we can have a strong economy and greater equality, individual liberty, and stronger communities.

In building a movement in the coming years, it is important to pick issues and reforms that give us an opportunity to: (1) expand the terms of public debate; (2) hold elected officials and candidates accountable on progressive economic issues; and (3) build powerful coalitions of labor, religious institutions, socially concerned business leaders, and community organizations. At each stage, we must stress the dangers of overconcentration of wealth and the need for a real democracy. We must shift the basic ideological framework from "free market capitalism is good; big government is bad," to "overconcentration of wealth and power are bad for our democracy, our economy, and our civil society."

Within each of the following sections, the proposals range from immediate to long-term and from the politically most doable to the most difficult. The last proposals within each section are the most far-reaching. Some might characterize them as Don Quixote–tilting-at-windmill solutions, but they attempt to fundamentally address the root causes of income and wealth inequality. Today, these proposals may seem quite ambitious; there are only a handful of leaders daring enough to discuss them. But if we do our jobs and build a movement advocating more initial reforms, these proposals will become common sense to most people.

Building a Real Democracy

The problems of inequality in the United States are rooted in a fundamental power imbalance with transnational corporations and large owners of capital on one side and everyone else on the other. In other words, inequality is fundamentally a democracy problem, in which the interests and rights of a wealthy minority and legal fictions called corporations supersede the interests and rights of the vast majority of citizens.

This power imbalance has led to a changing of the rules that govern our society and economy to benefit this minority. In organizing for change, we need to simultaneously organize for more people power and press for changes in the rules that worsen the wealth divide. The rules *can* be changed and corrected to ensure that prosperity is more evenly shared; it is within our power to insist that they are.

BUILDING WORKERS' POWER

The demise in the standard of living for working people is directly linked to the decline of union participation in the United States. Expanding the power of workers in the economy is essential to restoring democracy and building a fairer economy. Strengthening labor unions, worker centers, and working-class institutions and political organizations may be the most important thing we can do to build countervailing institutional power against concentrated corporate power and wealth.

The aim of unions, as articulated by the AFL-CIO, is to "achieve decent wages and conditions, democracy in the workplace, a full voice for working people in society, and the more equitable sharing of wealth in the nation." More poetically, the labor leader Samuel Gompers said in the early part of the twentieth century:

> What does labor want? We want more schoolhouses and less jails; more books and less arsenals; more learning and less vice; more leisure and less greed; more justice and less revenge; in fact more of the opportunities to cultivate our better natures, to make manhood more noble, womanhood more beautiful, and childhood more happy and bright.[2]

Unions have suffered severe setbacks in the last thirty years, largely due to a hostile antiunion political environment and the aggressive tactics of employers. The rules that govern the right to organize unions and protect workers have been undermined or not enforced. Employers use hardball tactics to intimidate employees involved in unionization drives, which, even if successful, often encounter stalling tactics from employers that delay union recognition.

RECLAIMING LABOR'S TARNISHED IMAGE.

For many years, the labor movement has been on the receiving end of a systematic and sustained antiunion propaganda campaign. Many people have negative feelings about organized labor, viewing it as corrupt or wasteful. Some see the union movement as historically discriminatory toward women, people of color, and new immigrants. While there may be elements of truth to some of these charges, it is essential that we mount an educational campaign about the value of the labor movement and its historical importance. It is imperative that we confront stereotypes about labor, acknowledge its limitations, and remind people of the tremendous role unions have played in the struggle for economic fairness.

STOPPING ANTIWORKER LEGISLATION. Each year, dozens of legislative proposals are introduced, aimed at diluting the power of workers and eroding their standards of living. The radical right has an agenda of weakening and rolling back existing labor laws. For example, there are strong efforts to undercut existing laws governing overtime pay.

Which side are you on?

Which side is your elected official on? The AFL-CIO maintains a list of all congressional representatives and their voting records on legislation important to workers. Visit it at: www.afl-cio.org.

DEFENDING AND ENFORCING EXISTING LABOR LAW. If existing labor laws were enforced in a timely way, many of the problems facing workers trying to organize unions would be addressed. Antiworker legislators and large corporations have put enormous resources into attacking and under-

mining existing labor law. Budget constraints at the National Labor Relations Board (NLRB) have prevented the agency from dealing efficiently with an expanding caseload. This results in backlogs and delays in enforcement and board decisions. The Occupational Safety and Health Administration (OSHA) has experienced similar attacks on its budget and capacity to enforce laws.

WORKPLACE ORGANIZING. A major arena for building power remains in the workplace. For many of us, it is where we spend a majority of our waking hours. Workers supposedly live in a democratic society, but many of their constitutional rights end at the workplace door. Even freedom of association is not protected within the workplace. As Elaine Bernard, director of the Harvard Trade Union Program, points out, growing inequality doesn't mean unions should abandon the struggle for greater rights and democracy in the workplace and work only on issues of inequality. There is a link between being involved in workplace organizing and advocating for public-policy change. According to Bernard, "Democracy and workers' rights in the workplace are crucial issues for organizing. And without greater levels of organization, inequality will continue to rise."[3]

RULE CHANGES TO STRENGTHEN THE RIGHT TO ORGANIZE. There are several immediate reforms that would strengthen the hands of workers choosing to unionize. Many of these policies already exist in Canada and Europe, where they have contributed to a climate that is more responsive to the concerns of working people and in which employers are less hostile to the rights of workers. One of the major differences between the United States and Europe is the latter's swift and efficient administration and enforcement of labor laws, instant recognition of unions, and protections for workers who are in disputes or on strike.

$ **STREAMLINE PROCESS OF DEALING WITH UNFAIR LABOR PRACTICES.** Unfair labor practices account for a great deal of the decline of U.S. unionization. Even with laws that protect workers who are fired for organizing, the enforcement process can take years. For many companies, firing workers, stalling on enforcement, and paying the costs of litigation and fines all improve the bottom line.

The balance of power in labor law enforcement needs to be changed. We need to streamline the processing of unfair labor practices along the lines of the European model. Workers claiming unfair labor practices would automatically qualify for hearings. Disputes could be resolved in one timely hearing rather than in the current three stages that involve judges of administrative law, the National Labor Relations Board, and the court system.

$ **INSTANT RECOGNITION.** In current union organizing drives, after a majority of employees in a workplace have signed union cards saying they want a union, they're not even halfway there. If an employer doesn't want to recognize the rights of the unionized workers, it can require an election, overseen by the National Labor Relations Board. In the time between a card-signing and an election, employees can be forced to attend employer-sponsored antiunion meetings, subjected to intimidation and firing, and exposed to threats that their plant will close.

Instant recognition or "card check" would allow a union to be recognized and in place once a majority of workers in a workplace have signed union cards. This system is in place in Canada and is one of the reasons why the rate of unionization there is over 32 percent, compared to 13 percent in the U.S.[4] Better yet, direct freedom of association would bypass the bureaucratic procedures currently in place.

$ **BAN ON STRIKEBREAKERS/REPLACEMENT WORKERS.** When workers go out on strike and risk their livelihood and security for safety, health, and wage issues, many private employers can legally hire replacement workers. A ban on the hiring of strikebreakers would give workers a stronger hand in their negotiations with employers.

$ **CHANGES IN SECONDARY BOYCOTT LAWS.** In a secondary strike or boycott, workers from another company, say a trucking company, might refuse to unload trucks containing beverages bottled by a company with striking workers. Under U.S. labor law, workers are now prohibited from joining in secondary strikes or boycotts, a form of worker solidarity that greatly enhances the chances of success for union demands.

SOCIAL UNIONISM AND DIRECT ACTION FOR WORKERS' RIGHTS. Changing the rules to strengthen the right of workers to organize is essential in rebuilding the labor movement as a countervailing power to organized money and corporate power. Yet, as we have seen, enforcement and recognition of workers' rights constitute another struggle entirely. Resorting to the bureaucratic maze of the National Labor Relations Board and the courts is extremely disempowering for workers, not only because these institutions tilt toward employers, but because of the stalling effect it has on organizing drives.

More and more, communities are creating their own tribunals and taking direct action to draw attention to and enforce workers' rights. Chapters of Jobs with Justice across the country have created "workers' rights boards" composed of respected members of the community including clergy, doctors, academic leaders, and elected officials. These boards hear disputes and publicize their rulings.

Resorting to direct action is a necessary and often effective tactic in bringing community pressure to bear on an employer. In the late 1990s, the workers at the Richmark curtain factory in Everett, Massachusetts, started a drive to join UNITE, the Union of Needletrade, Industrial, and Textile Employees. Most of the 120 workers at the plant were new immigrants from Latin America who were working under horrendous sweatshop conditions. When ten leaders of the union drive were fired, fifty of their coworkers courageously went on strike to defend their right to organize and to protest the firings.

The local Worker Rights Board contacted the employer to object to the treatment of workers, but its requests for meetings were rebuffed. UNITE and the local chapter of Jobs with Justice organized a public protest at the plant, enlisting over 300 community leaders to put pressure on Richmark. Thirteen community leaders were arrested in civil disobedience actions at the plant, including Father Robert Kennedy from St. Mary's on the Sea in East Boston, historian Howard Zinn, and several other community and labor leaders. The following day, Richmark's owner announced that he was reinstating fired workers and recognizing the union through a union-authorization card check verified by a local Roman Catholic priest. Direct action allowed the workers to bypass the election and the NLRB bureaucracy. Three months later, Richmark workers got their first contract, which included, for the first time, a 33 percent pay increase and paid sick leave. Just as importantly, they won dignity and respect.

In most worker-organizing efforts prior to the 1950s, organizing around the concerns of workers was not limited to organizing the workplace but included the formation of political clubs, block associations, women's organizations, fraternal clubs, and local religious congregations. Sometimes referred to as "social unionism," these organizations formed the backbone of a seamless network of institutions that supported workers, most visibly around struggles in the workplace for union recognition and rights. People understood how the dignity and rights of workers were essential for the advancement of the whole community.

What the Richmark example and other similar stories point to is the importance of strong labor-community ties. Religious congregations, student and faculty groups, and independent political organizations are finding ways to express solidarity with the struggles of workers. This is happening through the affiliated members of the National Interfaith Center on Worker Justice, organizations like Jobs with Justice, and new student-labor networks.

WORKER CENTERS. In many parts of the country, new worker organizations and community-based centers are bringing together unionized and nonunionized workers who share a certain bond by virtue of language, ethnicity, or type of employment. Many work in sectors that are not unionized or belong to ethnic groups unions have not succeeded in reaching out to. Worker centers are a form of community unionism that strengthens communities and workers, even when their workplaces are particularly hard to organize.

The Workplace Project on Long Island has focused on organizing immigrant workers who are severely exploited in their service occupations in restaurants, landscaping companies, manufacturing, and other service sectors. They won legislation at the state level to dramatically increase penalties for violating immigrant workers' rights.

The Chinese Staff and Workers Center was founded in 1979 to organize Chinese workers in many nonunionized businesses in New York City, including workers in the restaurant and garment industries in New York's Chinatown.

TEMP WORKER ORGANIZATIONS. As discussed earlier, more than 30 percent of the American labor force are people who work independently, including freelancers, independent contractors, temps, part-timers, contingent workers, and people who work from home. Across the country, there are national associations and local centers providing services and advocacy for this growing contingent workforce.

Working Today was formed in 1995 to promote the interests of independent workers, a broad-based membership with common interests, a sort of American Association of Retired Persons for workers who typically don't have a voice. It provides services for its 4,000 members, including health insurance, legal services, financial planning, and public-policy advocacy for the rights and needs of independent workers.

CO-DETERMINATION POLICIES. Ultimately, the voice of workers needs to be protected and institutionalized into the structure of the economy. This could take the form of what European countries call co-determination or co-management. Federal legislation in Germany requires that many corporations, by charter, must include representation of other stakeholders, including employees, on the governing boards of corporations.[5] In *Corporation Nation*, sociologist Charlie Derber writes that the United States is different from "virtually all European countries in its legal disenfranchisement of workers and other stakeholders." Most European countries have different rules that give broader stakeholder powers to workers, communities, and even consumers.

In Germany, for example, a codetermination charter requires that 50 percent of the board of directors of all large corporations be representatives chosen by the workers. Other German laws require "work councils," which are legally mandated representative bodies corporations must negotiate with before they introduce new technology, lay off workers, or change schedules.[6]

As discussed earlier in the section "Reining in Corporate Power," it is one thing to try to counter the money power of corporations with people power. It is more effective and powerful to transform the governance structure of corporations to institutionalize the interests of workers as stakeholders.

USING THE POWER OF LABOR'S CAPITAL. Through their pension funds and savings programs, workers own substantial wealth in this country. According to the AFL-CIO Center for Working Capital, workers' savings have grown in the past twenty-five years from $538 billion to $6 trillion, and now it represents the largest pool of investment capital in the United States.[7] Unfortunately, because of the ways in which these funds are invested, workers' own investments sometimes work against their interests. Union pension funds periodically find they are invested in companies firing U.S. workers while expanding operations overseas.

In 1997, the AFL-CIO established an Office of Investments and the Center for Working Capital to use the leverage of union pension-fund ownership to reform corporate governance structures and investment priorities. The center issues an annual scorecard rating the investment advisors who invest funds and vote proxies for unions. Investment firms that flunk the Working Capital scorecard by failing to invest and vote proxies in labor's interest will lose part of the hundreds of billions in total union pension fund business as labor-controlled funds look elsewhere. In addition to becoming more active as shareholders, many unions are looking at strategies to acquire substantial ownership interests in certain companies and sectors to influence their practices and hold them accountable to workers.

CONCLUSION: REALIGNING WORKERS' RIGHTS AND CORPORATE RIGHTS. The long-range goal is to redress the imbalance of worker power and corporate power. Today, corporations have the rights of free speech, freedom of association, privacy, and many other "rights of personhood." The rights of workers, however, end at the workplace door. What would it look like if workers had real freedom of association? What positive implications could this have for our democracy and economy?

Action Box: Labor Solidarity

AFL-CIO

815 16th Street, NW
Washington, DC 20006
Tel: (202) 637-5000
Fax: (202) 637-5058
Web: www.afl-cio.org and www.paywatch.org

Central labor body for the United States representing 13 million U.S. workers. Major programs include Labor Education, Voices@Work, Working Women, Research, Corporate Affairs, Organizing, and Public Policy advocacy.

Campaign on Contingent Work/ WorkCenter

33 Harrison Avenue
Boston, MA 02111
Tel: (617) 338-9966
E-mail: ccw@igc.org
Web: www.ccwglobal.org

Founded in 1996, CCW exists to help the 30 percent of Massachusetts (and U.S.) workers in contingent jobs—part-time, temp, day labor, contract, and on-call jobs among others—organize to win better pay, benefits, and working conditions.

Jobs with Justice

501 3rd Street, NW
Washington, DC 20001
Tel: (202) 434-1106
Fax: (202) 434-1482
Web: www.jwj.org

National network of community and labor coalitions fighting for workers' rights, with a strong commitment to direct action and forming local "workers' rights boards." Jobs with Justice coalitions now exist in over forty cities in twenty-nine states.

Labor Notes

7435 Michigan Avenue
Detroit, MI 48210
Tel: (313) 842-6262
Fax: (313) 842-0227
Web: www.labornotes.org

A monthly magazine that gives voice to rank-and-file workers. Every two years, *Labor Notes* sponsors a lively conference in Detroit, hosting workers from around the world.

National Interfaith Committee for Worker Justice

1607 West Howard Street, Suite 218
Chicago, IL 60626
Tel: (773) 381-2832
Fax: (773) 381-3345
E-mail: nicwj@ipc.apc.org
Web: www.igc.org/nicwj

National network of people of faith who educate, organize, and mobilize the religious community in the United States on issues and campaigns that will improve wages, benefits, and working conditions for workers, especially low-wage workers.

Working Today

P.O. Box 1261
Old Chelsea Box Station
New York, NY 10113
Tel: (212) 366-6066
Fax: (212) 366-6971
E-mail: working1@tiac.net
Web: www.workingtoday.org

National membership organization that promotes the interests of people who work independently— a diverse group that now makes up nearly 30 percent of the American labor force. Its members are freelancers, independent contractors, temps, part-timers, contingent workers, and people working from home.

REMOVING THE INFLUENCE OF BIG MONEY FROM OUR DEMOCRACY

Who are to be the electors of the federal representatives? Not the rich, more than the poor; not the learned, more than the ignorant; not the haughty heirs of distinguished names, more than the humble sons of obscure and unpropitious fortune. The electors are to be the great body of people in the United States....

—JAMES MADISON, *THE FEDERALIST PAPERS*[8]

The core problem [with politics] is that there is too much money, period. This is now a club for millionaires. You either have to have lots of money or you're indebted to somebody for the rest of your life.

—FORMER SENATOR TOM DASCHLE, SOUTH DAKOTA[9]

Many rule changes will be impossible to effect without removing the influence of big money from our democratic process. Because efforts to reform our campaign-finance system have been very visible in recent years, there is more public awareness of how our democratic elections are financed.

As a result of a growing national resolve, Congress passed the Bipartisan Campaign Reform Act of 2002, major campaign finance reform often referred to by the names of its Senate sponsors: McCain-Feingold. The major provisions included

$ a ban on soft-money contributions to national political parties,

$ an increase in the amount an individual may contribute to a candidate from $1,000 to $2,000,

$ a restriction on the ability of corporations (including nonprofit corporations and labor unions) to run "electioneering" ads featuring names or likenesses of candidates, and

$ creation of "527" issue organizations that can raise nondeductible contributions for issue education, advertising, and voter mobilization.

But the 2004 election dramatized that the power of big money is tough to contain—and will find ways to subvert campaign-finance laws. For instance, the Democratic and Republican party conventions relied largely on donations from corporations and wealthy individuals. There is evidence that the estimated $103.5 million in unrestricted soft-money donations that paid for conventions in effect are no different than banned contributions to parties.[10]

The stage has been set for the next round of campaign-finance reforms. The principal sponsors of McCain-Feingold didn't wait until the 2004 election was over before they introduced legislation to tighten regulations on 527 "non-party" organizations. Their proposed bill would require 527s with substantial donations and a federal focus to register as political committees with the Federal Election Commission. It would also limit individual contributions to $25,000 and ban contributions from corporations and labor unions.[11]

Others have argued that the continued subversion of election laws makes full public financing of federal elections the only way to thwart the influence of big money. Federal laws must navigate a 1976 Supreme Court decision called *Buckley v. Valeo*, which ruled that mandatory limits on campaign expenditures would be a violation of the First Amendment right of free speech. It did, however, uphold the creation of a voluntary public-financing system that has never been fully implemented at the federal level.

One significant indicator of movement progress has been at the state and local levels, where terrific organizing is going on to reduce the influence of large private contributions. In 1996, the citizens of Maine passed a Clean Elections Law creating a framework for public financing of elections. Several years later, the composition of the state legislature has changed with the election of hundreds of "citizen legislators" who don't need to raise lots of money to get elected. In 2004, 80 percent of all candidates for state office ran on the clean-elections system. Arizona and Massachusetts passed similar laws in 1998, although the Massachusetts statute was gutted by its state legislature. By 2004, Vermont, New Mexico, and North Carolina had also passed clean-election laws. In these systems, candidates

who agree to voluntary spending limits and pass a number of initial thresholds gain access to public financing. If they run against a self-financing or privately financed candidate, they have access to matching public funds up to certain limits. In thirty-nine other states, there are campaigns to pass state clean-election laws.[12]

Those who have worked for some time on the issue of money and politics have identified a variety of concrete "rule changes" that would create a more equitable system of financing elections. These can be grouped as approaches that expand public accountability, restrict the influence of money, and create rules that proactively level the playing field.[13]

A. PUBLIC ACCOUNTABILITY APPROACHES.

One route is to increase public accountability through instant electronic filing and full disclosure that would let voters know more quickly how much funding each candidate is receiving and from whom. This would allow voters to be better-informed "consumers" regarding which special interests are supporting a particular candidate.

B. RESTRICTIONS TO ENSURE POLITICAL EQUALITY.

There are a range of restrictions aimed at creating a level playing field in politics. These include

$ **MAXIMUM CONTRIBUTION LIMITS.** Such measures limit the size of contributions and the influence of large donors. Unfortunately, this opens the door to the Jon Corzine, Steve Forbes, and Ross Perot phenomenon of wealthy individuals self-financing their campaigns, tipping the scales in favor of wealthy individuals.

$ **TIME LIMITS.** Time limits prohibit campaign fund-raising during legislative sessions, thus reducing the risk of pay-for-vote arrangements.

$ **CAMPAIGN SPENDING LIMITS.** Though the 1976 *Buckley v. Valeo* decision ruled against mandatory spending limits, it permitted voluntary spending limits, particularly when linked to public financing. Over eleven states have adopted this solution.

$ **CANDIDATE LOAN LIMITS.** Kentucky is the only state limiting by law how much a candidate can loan him or herself during a campaign.

$ **BAN ON POLITICAL ACTION COMMITTEE (PAC) CONTRIBUTIONS.** Organizations like Common Cause have pushed for bans on contributions from Political Action Committees, and a number of candidates for office have renounced PAC funds. This is not, however, a particularly effective strategy used alone. According to the Center on Responsive Politics, "banning PAC contributions alone, while leaving individual contributions untouched, will not reduce the disparity of political influence between large donors, small donors and non-donors."

$ **BAN ON BUNDLING.** Bundling refers to the pooling of smaller contributions by a central funding organization, which then exercises the influence of the special-interest group in a highly focused distribution of funds to election campaigns. Maximum contribution limits often accompany this proposal. Oregon, Missouri, and Washington State all have some form of prohibition on bundling.

$ BAN ON WAR CHESTS. This prohibits the practice of carrying over money raised from a prior campaign to another election cycle. Montana and Missouri passed these bans, but they have been challenged as unconstitutional in the courts.

$ BAN OR RESTRICTIONS ON OUT-OF-DISTRICT CONTRIBUTIONS. Such laws bar contributions from people outside the office-seeker's district. Oregon passed such a ban in 1994, but it was declared unconstitutional and is limited in its effectiveness in reducing inequity in campaign funding.

$ BAN OR RESTRICTIONS ON SOFT MONEY. The 2002 campaign-finance reform dealt in part with "soft money" contributions to political parties. But soft money also includes contributions to think tanks, not subject to restrictions on gift size, including "think tanks" funded by tax-exempt contributions like Steve Forbes's "Institute for Hope, Opportunity and Growth," whose real, unstated mission was to publicize the policies and activities of candidate Forbes. More money is now pouring into soft-money vehicles on the state level, allegedly to help with activities like voter registration and education.

C. PROACTIVE APPROACHES TO POLITICAL EQUALITY. There are a range of other approaches aimed at leveling the playing field by proactively creating new rules and systems for campaign finance. These include

$ FREE OR REDUCED-RATE BROADCAST TIME AND POSTAGE. The cost of radio and particularly television advertising has pushed the cost of campaigning sky-high. Between 1955 and 1968, broadcast media campaign expenses increased from $10 million to $60 million for presidential elections. In the 2004 presidential campaign, the media costs rose to an unprecedented $400 million. Free or reduced time will have to be subsidized by taxpayers, or by radio and TV stations—not an easy sell in either case.

$ CONTRIBUTION TAX CREDITS AND TAX DEDUCTIONS. One approach to leveling the playing field is to encourage more donations from lower- and moderate-income people by giving a tax credit or deduction for contributions up to $50. Such a system is currently in place in Oregon and Oklahoma, but has not significantly altered the status quo.

$ CONTRIBUTION VOUCHERS. Similar to tax credits and deductions, all voters would have a limited number of voucher dollars they could give to the campaigns of their choice. Such an approach is being explored in Wisconsin, though a prohibition on larger gifts may be subject to constitutional constraints.

$ PARTIAL PUBLIC FINANCING. As of 2004, a growing number of states, including Maine, North Carolina, and Arizona, have some kind of partial public financing.[14] Since 1976, the federal government has provided limited public funding to presidential candidates. Combined with some form of reduced or free radio and TV time, this strategy could be quite effective in ensuring fair access to the political process.

$ FULL PUBLIC FINANCING. This proposal has the greatest long-term rewards if combined with agreements by candidates not to accept private money (personal funds included) during campaign periods and a requirement to collect a minimum number of small "qualifying contributions" from the candidate's own district.

Since many other reforms and rule changes designed to build a fairer economy will not succeed unless there is greater democracy, it will be important to support the movement working to remove money from politics. Some of the tactics to remove the influence of money from politics include:

EDUCATION. Broad public-educational campaigns about the problems of big money in politics are essential. Given the setbacks to federal campaign-finance reform, it is important to promote successful state and local reforms and prepare the way for stronger grassroots pressure at the federal level.

BALLOT INITIATIVES AND STATE LEGISLATIVE INITIATIVES. While avenues to federal reform may be blocked, popular initiatives and state legislation open powerful arenas for prodemocracy activists. In Massachusetts, the clean-election campaign sponsored by Mass Voters for Fair Elections enlisted over 6,000 volunteer campaign workers to collect signatures for ballot questions, drop literature, question candidates, and work the polls on election day.[15]

MOVEMENT-BUILDING. State and local campaigns undergird the basis of a broader movement of organizations and individuals working on this issue. Coalitions bringing together religious groups, labor, business, campaign donors, grassroots activists, and others have begun to build the power to hold candidates accountable on these issues. Elected federal representatives from states with public financing laws have become the strongest advocates for federal policy changes. Most states now have state-level organizations working on campaign-finance reform. There are over ninety such organizations around the country.[16]

What we learn from this is the importance of (1) grassroots education and consciousness-raising activities; (2) finding many roles and ways for people to take action; (3) the need for organizations at the local, state, regional, and national levels; and (4) the importance, for movement-building, of waging campaigns, even when they don't win immediate victories.

Action Box: Getting Money Out of Politics

Americans for Campaign Reform

5 Bicentennial Square
Concord, NH 03301
Tel: (603) 227-0626
Fax: (603) 227-0625
Web: www.just6dollars.org

Americans for Campaign Reform is working to build a grassroots movement to press for publicly financed elections.

Center for Responsive Politics

1320 19th Street NW, Suite 620
Washington, DC 20036
Tel: (202) 857-0044
Fax: (202) 857-7809
Web: www.opensecrets.org

The Center for Responsive Politics is a nonpartisan, nonprofit research group based in Washington, D.C., that tracks money in politics and its effect on elections and public policy. The center conducts computer-based research on campaign-finance issues for the news media, academics, activists, and the public at large. The center's work is aimed at creating a more educated voter, an involved citizenry, and a more responsive government.

Common Cause

1250 Connecticut Avenue NW
Suite 600
Washington, DC 20036
Tel: (202) 833-1200
Fax: (202) 659-3716
Web: www.commoncause.org

A national citizen's lobbying organization promoting open, honest, and accountable government, CC works against corruption in government and big-money special interests.

Fannie Lou Hamer Project

P.O. Box 117
Kalamazoo, MI 49004
Tel: (888) 287-FLHP
Fax: (888) 285-3548
Web: www.flhp.org

Founded in 1999, the FLHP strengthens democracy through bringing justice and equity to the campaign-finance system. Issues of concern include how our current system of campaign-finance reform disenfranchises people of color.

Public Campaign

1320 19th Street NW, Suite M1
Washington, DC 20036
Tel: (202) 293-0222
Fax: (202) 293-0202
Web: www.publiccampaign.org

A national organization dedicated to sweeping reforms to reduce the role of special-interest money in American elections and the influence of big contributors in American politics. Public Campaign works with citizen groups around the country to support public financing of elections.

BUILDING INDEPENDENT POLITICS

Economic inequality is growing, yet virtually no elected leaders have made this a significant political issue. In the past, the fact that more than half the population was losing ground economically would have provided fertile ground for elected leaders interested in the issues of progressive populist politics. But today, as big money dominates politics, the distinctions between the two major political parties in this country are diminishing. With both parties looking more and more alike, there is little public discussion about a wide range of substantive issues affecting a majority of Americans.

When was the last time you heard elected officials talk meaningfully about the increase in working hours and the impact on families, or the need for rethinking schools and child care in the face of our changing economy? What about overcrowding in prisons? Increasing college debt load and the pressure on students to go into career tracks based on the ability to repay loans? When was the last time you heard a politician talk about the moral imperative of eliminating poverty in America? These issues are clearly not scoring high in candidate focus groups with their wealthy donors, and it's not because they're not important—or because voters don't care. In fact, a large constituency exists to support a progressive economic agenda.

To the extent that any of these issues have reached public awareness, it is largely through independent political organizations and parties that have raised issues and organized people to hold elected officials accountable. Independent political organizations give rise to candidates independent of the big-money donors and corporation-dominated agenda.

Third-party efforts in this country have always faced tremendous challenges, especially at the national level. The Populist Party of the late nineteenth century was a significant independent force that was co-opted when the Democrats ran William Jennings Bryan for president in 1896. In 1992, Reform Party candidate H. Ross Perot tapped into voter frustration, winning 19 percent of U.S. voters in the presidential election. Tremendous opportunities exist in local and state-level politics, where over 80 percent of elected positions are nonpartisan races and the costs of participation are much lower.

Part of building countervailing power is to build independent political organizations that function either explicitly or in practice as political parties. Their role is to present candidates and political positions independent of the Democratic and Republican procorporate orthodoxy. Like political parties of the past, only more inclusive, independent progressive organizations can recruit and educate members and candidates, research and develop issues, mobilize a base of voters and campaign workers, and hold elected officials accountable.

One example is the Rainbow/PUSH Coalition (RPC), a multiracial, multi-issue, international membership organization founded by the Reverend Jesse L. Jackson Sr. The RPC is a progressive organization "working to move the nation and the world toward social, racial and economic justice." To date they have registered hundreds of thousands of voters; assisted in the election of hundreds of local, state; and federal officials; mediated labor disputes, and negotiated economic covenants with major corporations resulting in hundreds of minority-owned franchises and car dealerships and other business opportunities. RPC is dedicated to improving the lives of all people by focusing on cures for social, economic, and political ills. Their issues include jobs and economic empowerment, employee rights and livable wages, educational access, fair and decent housing, voter registration and civic education, election law reform, gender equality, affirmative action and equal rights, and environmental justice.

These organizations can function as subgroups within the Democratic Party or as independent party formations. Progressive alliances can function, in the words of the late Senator Paul Wellstone (D–Minn.), as the "democratic wing of the Democratic Party," in contrast to the centrist Democratic Leadership Council with its support for liberalized free trade, corporate tax cuts, and punitive welfare reform. These progressive alliances need the power to withhold support and run their own candidates to challenge procorporate candidates. The Christian Coalition, with its national candidate endorsement arm and voter education capacity, combined with its local ward and precinct operations, serves as a parallel force within the Republican Party.

A number of notable independent political party efforts, like the New Party, the Labor Party, and the Green Party, have successfully run candidates at the local level and won nonpartisan races for school boards, city councils, and higher office. In some states and jurisdictions, they have achieved independent ballot status and run their own candidates or endorsed progressive Democrats. The New Party has also endorsed Democratic candidates for office and then delivered a bloc of independent campaign volunteers and voters who the candidate knows are affiliated with the New Party. As of mid-2004, the New Party had run candidates in over 400 elections, winning more than 300 of them.[17]

In November 1998, the Working Families Party in New York State achieved independent ballot status. New York is one of ten states that allow "fusion," by which a single candidate can run on several different party lines. This enables independent parties to build loyalty and clout when endorsing major party candidates without playing spoiler by drawing votes from the lesser of two evils. A 1997 Supreme Court decision was a setback for the expansion of fusion to other states, unfortunately complicating and limiting the possibilities for third-party growth.

Independent political organizations are a critical part of the infrastructure of progressive power. They train leaders, promote issues that are not initially or currently being addressed, participate in media discussions, and build political power.

Action Box: Building Independent Politics

The Greens/Green Party USA

P.O. Box 1134
Lawrence, MA 01842
Tel: (978) 682-4353
E-mail: gpusa@igc.org
Web: www.greens.org

National alternative political party running candidates concerned about the natural environment and sustainable economics. In addition to running candidates, they educate, organize, and promote sustainable living.

Independent Progressive Politics Network

P.O. Box 1401
Broomfield, NJ 07003
Tel: (973) 338-5398
Fax: (978) 338-2210
E-mail: indpol@igc.org
Web: www.ippn.org

Building a unified, independent, progressive alternative to the corporate-controlled Democratic Party.

Labor Party

P.O. Box 53177
Washington, DC 20009
Tel: (202) 234-5190
Fax: (202) 234-5266
E-mail: info@thelaborparty.org
Web: www.labornet.org/lpa

A progressive labor party formed to give political voice and run candidates concerned about the interests of America's working families.

New Party

88 3rd Avenue, Suite 313
Brooklyn, NY 11217
Tel: (718) 246-3713
Fax: (718) 246-3718
Web: www.newparty.org

A progressive independent political organization building local chapters around the country. By starting small and thinking long-term, they aim to build a multiracial, lively, and creative political organization that can, over time, break the stranglehold that corporate money and corporate media have over our political process.

Working Families Party

88 3rd Avenue
Brooklyn, NY 11217
Tel: (718) 222-3796
Fax: (718) 246-3718
Web: www.workingfamilies
party.org
E-mail: wfp@workingfamilies
party.org

The WFP is a grassroots, community- and labor-based political party with chapters throughout New York State. The goal of the Working Families Party is to more forcefully inject the issues of working-class, middle-class, and poor people—like jobs, health care, education, and housing—into public discourse, holding candidates and elected officials accountable on those issues.

Rainbow/PUSH Coalition

930 East 50th Street
Chicago, IL 60615
Tel: (773) 373-3366
Fax: (773) 373-3571
Web: www.rainbowpush.org

A progressive organization of workers, women, and people of color building the power to make the American Dream a reality.

Real Choice

Web: http://home.earthlink.net/
~realchoice

Real Choice is an Internet website providing information on reaching various third parties currently active in the United States.

Reform Party USA

P.O. Box 9
Dallas, TX 75221
Tel: (972) 450-8800
Fax: (972) 450-8821
Web: www.reformparty.org

Committed to reforming the political system by reestablishing trust in government by electing ethical officials. Dedicated to fiscal responsibility and political accountability.

Reining in Corporate Power

In the last few years, corporate scandals have rocked the U.S. economy. Starting with Enron and WorldCom, rogue corporations have brazenly broken laws, betrayed accounting standards, and usurped public power. In 2002, this prompted a brief window of corporate governance reforms and legislation such as the Sarbanes-Oxley Public Company Accounting and Investor Protection Act (as discussed on p. 172). But these reforms essentially tinkered with relatively minor governance matters compared to the overwhelming problems of corporate power in our democracy.

Concentrated corporate power has been the engine of economic inequality. To reduce inequality, we must not only build people's power as a countervailing force, but also transform the nature of corporations themselves. At the root of many of the rule changes that have worsened inequality is unchecked corporate power implementing narrow agendas. We need to change the rules that govern corporate behavior to prevent harms and limit the way in which corporations are usurping power in our democracy. But we also need to "end corporations as we know them" by dramatically changing who controls them, expanding the diversity and power of stakeholders who determine corporate priorities and activities.

It is possible to be pro-business but anti-corporate. In this book, we draw attention to the powerful harms that have been caused by concentrated corporate power and a system of rules that rewards unbridled corporate behavior even when it is counter to the common good. Any sustainable economy has a wide range of public and private enterprises. Many of the reforms proposed in this section actually strengthen business enterprises. Charles Derber writes about the vision of a new progressive populism in the private market:

> Populists start with a challenge to the values of the unfettered market—a challenging voice in the name of democracy. But it is not opposed to markets per se, and seeks to show that democratic reforms can help preserve a more sustainable market order. Populists seek to keep markets in their place, but also to help them function better in areas where they belong. By remodeling markets on social principles, the new populism seeks to revive democracy and strike a more appropriate balance between markets, government, and civil society.[18]

The process of transforming corporations has several stages. The first is checking corporate power and containing future harms. Advanced reforms are aimed at changing the governance of corporations and reasserting wider democratic controls.

INITIAL ACTIONS TO CHECK CORPORATE POWER

There is a growing number of campaigns focused on holding large corporations accountable for the damage they have caused. Many of these campaigns respond to individual corporate harms that companies may have caused, such as tobacco poisoning, environmental degradation, or employment of workers in sweatshop conditions.

There is an emerging analysis, born from the experience of activists who have spent their lives fighting corporate crimes, of how corporations acquired so much power in the first place.[19] Campaigns that challenge corporate harms need to incorporate this analysis, while pushing for reforms within the current legal and political context.

SHAREHOLDER ACTIONS. In the mid-1960s, a Catholic religious order, the Sisters of Loretto, filed a series of shareholder resolutions with the Blue Diamond Coal Company concerning their environmental and labor practices in Appalachia. This marked the beginning of a new era in shareholder activism as the good sisters doggedly pursued the management of Blue Diamond and drew tremendous publicity to the issue of strip-mining at shareholder meetings and in the media.

In the last three decades, socially active organizations have used the shareholder resolution as a tool to pressure corporations. However, because of the corporate proxy voting system, heavily weighted to favor management, shareholder resolutions rarely win a majority. A share-holder campaign that garners 7 percent of the vote would be considered highly successful. But, even when they lose, shareholder resolutions affect the behavior of individual corporations because of the adverse publicity they attract.

To be politically successful, shareholder reso-lutions must be part of larger campaigns using a multitude of tactics. In the 1980s, organizations working to end apartheid in South Africa pres-sured hundreds of corporations to adopt the "Sullivan Principles" and other codes of conduct in their business with South Africa, or to remove their operations completely from the country.[20] The divestment movement was key in support-ing domestic movements within South Africa in the struggle to end apartheid.

Shareholder pressure is starting to create a new social contract around downsizing and executive pay. In 1997, United States Trust Com-pany of Boston filed a shareholder resolution with AT&T, calling for a freeze on executive com-pensation during periods of downsizing. This was in response to the 100 percent pay increase that AT&T CEO Robert Allen received just as AT&T laid off 49,000 workers in 1996 (according to one office joke, AT&T means "Allen and Two Temps"). The resolution garnered 14 percent of shareholder votes, a minor revolution in the undemocratic world of corporate proxies. In the ensuing year, AT&T brought in a new CEO and reviewed compensation policies. In January 1998, AT&T announced 10,000 additional layoffs—but indicated this time that they were freezing salaries and bonuses for top managers.

Half a Billion Votes for Sustainability

Each year, hundreds of social-issue share-holder resolutions are introduced at companies. To view lists of many of these resolutions, visit the Interfaith Center on Corporate Responsibility (www.iccr.org).

In 2004, the United Methodist Church introduced a resolution with Wal-Mart, calling on the company to report on its environmental, economic, and social sustainability. The resolution received over 14 percent of the vote, highly significant given that most institutional investors automatically vote "for management."

2004 Shareholder Resolution—Wal-Mart Stores, Inc.

Whereas, we believe that Wal-Mart as the world's largest company aspires to be a good employer, a trusted corporate citizen and a valued member of communities where it does business. To sustain these commendable goals in a global economy, we believe, requires adoption and imple-mentation of practices designed to protect human rights, worker rights, land and the environment. It is our expectation that Wal-Mart will be a leader in social and environ-mental, as well as economic performance.

Companies are beginning to publish sustainability reports and are taking a long-term approach to creating shareholder value through embracing opportunities and managing risks derived from economic, environmental and social developments. We believe sustainability reporting should be included in our company's annual report.

According to Dow Jones Sustainability Group, sustainability includes: "Encouraging long lasting social well being in communities where they operate, interacting with different stakeholders (e.g. clients, suppliers, employees, government, local communities and non-governmental organizations) and responding to their specific and evolving needs thereby securing a long term 'license to operate,' superior customer and employee loyalty and ultimately superior financial returns" (www.sustainability-index.com; March 2000). As shareholders, we are troubled about the number of lawsuits filed against our company related to labor violations and sex discrimination and the negative press that this has attracted (*BusinessWeek*, 10/6/03). We are also concerned about the number of negative articles in the press, such as the recent publicity surrounding some contractors cleaning Wal-Mart stores, the number of issues that are the subject of these articles and the fact that these articles are in the serious business press, including *The Wall Street Journal* and the *Financial Times*.

We need assurances that the Board of Directors and top management are undertaking a serious examination of the company's overall strategy and its impact on various stakeholders including the environment thus preserving the company's reputation and its license to operate.

We believe corporate sustainability includes a commitment to healthy communities and a healthy environment including paying a sustainable living wage to employees in the United States and every country where our company operates. Workers need to have the purchasing power to meet their basic needs.

The sustainability of corporations, we believe, is connected to the economic sustainability of their workers and the communities where corporations operate and sell products and the environmental viability of the planet. Effective corporate policies can benefit both communities and corporations.

Resolved: shareholders request the Board of Directors to prepare at reasonable expense a sustainability report. A summary of the report should be provided to shareholders by October 2004 [Note: Since the resolution did not win, no such report was conducted].

> We believe the report should include:
>
> 1. The company's operating definition of sustainability.
> 2. A review of current company policies and practices related to social, environmental and economic sustainability.
> 3. A summary of long-term plans to integrate sustainability objectives throughout company operations.

RESPONSIBLE CONSUMER ACTION. While shareholder actions represent the voice of the "owners" of companies, another powerful stakeholder group that corporations respond to is consumers. Organizers have employed consumer educational campaigns and boycotts as a means to pressure companies around particular behaviors. One well-known example was the international boycott of Nestlé Company during the 1970s over its unscrupulous practices in marketing infant formula products in developing countries. The boycott forced Nestlé to stop deceptive promotion of infant formula and persuaded the company to sign one of the first corporate "codes of conduct."[21]

In the 1960s and '70s, César Chávez and the United Farm Workers successfully appealed to consumers in their campaign for union recognition with grape and lettuce growers. Boycotts of textile products manufactured by the J.P. Stevens Company drew national attention to the company's hardball anti-union tactics.

Research does show that a critical mass of consumers will avoid products made by companies with bad environmental records, unfair labor practices, and cozy relationships with governments that violate human rights. Consumers will even pay more for products that are certified in some manner as "green," "union-made," and "sweatshop free."

Like shareholder actions, consumer actions such as boycotts are most effective when they are tied to larger campaigns using multiple tactics. To reach consumers directly, campaigns against U.S. and international sweatshop labor have employed action protests at store doorways. However, consumer choice actions must go beyond the framework of individual action to succeed in changing corporate behavior.

SOCIALLY RESPONSIBLE INVESTING. Pressuring corporations by using public shareholder campaigns to withdraw capital investment has evolved into a full-time, generally accepted wing of the larger investment-management profession.

A growing number of investors want some social conditions applied to the investment of their money. Increasing amounts of money, over $2.14 trillion in 2003, were managed according to social criteria.[22] Much of the volume of activity is involved in screening out corporations that cause "social injuries" and searching for the "relatively clean" investment options.

A much smaller amount of money is actually rechanneled into "community" or "alternative investments," such as affordable housing, worker-owned enterprises, and consumer cooperatives that are rebuilding a new economy on fundamentally different principles and values. This is essential in building a fairer economy, as discussed on pages 217–222.

LAYING GROUNDWORK FOR MORE FUNDAMENTAL CORPORATE REFORMS. Each of the approaches described above is important in addressing the specific harms caused by individual corporations. Yet they fail to go beyond a limited corporate accountability framework with its emphasis on stopping individual corporate harms. The next reforms focus on broader actions to reassert public-interest controls and sovereignty over corporations.

DEMOCRATIZING CORPORATIONS: CORPORATE GOVERNANCE REFORMS

Corporations guilty of ruthless downsizing, excessive compensation, and short-term fixes are quick to say that they are acting in the interests of shareholders, responding to their severe demands. It is true that many institutional investors on Wall Street force companies to operate on short-term horizons in terms of profitability. But to blame shareholders in general, many of whom have limited powers to affect the direction of corporate management, is disingenuous. The Sarbanes-Oxley Public Company Accounting and Investor Protection Act of 2002 instituted elements of needed reforms, some of which are described below.

PROHIBIT SELF-DEALING. Many large companies have boards of directors filled with insiders, often composed of chief executive officers of other peer corporations. Many do not provide real accountability in issues such as setting executive compensation. In 2002, the Sarbanes-Oxley legislation spelled out new rules on corporate governance, including provisions prohibiting board members from having business dealings with the corporation or working for the auditing firm.[23]

EXPAND STAKEHOLDER REPRESENTATION. Another powerful reform would be to expand governing boards to make sure all stakeholders are represented, not just capital investors. These other stakeholders include employees, consumers, and members of the communities where corporations operate. Many European countries mandate by law representation of these other interest groups on corporate boards. This practice is called co-determination, discussed on pages 155–156.

DEMOCRATIZE CORPORATE SHAREHOLDER/ STAKEHOLDER GOVERNANCE. It is a myth that shareholders own and control their corporations. There is a big difference between ownership and decision-making control. Many shareholders are essentially disenfranchised by a system dramatically tilted in favor of management. Shareholders can propose resolutions that are put before the shareholders in the form of proxies or ballots. Most shares are controlled by mutual funds and institutional investors who vote almost automatically "for management."

Most individual shareholders don't have a direct vote. It's as if the owners of large apartment buildings were allowed to cast votes for all their tenants in presidential elections.

One meaningful reform has occurred in the last few years. For over a decade, shareholder groups have advocated for an "Investor Right to Know" law requiring mutual funds and institutional investors to disclose to their clients how they voted on shareholder resolutions. In 2002, the Securities and Exchange Commission approved new rules requiring mutual-fund disclosure.

Other proposed reforms could include

$ **Rules and regulations governing shareholder resolutions and actions should be neutral, not biased in favor of management.**
$ **Shareholders should be able to put forward contested candidates and slates in board elections.**
$ **Shareholder resolutions should be binding on the corporation, not just advisory.**

CORPORATE DISCLOSURE. In exchange for being granted state charters giving them the right to exist and reap profits, corporations should have more stringent reporting and disclosure requirements. Corporations operate today with little or no public scrutiny, ostensibly justified by the need to protect trade secrets. Property law has evolved to grant corporations a right to privacy, similar to that enjoyed by human beings. There is no legal or moral reason why corporations, which are, after all, allowed to exist only at the pleasure of the people, should not have to disclose information in the public interest. Some matters of public interest for disclosure include the amount of taxes paid, government subsidies received, wages and salaries for all employees, and citations for breaking the law.

EXPANDING THE PEOPLE'S SOVEREIGNTY: ELIMINATING CORPORATE RIGHTS

The most far-reaching transformation should be the elimination of powerful transnational corporations as they are currently constituted. These global corporations, with no accountability to community or nation-state, pollute our environment, steal our democracy, plunder our treasuries, grind down our workers, poison our culture, obliterate our memories, define our realities, and reduce all our human tendencies to consumption.

Worse yet, we accept their existence and surrender our sovereignty to them, allowing them to commit immeasurable harm to our planet. Our minds have been so colonized by this most modern form of human domination and subjugation that we don't even recognize the extent to which we have given up what belongs to all of us.

The postcorporate world will still have businesses, many of them large-scale with thousands of employees.[24] But they will be much more accountable to communities, workers, consumers, and the public interest. There are several other fundamental actions that reflect the reassertion of democratic rights over corporations and an end to corporate rule.

FEDERAL CHARTERING OF CORPORATIONS. Corporations are presently chartered at the state level. There are wide disparities in regulation and charter oversight from state to state. An enormous percentage of multinational corporations is chartered in the state of Delaware because of its low taxes and lax regulatory environment.

Placing democratic controls on corporations is difficult on a state-by-state basis because of the way states are pitted against one another in a deregulation race to the bottom. One remedy would be to require corporations to be chartered both at the state and federal levels, with uniform disclosure and accountability standards. This requirement might be limited to corporations over a certain size operating multinationally or conducting a certain percent of their business in different states.

The national progressive populist organizing effort Alliance for Democracy has formed a national committee to "prepare a model federal law defining, chartering, and controlling interstate corporations." Once a draft statute has been developed, the Alliance aims to conduct an educational campaign and congressional hearings in support of federal charters.

ELIMINATE PERSONHOOD RIGHTS FOR CORPORATIONS. We must challenge judicial doctrines that give corporations expanded rights generally accorded only to people—free speech (including political contributions), privacy rights, and others. We must strictly circumscribe the rights of corporations, placing human rights and the rules instituted by democratically elected governments above the interests and rights of corporations.

EXPAND HUMAN RIGHTS IN RELATION TO CORPORATIONS. We must expand the Bill of Rights to include employees in corporations (free speech, freedom of assembly), citizens in shopping malls, and so on. We must eliminate the current bias in property law giving corporations more rights and powers in the workplace than people.

CHANGE CORPORATE CHARTERS TO REDEFINE ACCEPTABLE PRACTICES AND BEHAVIORS. We must amend state corporation codes to ban corporations from owning other companies and operating with unlimited powers, and to outlaw certain behaviors and revoke corporate charters of outlaw corporations.

As discussed in Chapter 3, the early-nineteenth-century precursors of the modern corporation were chartered by state legislatures to perform circumscribed activities tied to a public purpose. These charters would have to be renewed every few years if the corporations' owners wanted them to continue to exist. There are repeated examples of charters not being renewed or revoked for the corporation's failure to obey the law or serve the public interest. Ralph Nader wrote about one case:

> In 1815, Massachusetts justice Joseph Story ruled in the case of *Terrett v. Taylor* that a private corporation that misused its franchises could have its charter revoked under a procedure known as "quo warranto" (by what authority). Justice Story said that such a risk of revocation was "a tacit condition annexed to the creation of every such corporation."[25]

In California, a coalition of thirty public-interest organizations has presented overwhelming evidence to the state's attorney general alleging that the corporate charter for Unocal, a large oil conglomerate, should be revoked. They document Unocal's environmental devastation, unethical and unfair treatment of workers, usurpation of political power, the undermining of U.S. foreign policy, and violations of environmental and labor laws. Unocal's pipeline construction project in Burma has drawn the attention of international human rights organizations because the military regime has reportedly seized land, forcibly relocated villages, and used forced labor of children and the elderly to build it. Under California state law, the attorney general has a legal duty to go to court to revoke a corporation's charter if it is abusing private powers granted by the state.[26]

Five days after the petition was filed, the California attorney general rejected the petition. But Unocal opponents aim to appeal the case. Loyola Law School Professor Robert Benson, who is leading the challenge, indicated that corporate reformers are not naïve enough to think that they will break up Unocal any time soon. "Our fundamental goal," said Benson, "is to change the public discourse and the media perception of the power of corporations versus people, to float the idea that people are sovereign over corporations."[27]

In 1998, Eliot Spitzer, the attorney general of New York State, asked the court to revoke the charters of two tobacco industry "research" corporations. Spitzer indicated that he would broaden the powers of people over corporations, instituting the "death penalty" for repeat lawbreaking corporations. In a 1998 statement, Spitzer explained his position: "When a corporation is convicted of repeated felonies that harm or endanger the lives of human beings or destroy our environment, the corporation should be put to death, its corporate existence ended, and its assets taken and sold at public auction."[28]

More challenges lie ahead. An Alabama judge filed a complaint in state court demanding that the corporate charters of the five major tobacco companies be revoked because of their violation of dozens of laws. *Adbusters* magazine and other groups are launching a campaign to revoke the charter of tobacco giant Philip Morris.

BAN CORPORATIONS FROM OUR DEMOCRACY. We must exclude business corporations and their trade associations from elections, lawmaking, education, and public-policy debates over community values, legal philosophy, and policy. This would address both the financing of elections and the influence-peddling process once people are elected.

Action Box: Reining in Corporate Power

180 Movement for Democracy and Education

Web: www.corporations.org/democracy

180 is dedicated to building a campus-based movement for political empowerment and participatory democracy through education and organizing.

Alliance for Democracy

681 Main Street
Waltham, MA 02451
Tel: (781) 894-1179
Fax: (781) 894-0279
E-mail: peoplesall@aol.com
Web: www.afd-online.org

AFD works to free all people from the corporate domination of politics, economics, the environment, culture, and information, and to establish true democracy and a just society with a sustainable, equitable economy. It has fifty-two chapters across the country.

Center for Commercial-Free Public Education

360 Grand Avenue, Suite 385
Oakland, CA 94610
Tel: (510) 268-1100
Fax: (510) 268-1277
E-mail: unplug@igc.org
Web: www.commercialfree.org

The Center for Commercial-Free Public Education is a national nonprofit organization that addresses the issue of commercialism in our public schools. The center provides support to students, parents, teachers, and other concerned citizens organizing across the United States to keep their schools commercial-free and community-controlled.

Council on Economic Priorities

30 Irving Place
New York, NY 10002-2386
Tel: (212) 420-1133
Fax: (212) 420-0988
E-mail: cep@echonyc.com
Web: www.cepnyc.org

The council was founded in 1969 as a public-service research organization, dedicated to the accurate and impartial analysis of the social and environmental records of corporations. CEP is committed to making information on corporate social responsibility available to millions of consumers, investors, policy makers, and businesses.

Interfaith Center for Corporate Responsibility

475 Riverside Drive
5th Floor, Room 550
New York, NY 10115
Tel: (212) 870-2294
Fax: (212) 870-2023
E-mail: info@iccr.org
Web: www.domini.com/IRRC.html

The Interfaith Center on Corporate Responsibility (ICCR) is the leading organization in the shareholder resolution process, instrumental in coordinating resolutions co-filed by different investors. While ICCR's members are faith-based organizations, its broader constituency includes many nonreligious groups that look to it for guidance on social issues.

Social Investment Forum

1612 K Street NW, Suite 600
Washington, DC 20006
Tel: (202) 872-5319
Fax: (202) 822-8471
E-mail: info@socialinvest.org
Web: www.socialinvest.org

The Social Investment Forum is a national nonprofit membership association dedicated to promoting the concept, practice, and growth of socially and environmentally responsible investing. Its members include over 500 social-investment practioners, including financial advisors, portfolio managers, banks, mutual funds, community development loan funds, foundations, researchers, and analysts.

Co-op America

1612 K Street NW, Suite 600
Washington, DC 20006
Tel: (800) 58-GREEN or (202) 872-5307
Fax: (202) 331-8166
E-mail: info@coopamerica.org
Web: www.coopamerica.org
National Green Pages Web: www.greenpages.org

A national organization that provides economic strategies, organizing power, and practical tools for businesses and individuals to address today's social and environmental problems.

Program on Corporations, Law and Democracy

P.O. Box 246
S. Yarmouth, MA 02664-0246
Tel: (508) 398-1145
Fax: (508) 398-1552

POCLAD is working to address the root causes of corporate domination through education and support for local organizing.

INFACT

256 Hanover Street
Boston, MA 02113
Tel: (617) 742-4583
Fax: (617) 367-0191
E-mail: infact@igc.apc.org
Web: www.infact.org

INFACT is a national grassroots organization whose purpose is to stop life-threatening abuses by transnational corporations and increase their accountability to people around the world.

Transnational Resource and Action Center

P.O. Box 29344
Presidio Building 1016, Second Floor
San Francisco, CA 94129
Tel: (415) 561-6567
Fax: (415) 561-6493
Web: www.corpwatch.org

TRAC works to educate people in the United States and around the world about the social and environmental impacts of corporate globalization, inspiring them to take action. It strives to help build an alternative form of grassroots globalization by creating local, national, and international links for democratic control over corporations, human rights, and environmental justice.

Stakeholder's Alliance

1735 S Street NW
Washington, DC 20009
Tel: (202) 797-0606
Fax: (202) 265-6245
Web: www.essential.org/capp

The Alliance is an association of organizations and individuals that promotes the interests of corporate stakeholders. It acts to hold corporations fully accountable to all stakeholders for their actions.

Changing the Rules to Build a Fair Economy

There is a chicken-and-egg relationship between building power and changing the rules of our economy to build a more equitable society. Without more people power, it will be difficult to enact rule changes to reduce inequality. At the same time, certain rule changes will help reverse the "wheel of misfortune," enable ordinary people to have more time and power, and lay the groundwork for more people power.

One way to think about this section is to ask: "If ordinary people had more power, what rule changes might they enact?"

Global Trade and Investment Rules

In Chapter 3, we discussed ways in which the global economic system, with its emphasis on unbridled free trade, contributes to economic inequality in the United States (and elsewhere), eroding our democracy and worsening the lives of low- and moderate-income people around the world.

It is clear that we cannot solve the problem of economic inequality in the United States without addressing the new rules and institutions that govern the global economy. The popular slogan of the last two decades, "think globally, act locally," reflects a luxury that we no longer have. We must now "act locally and act globally." Grassroots activists trying to improve conditions for workers and the natural environment cannot succeed in their efforts without reforming the rules

of the new global game. Neither can community-based development institutions working to gain control over the local economy.

Changes in the global economic and power structure require that grassroots citizens' movements around the world be involved in issues related to trade, international investment, raising human rights and environmental standards, and building citizen alliances to counter the power of transnational corporations.

The range of activities to address globalization include education, building coalitions and movements across borders, pressing to transform trade and investment agreements, and canceling the international debt burden on many countries in the southern hemisphere. We need to rethink the rules governing the global economy and begin to put in place a new set of rules.

EDUCATION ABOUT THE GLOBAL ECONOMY. Most people in the United States are woefully uninformed when it comes to the rest of the world. When women from all around the world gathered in Beijing, China, for the 1996 Women's Conference, many representatives from the United States reported being embarrassed by their lack of understanding about the global economy.[29] Rural Malaysian farmers and slum dwellers from Calcutta, without formal literacy or access to the media, knew more about the workings of the global economy and the policies of the International Monetary Fund than most of the North American participants. We must remedy this by dramatically increasing our understanding and analysis of the global economy. Educating ourselves and others is an essential action step at this stage of movement-building.

What is NAFTA?

Implemented in 1994
US - Canada - Mexico

• Not just "Trade" but Investor Rights
• Toothless "Side Agreements" on Labor & Environment
• Race to the Bottom:
 - wages
 - workers rights
 - environmental protections
 - democratic rights

FAIR TRADE. It is not antitrade or anti-investment to oppose some agreements such as NAFTA, the Free Trade Area of the Americas, and those negotiated by the World Trade Organization. Advocating speed limits does not mean that one is "anti-automobile." The U.S. economy has been integrating into the global economy from the country's inception and will continue to do so. However, the rules of how we participate should not be written solely for the benefit of investors and global corporations.

If there were a fairer distribution of power in this country, then the interests of consumers, workers, communities, and the environment would also be more significantly represented in these agreements. Agreements would be written to raise standards, not fuel a race to the bottom—

the rapid lowering of standards as the result of global competition. We can imagine what trade agreements that promote the economic "high road" might look like: unrestricted trade between nations with high labor and environmental standards; social tariffs on products made in countries with gross human-rights violations and low environmental standards. Countries would have the ability to impose emergency sanctions in the face of "product dumping" from nations that restrict the right to organize and maintain low wages and environmental protections.

We must organize to oppose future trade and investment agreements like the Multilateral Agreement on Investment (MAI) that would dramatically increase the power of transnational corporations at the expense of human rights. Even if the MAI treaty doesn't move ahead in its original form, corporations will continue to push for its objectives. In the same way corporations in the 1880s attained the rights of personhood in their successful journey to expand their rights, today they want to attain the powers of nation-states.

In the coming years, we can expect a number of developments on the free-trade agenda:

$ **an attempt to pass a Central America Free Trade Agreement (CAFTA),**

$ **attempts to expand NAFTA-like trade agreements with other Latin American countries such as the Free Trade Area of the Americas,**

$ **new free-trade agreements with Asian and African countries,**

$ **a push to include more human rights-violating countries like China in free-**

**trade organizations like the World Trade
Organization,**

$ **new rounds of trade and investment
agreements negotiated through the World
Trade Organization, and**

$ **attempts to place provisions of the MAI in
future trade and investment agreements.**

The United States is one of the few countries that must bring trade treaties back to its elected governments for ratification. This gives U.S. fair trade activists an opportunity to pressure our elected officials about the terms of these global agreements.

There are now opportunities to reshape the terms of trade agreements that legislate new standards. In 1998, proponents of a NAFTA-style procorporate trade bill for Africa were gathering momentum in Congress. The African Growth and Opportunity Act offered African nations trade benefits with the United States, but required them to cut social spending and food subsidies, privatize public assets, and cut corporate taxes. Additional conditions required African nations to eliminate national laws that restrict foreign ownership of land, farms, mines, and other enterprises, and to adopt free-trade agricultural policies that would jeopardize food security.

Fair-trade activists rallied and proposed countertrade legislation. The HOPE for Africa bill, introduced by Rep. Jesse Jackson Jr. (D–Il.) in March 1999, takes a "lifting standards" approach to trade, rather than a race to the bottom. With over sixty cosponsors, it offered broad market access for African goods but encouraged countries to meet internationally recognized environmental and labor rights and worker safety standards.

The HOPE for Africa proposal was concerned with who stood to benefit from economic growth, aiming to keep more value in African communities rather than letting it flow out to absentee-owned global corporations. The bill proposed that companies that benefit from trade preferences must have 51 percent African ownership and hire 80 percent African workers. It included debt relief, ensuring that no African country would have to pay more than 5 percent of its annual export earnings for debt. It restored U.S. development aid to 1994 levels and targeted assistance to address the AIDS epidemic. The procorporate African Growth and Opportunity Act was silent on the matter of debt, AIDS, and the restoration of U.S. development aid.[30] The HOPE for Africa bill passed the House but died in the Senate in 1999. However, President Clinton revived the legislation in the Africa Trade and Development bill that incorporated some elements of HOPE and was passed into law on May 18, 2000.

The HOPE for Africa proposal was an example of trade legislation that was a radical departure from the previous one-sided debate. It demonstrated the possibilities for proactive and positive fair-trade legislation. It offered a vision of the way trade practices can strengthen, rather than undermine, community standards and aspirations.

**BUILDING CROSS-BORDER ORGANIZING
EFFORTS.** One important part of building a fair economy in the United States is to build greater global security and fairness. Our security is now completely interwoven with the prospects of people all around the planet. Transnational

corporations are pushing workers in each nation in a race to the bottom, pitting communities against one another in terms of who will offer the lowest wage and the least restrictive health and environmental standards. Global capitalism has, on the one hand, brought us to the brink of economic and environmental imbalance. On the other hand, it has created the conditions necessary for global citizenry and solidarity.

There are constituencies in the United States opposed to free trade policies for reasons of wanting our country to go it alone. Economic nationalists like Pat Buchanan advocate for a "closed border" protectionist stance to protect jobs and markets within the United States; the rest of the world be damned.[31] The progressive populist approach advocates remaining interconnected with people all over the world and, out of long-term self-interest and solidarity, lifting standards everywhere.

We need to reach across borders and build relationships with grassroots movements around the planet as they challenge the negative impacts of globalization. This is difficult to do as isolated individuals. To respond to the power of global corporations, we need to build parallel international organizations. Some of us are already part of organizations that cross borders, but we are only beginning to tap them as sources of insight and power in building a fair economy at the global level. One ongoing effort to build a citizens' alternative to globalization is the annual World Social Forum, which has taken place in Brazil and India in recent years as a counterconference to the World Economic Forum, an elite gathering of global corporate leaders. These events have produced a whole vision of alternatives to corporate globalization.[32]

Labor, religious, and civic organizations don't generally think of themselves as institutions operating in a global context, but they are. They could do more to build their power as global institutions. Actions can take the form of hosting international delegations of activists, communicating by e-mail and Internet, responding to action notices from global advocacy organizations, and participating in campaigns, like those aimed at pressing companies with sweatshops around the world and maquiladora assembly factories along the Mexican border.

POLITICAL AND CONSUMER ACTIONS. Two ways people in the United States can express their international solidarity are through consumer boycotts and preferential purchasing of fairtrade items. Organized consumer boycotts have helped to improve working conditions at the Hanes pants factories in Guatemala and El Salvador. Worldwide boycotts of Nike shoes forced that company to end child labor practices in Vietnam, where, as the organizer's slogan declared, "every day is bring-your-daughter-to-work day."

On campuses across the country, students are demanding that clothing emblazoned with college logos not be made in sweatshops. Colleges make a lot of money licensing their names to apparel makers, many of whom outsource the manufacturing to companies with overseas operations. Students at Duke, Georgetown, the University of Wisconsin, and twenty other schools have undertaken campaigns that have included protests, sweatshop fashion shows, rallies, teach-ins on sweatshops, and sit-ins at administration offices.[33]

DEBT CANCELLATION MOVEMENT. There is a worldwide movement of religious organizations and concerned people seeking the cancellation of international debts. They are particularly concerned about fifty-two countries in the southern hemisphere that are heavily indebted and forced to divert scarce government resources away from education, health care, and other vital services in order to repay foreign debts. As of 2004, these fifty-two countries owed $375 billion to the wealthy countries. Every day, sub-Saharan Africa pays $27 million to the rich world in debt service.[34]

In Africa, each child indirectly inherits an average of $379 in debt at birth. In the Congo, the dictator Mobutu borrowed $8.5 billion from international financial institutions, most of which went into his personal fortune. Today, every person in the Congo owes $283 toward the country's external debt. In Nicaragua, each child is born owing over $2,000, while average yearly income is only $390. These debts force nations onto a crushing treadmill of making interest

payments rather than investing in their citizens and building their communities.

Some people ask, why should these countries be let off the hook? In reality, much of this money was borrowed by corrupt or undemocratic governments for projects that didn't help the broader citizenry. The cost of canceling the debt will not be significant for ordinary citizens in the northern nations. Jubilee UK estimated it would cost each British taxpayer about $3.50 a year to cancel debts directly owed to Britain. If every penny of the debt was cancelled, the maximum loss to the rich countries would be about $21 per taxpayer.[35]

Citizens who live in northern lender nations have a self-interest in canceling this debt, because the negative consequences on people in the global south "boomerang" back on lender countries. A large debt burden motivates many poor countries to lower labor standards in an effort to attract foreign currency and investment to earn hard currency to repay loans. Citizens in heavily indebted countries are so impoverished that they cannot afford to purchase U.S. exports and products, contributing to the massive U.S. trade deficit. This leads to lower U.S. wages, increased poverty, and greater job insecurity, factors that contribute to greater inequality in the United States. The largest debtor countries, out of desperation to pay back interest, ravage the environment through logging, clear-cutting, strip-mining, deforestation, and unrestrained pollution. These environmental problems know no borders. Citizens in lender nations end up subsidizing bad bank loans in their countries and military interventions to maintain stability caused by violent conflicts and wars using weapons purchased with global loans.[36]

In the summer of 2005, it is quite likely that a major initiative to provide debt relief to thirty heavily indebted countries will pass at the G-8 Summit in Scotland. This will be a victory after a decade of efforts by organizations like Jubilee.

NEW RULES FOR THE GLOBAL ECONOMY. Ultimately, the rules of the global economy need to be changed to stop the negative impact of unregulated economic globalization. After the Asian financial crisis triggered a U.S. stock market plunge in September 1998, even the boosters of global capitalism started to publicly suggest that there might be a need for a new global "architecture" to address the volatility of the system. Some, like Jeffrey Sachs from the Earth Institute at Columbia University, one of the high priests of unbridled markets, suggest that there is a need for "speed bumps" to slow the movement of investment dollars in and out of "emerging markets."[37]

Citizens and civil society organizations need to be involved in broad discussions about what the rules of the new global economy should look like. For several years now, members of the U.S. Congressional Progressive Caucus have filed what they call the Sustainable Global Economy Act. While this legislation will not pass in the short term, it lays out a good roadmap for reform.

The legislation calls for a national dialogue, sponsored by a federal Commission on Globalization. It urges a series of Bretton Woods–type conferences, with representation of civil society organizations, to forge recommendations for a Global Sustainable Development Agreement. It calls on the U.S. government to develop and implement a strategy to restructure the international financial system to avoid global recessions, protect the environment, ensure full employment, reverse the polarization of the wealthy and everyone else, and support the efforts of different jurisdictions to mobilize and coordinate their economic resources.

Concrete elements of the act include

$ **Imposing an internationally coordinated tax on foreign-currency transactions, sometimes referred to as the "Tobin Tax."[38] This would discourage the frenzied currency speculation that can make or break a developing country's economy overnight.**

$ **Renegotiating NAFTA, GATT, and World Trade Organization (WTO) agreements with stronger representation of civil society interests to encourage just and sustainable development.**

$ **Creating international public-investment funds for sustainable development.**

$ **Creating international institutions to perform functions of monetary regulation currently performed, inadequately, by central banks.**

$ **Reorienting the International Monetary Fund (IMF), World Bank, and other international financial institutions away from the imposition of austerity reforms and toward support for labor rights, environmental protection, rising living standards, and encouragement for small and medium-sized local enterprises.**

$ **Terminating all IMF activities except those fulfilling its original mandate of addressing short-term external trade imbalances.**

$ **Establishing a binding United Nations Code of Conduct for Transnational Corporations, including regulation of labor, environmental, investment, and social behavior.**

$ **Instituting mechanisms to hold corporations incorporated or operating in the U.S. liable for harms caused abroad.**

Action Box: Globalization Action Organizations

50 Years Is Enough Network
1025 Vermont Avenue NW
Washington, DC 20005
Tel: (202) IMF-BANK
Fax: (202) 879-3816
E-mail: wb50yearsAigc.apc.org
Web: www.prairienet.org/acas/50years.htm

A coalition of over 100 citizens' groups, representing five million Americans, joined in the common cause of bringing democratic reform to the operations of the World Bank and International Monetary Fund and halting the socially and environmentally destructive policies of these institutions. It has over 185 international partner organizations in some sixty-five countries.

Canadian Centre for Policy Alternatives

251 Laurier Avenue West, Suite 1004
Ottawa, Canada K1P 5J6
Tel: (613) 563-1341
Fax: (613) 233-1458
E-mail: brucec@policyalternatives.ca
Web: www.policyalternatives.ca

The Centre is an independent Canadian organization founded in 1980 to promote research on economic and social policy issues from a progressive point of view.

Global Exchange

2017 Mission Street, Suite 303
San Fransisco, CA 94110
E-mail: membership@globalexchange.org
Web: www.globalexchange.org

Global Exchange is a nonprofit research, education, and action center dedicated to promoting people-to-people ties around the world. Since its founding in 1988 it has striven to increase global awareness among the U.S. public while building international partnerships around the world.

Global Justice

1225 Connecticut Avenue NW, Suite 401
Washington, DC 20036
Tel: (202) 296-6727
Fax: (202) 296-0261
Web: www.globaljusticenow.org

Global Justice was founded in 2001 to mobilize students to advocate for political and social change on global AIDS and other issues of global justice. They have a presence on over 200 campuses.

Global Trade Watch Public Citizen

215 Pennsylvania Avenue SE
Washington, DC 20003
Tel: (202) 546-4996
Fax: (202) 547-7392
Web: www.citizen.org/pctrade/tradehome.html

Global Trade Watch is the division of Public Citizen that fights for international trade and investment policies promoting government and corporate accountability, consumer health and safety, and environmental protection through research, lobbying, public education, and the media. Global Trade Watch is on the cutting edge of research and advocacy in the field of international trade and investment. Public Citizen is a national consumer and environmental organization founded by Ralph Nader in 1971.

Grassroots International

179 Boylston Street, 4th Floor
Jamaica Plain, MA 02130
Tel: (617) 524-1400
Fax: (617) 524-5524
Web: www.grassrootsonline.org

Grassroots International promotes global justice through partnerships with social-change organizations. They work to advance political, economic, and social rights and support development alternatives through grant-making, education, and advocacy.

Institute for Agriculture and Trade Policy

2105 1st Avenue S
Minneapolis, MN 55404
Tel: (612) 870-0453
Fax: (612) 870-4846
Web: www.iatp.org

The Institute for Agriculture and Trade Policy's mission is to create environmentally and economically sustainable rural communities and regions through sound agriculture and trade policy. They assist public-interest organizations in coalition-building and influencing both domestic and international policy making through monitoring, analysis and research, education and outreach, and information systems management.

International Forum on Globalization

1555 Pacific Avenue
San Francisco, CA 94109
Tel: (415) 771-3394
Fax: (415) 771-1121
E-mail: ifg@ifg.org
Web: www.ifg.org

The International Forum on Globalization (IFG) is an alliance of sixty leading activists, scholars, economists, researchers, and writers formed to stimulate new thinking, joint activity, and public education in response to the rapidly emerging economic and political arrangement called the global economy.

Jubilee USA

222 East Capitol Street NE
Washington, DC 20003-1036
Tel: (202) 783-3566
Fax: (202) 546-4468
E-mail: coord@j2000usa.org
Web: www.j2000usa.org/j2000/
International Web Sites: www.jubilee2000uk.org has research on debt crisis; http://www.jubileedebt campaign.org.uk/ has campaign information.

Jubilee is an international organization working to eliminate the crushing international debt on countries in the global south. There is both a strong U.S. organization and an international effort based in England.

National Labor Committee

275 7th Avenue, 15th floor
New York, NY 10001
Tel: (212) 242-3002
Fax: (212) 242-3821
Web: www.nlcnet.org

The National Labor Committee (NLC) is a human-rights advocacy group that focuses on the promotion and defense of workers' rights. Through establishing long-standing working relationships with nongovernmental, human-rights, labor, and religious organizations, the NLC puts a human face on the global economy. The NLC educates and actively involves the public in actions aimed at ending labor abuses, improving living conditions for workers and their families, and promoting the concept of a living wage.

Oxfam America

26 West Street
Boston, MA 02111
Tel: (617) 482-1211
Fax: (617) 728-2594
E-mail: info@oxfamamerica.org
Web: www.oxfamamerica.org

Oxfam International is a confederation of twelve organizations working together with over 3,000 partners in more than 100 countries to find lasting solutions to poverty, suffering, and injustice.

Third World Network

228 Macalister Road, 10400
Penang, Malaysia
Tel: 60-4-2266728 / 2266159
Fax: 60-4-2264505
E-mail: twn@igc.apc.org or twnet@po.jaring.my

The Third World Network is an international network of organizations and individuals involved in issues relating to development, the Third World, and north-south issues. Their objectives are to conduct research on economic, social, and environmental issues pertaining to the global south; to publish books and magazines; to organize and participate in seminars; and to provide a platform representing broadly southern-hemisphere interests and perspectives to an international audience such as UN conferences.

Transnational Resource and Action Center

P.O. Box 29344
Presidio Building 1016, Second Floor
San Francisco, CA 94129
Tel: (415) 561-6568
Fax: (415) 561-6493
E-mail: corpwatch@igc.org
Web: www.corpwatch.org

TRAC works to educate people in the United States and around the world about the social and environmental impacts of corporate globalization, inspiring them to take action. TRAC strives to help build an alternative form of grassroots globalization by creating local, national, and international links for human rights, environmental justice, and democratic control over corporations.

United for a Fair Economy

29 Winter Street
Boston, MA 02108
Tel: (617) 423-2148
Fax: (617) 423-0191
E-mail: info@faireconomy.org
Web: www.faireconomy.org

United for a Fair Economy has developed a number of popular education programs about the global economy.

Reducing Wage Inequality

A number of the remedies discussed in this chapter address wage and income disparities, including reforms in the Federal Reserve, global trade policy, and others.

The overall decline in wages since the early 1970s is directly linked to the decline of unionization in the United States. With the erosion of labor's clout, laws and regulations protecting minimum-wage standards have been weakened and the disparities between highest-, average-,

and lower-paid workers have accelerated. Grassroots organizations are focusing on wage issues at the local level and even on the campus level, while legislators at the federal level try to raise the minimum wage to keep pace with inflation. This section examines some of these efforts and discusses ways to up the ante on the wage-inequality debate.

INCREASING STATE AND FEDERAL MINIMUM WAGES. The minimum wage has historically played an important role in raising the earnings of low-wage workers (which also helps workers the next few rungs up the economic ladder).

Unfortunately, the policy debate over the issue has focused almost exclusively on the risk of job loss, despite the fact that recent research demonstrates that such job loss effects are either nonexistent or negligible. Given these findings, too little attention has been paid to the question of who benefits from the increase in the minimum wage. Analysis done by organizations such as the Economic Policy Institute reveals that benefits of the minimum wage go almost exclusively to those who need it the most: full- and part-time adult workers in lower-income families.[39]

The current minimum wage of $5.15 an hour—$10,712 a year—is not enough for a family with children to eke out a living. Raising the minimum wage is only a small step in closing the ever-growing gap. The minimum wage should be closer to a living wage that would lift a family of four over the poverty line. It should be raised to at least $8.10 an hour over the next two years and indexed annually to inflation so we don't need to wait for politicians to act in order to protect its buying power.[40]

With four more years of President Bush and most likely a Republican-controlled Congress, we will probably see further erosion of the spending power of the federal minimum wage. But a growing number of states are not waiting for Washington, D.C. to wake up. In 2004, several states, including Florida and Nevada, passed initiatives to raise their state minimum wages.

LOCAL LIVING-WAGE CAMPAIGNS. Across the country, coalitions have come together at state and municipal levels to advocate for living-wage ordi-

nances. Robert Kuttner, editor of the *American Prospect*, calls living-wage struggles "the most interesting (and under-reported) grassroots enterprise to emerge since the civil rights movement."[41]

In 1995, the city of Baltimore passed the first living-wage ordinance. As of November 2004, over 123 cities, counties, and universities have passed living-wage ordinances.[42] These include San Antonio, Boston, Chicago, and Milwaukee. Coalitions of labor, religious, and community activists have pushed successfully for the passage of living-wage ordinances. There are currently 119 active municipal living-wage campaigns organizing to institute laws that will require companies doing business with these cities to pay a living wage, usually pegged to the amount that would lift a family of three or four above the region's poverty level. Most ordinances include vendors, private contractors, and organizations receiving substantial public subsidies, including real estate developers who get housing-development subsidies.

These living wages range between $7.50 and $10.00 per hour, depending on the location. Unfortunately, wages typically based on the federally determined poverty line are usually not adequate. Estimates of the wages necessary to relieve a family from the need for food stamps, housing subsidies, and other forms of assistance are closer to $11 to $13 per hour, while complete economic self-sufficiency would require even higher wages.[43] A living wage based on the poverty line might be better termed a *survival wage*. But, at times, local campaigns must make political calculations about what has the potential for passage without ignoring the inadequacy of even living wages as they are often defined.

In 1996, Los Angeles passed a living-wage ordinance that required companies with county contracts or subsidies to pay $7.25 an hour plus $1.25 per hour for workers without private health insurance. The ordinance initially covered over 7,000 workers in a city where 35 percent of the workforce earns less than $7.00 an hour.

Living-wage proposals, as well as efforts to raise state and federal minimum-wage levels, all encounter the same concerns: Will raising the minimum wage hurt low-wage workers by increasing unemployment? Will increased wages force small employers out of business? Robert Pollin and Stephanie Luce, in their book, *The Living Wage: Building a Fair Economy*, draw on both historical evidence and an analysis of several communities that have passed living-wage ordinances to respond to these concerns.

Their verdict: Living-wage ordinances have not increased unemployment, nor placed undue burdens on small businesses. The positive effect of boosting the wages of a targeted number of low-wage workers is enormous, in many cases lifting people over the poverty line and expanding

health care, training, and vacation benefits. Taxpayers don't have to subsidize low-road companies by supplementing their low wages with food stamps, housing subsidies, and emergency-room health care for the uninsured. Even businesses benefit from increased morale and efficiency, more incentives to train employees, and reduced employee turnover.

Living-wage movements can also help revitalize urban communities. They offer an alternative to the "business-subsidy model" of urban revitalization in which cities and states outbid each other in offering tax breaks, infrastructure grants, and other forms of corporate welfare to lure companies and jobs to their communities. Living-wage ordinances are part of a high-road economic-development approach that raises wages, supports and expands existing businesses, and offers limited subsidies to companies that agree to provide long-term community benefits.

Many major community, religious, and labor organizations are taking up the living-wage issue. Such organizing is a good first step in focusing attention on disparities in pay between the highest-paid and average wage-earners.

Business Leaders for a Living Wage

For years, whenever Senator Edward Kennedy introduced legislation to raise the federal minimum wage, he looked for an employer to stand beside him in support of a modest wage hike. There was never a stampede. Eric Sklar, the founder of Burrito Brothers, a D.C.–based restaurant chain, was one of the exceptions.

In 1999, however, a project of United for a Fair Economy called Responsible Wealth launched Business Leaders and Investors for a Living Wage, an effort to rally employers and investors to support local living-wage efforts and federal increases in the minimum wage. Several hundred employers and top managers have taken a pledge to pay a living wage, while investors pledge to scrutinize companies for their practices related to wages and wage disparities.

Their argument: it's good for business. Paying workers a decent wage encourages loyalty, reduces employee turnover, and boosts productivity. High-road businesses that want to pay their workers decently have a hard time competing with low-road businesses that pay poverty wages. Raising the minimum wage creates a level playing field where businesses compete in terms of other qualities, not who can squeeze their workers the most.[44]

FULL EMPLOYMENT. You can't earn wages if you can't find a job. Government policies should promote full employment and assure jobs for every American who needs one. This could be accomplished through Federal Reserve policies (discussed later) and a public works program, like the Works Project Administration during the 1930s, that guarantees a government job as a last resort.

ELIMINATING PUBLIC SUBSIDIES FOR WAGE INEQUALITY. The issue of wage inequality touches a lot of nerves, particularly excessive salaries paid to CEOs and other professionals. As discussed earlier, the disparity between highest and average workers in the United States now exceeds 400 to one. Most people are incensed by the arrogance of top managers paying themselves multimillions while overall paychecks remain flat and workers are downsized. The public is even more outraged when they learn that corporations reduce their taxes by deducting CEO salaries. As a result, other taxpayers pick up the revenue slack caused by excessive paychecks. One broadly popular reform denies corporations the right to deduct the excessive pay of top managers from corporate profits.[45]

Currently, the Internal Revenue Code allows all businesses to deduct "reasonable salaries and benefits" as a cost of doing business. "Reasonable," however, is not defined. A 1993 congressional reform to cap the deductibility of salaries at $1 million is so full of loopholes that it is virtually useless. If the directors of a corporation declare that the pay of their top managers is "perform-ance-based," they avoid the cap.

Congressman Martin Sabo (D-Minn.) and others in Congress have taken the lead in advocating for a definition of "reasonable" that caps the deduction for executive pay at twenty-five times that of the lowest-paid worker in a firm. Under such a provision, companies could reduce their tax liability by raising the wage floor or reducing top pay.

Eliminating the deductibility of pay accomplishes a number of things. One, it sets a social norm: corporations cannot expect tax subsidies for excessive and unequal pay. Two, it stimulates an important national debate about what the appropriate gap between highest- and lowest-paid workers should be. Finally, it generates revenue from corporations that have chosen to heap their profits on a limited few rather than distribute them widely to all workers. The amount of potential revenue is not insignificant. If the Income Equity Act had been applied to only the top two executives at the 365 companies covered in the annual *Business Week* pay survey, the U.S. Treasury would save over half a billion dollars a year.[46] Subsidizing these excessive salaries through the tax code is a form of corporate welfare.

Monumental Pay Cap

The Washington Monument is 555 feet tall. Say it signifies the 2003 average compensation for CEOs in the Fortune 500. The average worker salary would only be sixteen inches tall, representing a ratio of 419 to one. In 1965, the worker's monument was thirteen feet, six inches tall, representing a ratio of forty-one to one.

In April 1998, hundreds of people from around the country came to Washington for a forum and lobby day to close the wage gap. They lobbied Congress to raise the minimum wage and eliminate the deduction that corporations can take for excessive compensation. They brought a replica of the average worker's Washington Monument to place beside the real Washington monument for some perspective. It conveniently fit into the overhead compartment of their airliner. Just a few years ago, protesters would have had to bring the monument replica in a pick-up truck. At this rate, in a few years' time they'll be able to fit the worker's Washington Monument in a handbag.

A WASHINGTON MONUMENT PERSPECTIVE ON PAY: THE AVERAGE C.E.O. NOW MAKES 419 TIMES THE SALARY OF THE AVERAGE WORKER.

MINE! ALL MINE!

C.E.O. PAY

AVERAGE WORKER PAY

United for a Fair Economy · 4/17/98

EXPANDING NOTION OF WAGE RATIO. The Income Equity Act would limit the deductibility of excessive compensation to salaries that do not exceed twenty-five times the salary of the lowest-paid worker in a firm. Another set of reforms would broaden the establishment of reasonable ratios between highest and lowest pay to other aspects of public policy.

$ LIMIT WAGE DISPARITIES IN CHARITABLE CORPORATIONS. A number of so-called charitable nonprofit corporations have enormous disparities in their wages. Some nonprofit health-care providers pay their CEOs 150 times the wages of the lowest-paid workers

in their hospitals and care facilities. Through our tax code, we grant special status and subsidies to certain types of corporations so that they can operate in the public interest. These are charitable, nonprofit corporations, often with the Internal Revenue Status of Chapter 501(c)3 corporations. The benefits that flow to these entities include lower-cost postage, exemption from sales tax, and the valuable ability to allow contributors to take tax deductions for contributions. These benefits cost the state and federal treasuries billions of dollars, but in principle these charitable corporations are performing valuable services that relieve burdens on government and serve the common good at once.

Following the principle that the public sector should not subsidize excessive inequality, we propose amending the definition of charitable corporations to include a maximum permissible wage ratio. We propose that corporations granted not-for-profit charitable status have a maximum ratio between highest- and lowest-paid workers of eight to one.

$ LINK POLITICIAN PAY TO RATIO OF MEDIAN INCOME. How do we ensure that our elected leaders have a direct stake in the uplift of all, not just the wealthy? What if congressional pay could never exceed three times the median household income? If congressional pay increased or decreased based on the real fortunes of the median U.S. family, it would create direct incentives for elected officials to think about lifting the income floors of all Americans.

$ INCORPORATE WAGE RATIOS INTO COLLECTIVE BARGAINING AGREEMENTS. Unions could enforce a reduction in inequality by advocating wage ratios in their collective bargaining agreements. Contracts could specify that when senior management wants to lift their own paychecks, the wage floor would also rise by a certain ratio. Trade unionists in other countries have negotiated such agreements; in the United States, the United Electrical Workers union has pressed for such provisions.

$ NEW PROSPERITY INDEXES BASED ON INCOME RATIOS. The commonly used economic indicators in the United States fail to adequately measure genuine economic sustainability and health. There are hundreds of indicators used by the United Nations that are a more accurate measure of human welfare and economic strength. The ratio between top and bottom wage-earners should become incorporated into regional and national indicators.

$ LINK THE TOP MARGINAL TAX RATE TO A WAGE RATIO. To reduce the most extreme forms of inequality, the top marginal tax rates could be linked to a ratio of the median household income. A top tax rate of 70 percent would apply to income that exceeds ten times the median income. Such a policy would lay the groundwork for the maximum wage proposal discussed below.

$ CAPPING EXCESSIVE INCOME. One way to put an absolute brake on excessive inequality is to cap incomes. In ancient Greece, Plato argued that the city's richest citizens should not have more than four times the wealth of the poorest citizen. Aristotle reasoned that the ideal gap was five to one. In the Torah and Old Testament teaching about the Jubilee, the righteous community would address excessive inequality by a forgiveness of debts and a redistribution of land every forty-nine years. Ancient philosophers recognized that too great a level of inequality would undermine the community of the faithful and that inequality carried from generation to generation is problematic.

Proposals to reduce wage disparities range from increasing marginal tax rates to a maximum wage, at which point income exceeding a maximum is taxed at a 100 percent level. In his book *The Maximum Wage*, labor writer Sam Pizzigati proposes a "ten times rule" under which income exceeding ten times the minimum wage would be taxed away. He points to historical precedents such as Franklin Roosevelt's call for a 100 percent tax on all individual income over $25,000—a sum equal to over $200,000 today. By the end of World War II the top marginal tax rate on the very rich was 91 percent.[47]

According to Pizzigati, there are many benefits of a maximum wage linked to a minimum wage. While taxes on the top are increased, taxes on everyone else would be reduced, putting more money in the pockets of people who work for wages. It would also reduce the speculation in the economy stemming from overconcentrations of wealth. "Money is like manure," Pizzigatti writes. "It only does good when you spread it around. Which investment of a million dollars, after all, stimulates more jobs? One billionaire laying out a million for a Rembrandt or a thousand regular folks buying home computers for kids?"[48]

A high marginal tax rate or maximum wage would ensure a high level of social solidarity, as the wealthy would have a direct financial stake in seeing the minimum wage and the income of their lowest-income neighbors rise. "The richest and most powerful Americans would have a vest-ed interest in improving the well-being of the poorest and least fortunate Americans," according to Pizzigati. For every dollar of increase in the minimum wage, the folks at the top would get to keep ten dollars.

While actions dealing with wages and income are imperative, the issues of inequality we have discussed won't be adequately addressed until we focus on assets or wealth.

Action Box: Closing the Wage Gap

AFL-CIO

815 16th Street NW
Washington, DC 20006
Tel: (202) 637-5000
Fax: (202) 637-5058
Web: www.afl-cio.org

The AFL-CIO is the central labor body for the United States, representing thirteen million U.S. workers. Major programs include labor education, Voices@Work, working women, research, corporate affairs, organizing, and public policy advocacy.

Association of Community Organizations for Reform Now (ACORN)

2101 South Main Street
Little Rock, AR 72206
Tel: (501) 376-7151
Fax: (501) 376-3952

ACORN is a grassroots coalition of low- and moderate-income people organizing to build power and influence at the local level. There are 120,000 ACORN member families, organized into 600 chapters in forty-five cities, which have been involved in twenty living-wage campaigns in eight years.

Living Wage Resource Center

1486 Dorchester Avenue
Boston, MA 02122
Tel: (617) 740-9500
Fax: (617) 436-4878
Web: www.livingwagecampaign.org

The Living Wage Resource Center was established in 1998 to track the living-wage movement and provide materials and strategies to living-wage organizers nationwide.

Business Leaders and Investors for a Living Wage

c/o Responsible Wealth
29 Winter Street
Boston, MA 02111
Tel: (617) 423-2148

National network of business leaders and investors who are publicly expressing support for increased state and federal minimum wages and local living-wage campaigns.

Wealthy Individuals Who Say "I Didn't Do It Alone" Shed Insights into Wealth Creation

"Self made men, indeed! Why don't you tell me of the self-laid egg?"—Francis Lieber

During the political battle over preserving the federal estate tax, an interesting thing happened. Thousands of multimillionaires and billionaires signed a petition, sponsored by UFE's Responsible Wealth project, to maintain the estate tax. The fact that there were wealthy people who would endorse paying a tax was news in itself. But underlying their support for a tax on accumulated wealth is a new way of looking at society's contribution to wealth creation and a reevaluation of the American success narrative.

Some commentators argued that this "billionaire backlash," as Newsweek called it (see p. 209), was rooted in unselfishness or class betrayal. But for many of the individuals who signed the petition, it was a matter of simple accounting: "We owe something back to the society that created opportunities for us."

The notion that wealthy individuals might have an obligation to pay something back to society is a radical departure from today's individualistic, antigovernment ethos. Many successful people view government and society as irrelevant to their good fortune, or worse, as a hindrance. They attribute their success solely to their own character, values, and performance. A 2004 report published by Responsible Wealth took on this "great man theory of wealth creation."

Relying on interviews with wealthy supporters of the estate tax, United for a Fair Economy published "I Didn't Do It Alone." The report amplifies the voices of several individuals who counter the myth and reflect on the role of society, privilege, historical timing, and luck in their success, in addition to their own moxie, creativity, and hard work. Those profiled in the report discuss such factors as the role of U.S. property law and patents, public investment in education and technology, orderly and regulated investment markets, and other factors in creating a fertile ground for their wealth creation.

Investor Warren Buffett observes that his skills are "disproportionately rewarded" in the U.S. marketplace. He reflects that if he were attempting to do business in another country, without our system of property laws and market mechanisms, "he would still be struggling thirty years later."

Amy Domini, founder and president of Domini Social Equity Fund, believes she owes her success in part to basic government-provided public infrastructure. "Getting my message out over the public airwaves has allowed me to be far more successful than if I had been born in another time and place," she said in a 2004 interview. "The mail runs on time, allowing me to communicate with existing and potential shareholders, and the rise of the publicly financed Internet has lowered the costs of these communications still further. I can fly safely—and most often conveniently—throughout the country, sharing my ideas and gaining new clients, again thanks to a publicly supported air-travel system."

Venture capitalist Jim Sherblom was the chief financial officer of biotech wonder company Genzyme when it went public in 1986. He estimates that the stock market, a socially financed and regulated institution that provides enormous liquidity for private companies, created 30 to 50 percent of the value of the company. The stock market's liquidity and trust depend enormously on societal institutions that regulate, ensure transparency, and enforce fair transactions. If there is any doubt about this, consider how the accounting scandals behind Enron and WorldCom affected the value of dozens of publicly owned technology companies. Hundreds of billions of dollars in wealth vanished overnight. Cook the books, shake the public trust, and watch the wealth disappear.

New York–based software designer Martin Rothenberg argues that his "wealth is not only a product of my own hard work, but resulted from a strong economy and lots of public investment in others and me." He credits his New York City public technical school for his early education, and the GI Bill and government-backed student loans for funding his university degree. Later, government investment directly supported the lab research that led to his establishing a company that he later sold for $30 million.

Our society needs a new narrative of success, one that shows a more complex reality: that societal forces are important in fostering success. This is no small challenge, for the American self-made success narrative is deeply rooted. But wider recognition of the social roots of wealth should lead to a deeper understanding of the need to pay taxes and invest in public goods and services.

The mythology of self-made success would not be such a problem if it were a matter of simple personal self-delusion. But this worldview, held by many who hold great power and influence in our society, has serious consequences for the kind of society we have, and for our commitment to equality of opportunity.

From this creed of individual achievement, it is a short distance from "I made this money myself" and "It's all mine" to "Government has no business taking any part of it." If one really believes "I did it all myself," then any form of taxation quickly becomes a form of larceny.

Perhaps the myth-makers understand what is at stake here. If luck, privilege, and societal investment are more important in determin-

ing success outcomes than individual character, then shouldn't the rules of the economy be organized to strengthen starting-gate equality and minimize the vagaries of luck?

These narratives have powerful implications for public policy. If society's role in wealth-creation is as big as this report suggests, then society has a claim upon these great fortunes and an obligation to foster a more level playing field.

Reducing the Asset and Wealth Gap

There are a variety of actions we can take to reduce the enormous gap in wealth ownership in America. Asset-building policies have been an integral part of U.S. history. The Homestead Act in the nineteenth century gave white settlers access to land—often land expropriated from Native Americans. During the years after World War II, the GI Bill enabled millions of Americans, primarily white men, to have a debt-free college education and access to low-interest mortgages.

Unfortunately, in recent years, our government has targeted its subsidies to those who don't need any help with asset-building. An estimated $175 billion in federal subsidies are directed to corporations in the form of tax loopholes, direct cash transfers, and subsidized access to public resources.[49] This misdirected "corporate welfare" benefits large corporations and affluent individuals. Government assistance

should be focused on nonaffluent households, small businesses, family farms, and democratic enterprises such as cooperatives. Immediate reforms are needed to enable low- and moderate-income families to earn, save, and invest more money in order to build asset security.

Thoughtful Americans are advancing a variety of proposals that would narrow the wealth gap, ranging from expanding worker ownership to creating universal asset-building accounts. What follows is a brief survey of some of these initiatives.

DEDICATED TAX-EXEMPT SAVINGS PROGRAMS. A politically popular way of promoting savings and asset-building is through Individual Retirement Accounts (IRAs), which exempt accounts from taxation at the front end or, like the Roth IRA, from the back end. Similar accounts have been proposed to enable people to save for home ownership, and individuals can withdraw, without penalty, $10,000 from an IRA for a first-time home purchase. A tax credit for college education went into effect in the late 1990s. Over the long run, we should make sure that tax policies encourage access to higher education and asset-building by low- and middle-income Americans rather than disproportionately subsidizing wealthier Americans.

INDIVIDUAL DEVELOPMENT ACCOUNTS (IDAS). IDAs are like individual retirement accounts (IRAs), but are targeted to low- and moderate-income households to assist them in asset accumulation. Participants in IDAs may have their tax-free deposits matched by public or private dollars. A number of private charities have financed pilot IDA programs through community-based organizations. A publicly funded IDA program, with matching funds based on income, would provide significant opportunities for asset-poor households to build wealth.[50] Participants could withdraw funds from IDAs in order to purchase a home, finance a small business, or invest in education or job training. Even small amounts of money can make a substantial difference in whether or not individuals get on the asset-building train.

BABY BONDS. One interesting proposal to reverse inequality trends over generations would be to create a "kids savings account" for children when they are born. In 2003, the British parliament created just such a program, which people refer to as the "baby bond." The idea is to provide every American child with $1,000 at birth, plus $500 a year for children ages one to five, to be invested either until adulthood or until retirement. Through compound returns over time, the account would grow substantially, provide a significant supplement to Social Security and other retirement funds, and enable many more Americans to leave inheritances to their children. That would strengthen opportunities and asset-building across generations.

Such universal accounts could be capitalized by a portion of estate-tax revenue levied on estates in excess of $10 million, redistributing a small portion of the largess of the top 0.5 percent to address the generational inequalities of wealth.

EXPAND EARNED-INCOME CREDIT AND RAISE NO-TAX THRESHOLD. As discussed later in the taxation section (page 203–210), progressive tax policies can enable working families to keep more money in their pockets. These include an expanded earned-income credit, an increased personal exemption, and a higher no-tax threshold.

AFFORDABLE HOUSING. Owning a home has long been considered a stepping stone to building assets. Public policies that increase access to home ownership include subsidized mortgages and mortgage insurance, down-payment assistance funds, second-mortgage subsidy programs, and grants and low-interest loans for home improvements and weatherization. Stricter enforcement of fair housing and community reinvestment laws would remove barriers to asset-building for people of color.

Home ownership is not the only tenure option that should be promoted, however, as it is not appropriate for all households at all stages of life. Nor should home ownership be considered the only "asset account" and "line of credit" for low-

and moderate-income families, as it has many risks. Access to decent and affordable cooperative and rental housing would enable many people to save and meet other financial security goals. Public subsidies should be targeted to "third sector" housing ownership that includes community land trusts, housing cooperatives, mutual housing, and other models that reduce housing costs and preserve long-term affordability.

A GI Bill for the Next Generation?

On June 22, 1944, President Franklin Roosevelt signed into law the Servicemen's Readjustment Act of 1944, known as the "GI Bill of Rights." Without the GI Bill, the American Dream would have never become real for millions of Americans. The GI Bill opened tremendous opportunities for veterans and their families and transformed America (see box on pages 117–118).

The GI Bill was one of the greatest investments made in our nation's history—and it almost didn't happen. Influential college presidents testified against it, complaining that millions of unschooled veterans would lower education standards and create millions of "educational hobos." Congressional conservatives tried to block it as too expensive and gave in only after concerted grassroots lobbying by the American Legion.

It's time to revitalize the American Dream and restore the foundation for a new century of progress. America needs a bold effort to expand opportunity, close the racial wealth divide, and ensure that college is affordable to all Americans.

Why can't we establish a GI Bill for the next generation? Like the housing and education programs after World War II, such an effort should not be restricted only to those who served in the military. A universal fund would provide grants for college and subsidized mortgages for all those who need them. This opportunity fund could be capitalized by a reformed federal estate tax, our nation's only tax on accumulated wealth. Much of that wealth has appreciated tax-free over generations. A reformed estate tax, completely exempting the first $2.5 million in wealth for an individual and $5 million for a couple, would generate almost a trillion dollars in revenue over the next two decades. Unfortunately, Congress is considering abolishing the estate tax, even at a time of war, sacrifice, huge budget deficits, and widening gaps in opportunity.

What would be more American than for those who have accrued tremendous wealth in our country to pay a small portion of their accumulated wealth to capitalize a fund for opportunity for the next generation?

BROADENING EMPLOYEE OWNERSHIP. In *The Ownership Solution*, Jeff Gates urges us to look beyond wage and job policies and expand the ownership stake that workers and their communities have in private enterprise. There is a range of public policies that could promote broader ownership and reward companies that share the wealth with employees, consumers, and other stakeholders. These include encouraging employee ownership through government purchasing, licensing rights, public pension plan investments, loans and loan guarantee programs, and so on.[51]

While the overall trend of wealth growth has been toward concentration, a significant exception is found among employee owners. As of 1998, more than 8 percent of total corporate equity was owned by nonmanagement employees, up from less than 2 percent in 1987. This ownership takes the forms of Employee Stock Ownership Plans (ESOPs), profit-sharing plans, widely granted stock options, and other forms of broad ownership. In 2004, according to the National Center on Employee Ownership, the average ESOP had about $45,500 in corporate equity, disregarding what they were able to save from their paychecks.[52] A second study of 102 ESOP companies in Washington State found that average employee-owned wealth was $32,000.[53]

POLICIES THAT ADDRESS THE OVERCONCENTRATION OF WEALTH. Many of the proposals described above are aimed at assisting people with very little savings and assets to increase their personal net worth. There will continue to be distortions, however, in who benefits from public policy unless we address the issue of the current overconcentration of wealth and power at the pinnacle of the population.

While there is some consensus that government should play a role in helping the assetless build a nest egg, there are strongly divergent views as to how to appropriately address the overconcentration of asset power. Many of these initiatives are discussed in the upcoming section on Fair Taxation (pages 203–210). They include: taxing capital gains at the same rate as wages, maintaining and expanding progressive inheritance and estate taxation, and taxing wealth.

Action Box: Reducing Wealth Inequality

Asset Development Institute/ Center on Hunger and Poverty

Brandeis University
Mailstop 077
Waltham, MA 02454-9110
Tel: (781) 736-8885
Fax: (781) 736-3925

The Center on Hunger and Poverty promotes policies that improve the lives of low-income children and families.

Corporation for Enterprise Development

777 North Capital Street NE, Suite 800
Washington, DC 20002
Tel: (202) 408-9788
Web: www.cfed.org

CFED is a nonprofit, nonpartisan organization that works to expand economic opportunity. It has led the effort to pilot, monitor, and federate different efforts with Individual Development Accounts and other wealth-building strategies.

National Center for Employee Ownership

1736 Franklin Street, 8th Floor
Oakland, CA 94612
Tel: (510) 208-1300
Fax: (510) 272-9510
Web: www.nceo.org

The National Center for Employee Ownership (NCEO) is a membership and research organization that serves as the leading source of accurate, unbiased information on employee stock-ownership plans (ESOPs), broadly granted employee stock options and related programs, and ownership culture.

National Low Income Housing Coalition (NLIHC)

1012 14th Street NW, Suite 610
Washington, DC 20005
Tel: (202) 662-1530
Fax: (202) 393-1973
E-mail: info@nlihc.org
Web: www.nlihc.org

The Coalition was founded in 1974 with the aim of ending America's affordable-housing crisis. Through education, organizing, and policy advocacy, it seeks to ensure decent affordable housing within healthy communities for everyone.

New America Foundation/ Asset Building Program

1630 Connecticut Avenue NW, 7th Floor
Washington, DC 20009
Tel: (202) 986-2700
Fax: (202) 986-3696
Web: www.newamerica.net

The purpose of New America's Asset Building Program is to significantly broaden the ownership of assets in America, thereby providing all Americans with both the means to get ahead and a direct stake in the overall success of our economy. This major new direction in public policy promises to be as successful in the twenty-first century as the Homestead Act was in the nineteenth century, and as the GI Bill and home mortgage deduction were in the twentieth century.

Shared Capitalism Institute

570 Cress Street
Laguna Beach, CA 92651
Tel: (949) 494-4437
Fax: (770) 451-4985
Web: www.sharedcapitalism.org

The Shared Capitalism Institute promotes broader
ownership—including employee and community
ownership—as a remedy to address growing
income and wealth disparities in the United States
and internationally.

United for a Fair Economy

29 Winter Street
Boston, MA 02108
Tel: (617) 423-2148
Fax: (617) 423-0191
E-mail: info@ufenet.org
Web: www.ufenet.org

The Racial Wealth Divide Program at UFE works to
educate the public about the root causes of the racial
wealth divide and coordinates public policy work to
close the wealth gap.

Fair Taxation

Unfair taxation is one of the factors that helps
foster and reinforce the income and wealth
divide in America. As we discussed earlier, the
special treatment and loopholes that exist for
holders of great wealth undermine the fairness
and progressivity of the tax system.

Tax policy will be a major issue in the coming
years because the radical right is focused on
bankrupting the federal government and states
as a way to force reductions in public spending.
There will be a need to defend the remaining
components of the progressive tax system and
stop further shifts in the tax burden from the
wealthy onto everyone else.

The resentment toward taxation is rooted in
the excessive individualism in our culture; a
desire to reap all the benefits without having to
pay the toll. It is a failure to recognize our interdependence and the necessity of solidarity for
our survival and well-being. Taxation is not only
the "price we pay for civilization," as noted by

Oliver Wendell Holmes; it is the price we pay for
community and solidarity.

Beyond broad taxation, the moral justifica-
tion for taxing great wealth at higher rates and
imposing an inheritance tax is that the wealthy
have benefited disproportionately from the
defense of property and the fertile ground created by public investment for private wealth. In the
words of Bill Gates Sr., it is a "payback to society, the price of building and protecting wealth in
the United States."

At stake is the question of what kind of society we want to become. Do we want to dismantle
the ladder of opportunity we have attempted to
build over the last half century? Do we want to
further polarize our country along the lines of
wealth and power?

DEFENDING PROGRESSIVE TAXATION. Progressive tax reforms should be founded on principles
of fairness, simplicity, and their adequacy in raising sufficient revenue to pay for government
services. In the coming years, right-wing forces

will be proposing a range of unfair tax policies at the federal level including a flat tax, the abolition of inheritance taxes, a national sales tax, and other schemes to further shift the tax burden from wealthy asset-owners to people who work for wages and salaries. Each proposal will be wrapped in a deceptive, pseudopopulist cloak, but as always, the bottom line is found in the distribution of tax benefits—who pays more and who pays less.

At the state level, the radical right is working to change state constitutions to limit the growth in public spending, tying the hands of legislatures that see the need to raise revenue. Through the Taxpayer Bill of Rights or TABOR laws, they attempt to constrain spending rather than address the root causes of state budget problems like runaway prescription-drug costs. In the end,

such laws force cuts in public services that erode the quality of life at the local level. Local coalitions are forming to fight these efforts (see the Action Box on page 210).

STOP THE TAX CHEATS BY ENFORCING THE TAX CODE. One of the ways that the radical right has undermined the progressivity of the federal tax system is by weakening enforcement on the wealthy. If you are a working poor person claiming the earned-income credit, the possibility of getting audited is nine times more likely than an investor with an oil and gas depletion tax shelter.[54] Journalist David Cay Johnston estimates that between $200 billion and $300 billion of revenue is annually lost to the U.S. Treasury because of wealthy individuals and corporations gaming the tax code with loopholes and avoidance shelters.[55]

Ambushing the Flat Taxers

It was Tax Day, April 15, 1998 in Boston. Two Republican Congressmen, Dick Armey of Texas and Billy Tauzin of Louisiana, came to Boston to promote their snake-oil proposals for a flat tax and national sales tax.

They set up the classic photo opportunity by inviting national TV and print media to the Boston Tea Party Ship Museum, where they planned to symbolically throw the entire IRS tax code into Boston Harbor. With the cameras rolling, they stepped up to the railing of

the Tea Party boat to heave an enormous trunk labeled "Tax Code" into the water.

Suddenly, from around the bow of the ship, two United for a Fair Economy (UFE) protesters appeared with a plastic baby doll, paddling in the precarious "Working Family Liferaft." They moved into position directly below where Armey and Tauzin were standing and pleaded "Please don't sink us with your flat tax! You'll drown us with your sales tax!" Meanwhile, UFE infiltrators on the Tea

Barrali, and baby doll Veronica into effervescent Boston Harbor.

Ambushed, Representatives Tauzin and Armey retreated to their limousine, which was surrounded by cheering members of the Rich People's Liberation Front, a UFE theater group holding signs that said, WE LOVE YOU, ARMEY AND TAUZIN!, TAX CUTS FOR US, NOT OUR MAIDS, FREE THE FORBES 400, and WE RICH LOVE THE FLAT TAX!

Party ship, dressed in fancy suits and dresses, started to chant "Sink them with the flat tax! Drown them with the sales tax!"

UFE staff approached all the media with press releases, explaining the symbolism of the protest and offering evidence of how both the flat tax and national sales tax would sink working families. Armey and Tauzin stood paralyzed on the boat. Their media "handlers" went nuts.

Then Armey and Tauzin threw the tax code trunk into the harbor, swamping the fragile liferaft and plunging Chris Hartman, Kristin

Simultaneously, images of the tipping Working Family Liferaft were broadcast across the planet through hourly runs on CNN and other national networks. The Reuters International story declared GOP TAX PHOTO OP BACKFIRES. The Associated Press reported PROTESTERS USE TAX DAY FOR BATTING PRACTICE. Rush Limbaugh chortled that he was glad the UFE protesters got wet. UFE staff conducted live TV interviews and radio feeds all afternoon describing the protest. The next day, the *Boston Globe* ran a three-photo sequence of the raft's demise.

Defensive battles have their limits, but in this case we should lay the groundwork for developing a broad public understanding and critique of the current inequities in the tax system.

PROGRESSIVE TAX CUTS. Since cutting taxes is acceptable in today's political climate, there are a number of tax initiatives that could help working families and lower-income people. Unfortunately, current tax-cutting has created enormous deficits that undermine the adequacy of existing tax systems. Any tax cut must pay for itself somehow. Proposing sound progressive tax policies is part of a good defense against regressive proposals.

These include

$ **EXPANDING THE EARNED INCOME TAX CREDIT.**
The initial earned income tax credit was
a politically popular initiative, winning the
praise of liberals and conservatives alike.
President Reagan called it the "best
pro-family, anti-poverty" program. The
credit is clearly targeted to lower-income
working families and could be expanded
to be both larger in amount and available
to higher-income households with incomes
of up to $50,000. As of 2004, eighteen
states have created state-level EICs—and
others should follow suit.[56]

$ **EXPANDING THE NO-TAX STATUS OR PERSONAL
EXEMPTION.** These tax proposals raise the
amount of income people could earn
before it is subject to taxation. Even
conservative tax-cutters like Steve Forbes
believe that a family of four should not
have to start paying federal income taxes
until their incomes exceed $36,000. This
is accomplished through a big exemption
for the "head of household" ($13,000)
and expanded personal exemptions for
every additional dependent.[57]

PROACTIVE FAIR TAXATION PROPOSALS. When
the political climate allows for progressive tax
proposals besides tax cuts, there are several that
should be pursued.

$ **TAXING CAPITAL GAINS LIKE WAGES.** The tax
burden has been increasingly shifted from
large-asset-owners onto wage-earners.
The Social Security payroll tax has taken
an increasingly bigger bite out of the paychecks of most wage-earners, especially
low- and middle-wage earners. The income

subject to Social Security tax is capped: In
2005 it was $90,000, and it gradually
rises each year. Meanwhile, taxes on capital gains have been substantially reduced.
A fair tax system would not favor income
from assets over income from wages.

Because of tax cuts in 1997 and 2003 that
benefited the rich by reducing the tax rate
on long-term capital gains from 28 percent to 15 percent, many workers now pay
a higher tax rate on income from wages
than wealthy investors pay on realized
capital gains. Billionaire investor Warren
Buffett was troubled by this gross
inequality. At an annual meeting of his
company, Berkshire Hathaway, Buffett
said, "The capital gains tax rate is just
about right. I don't think it's appropriate. . . to have me taxed at 28 percent if
I sell my Berkshire shares when someone
who's trying to find a cure for cancer is
taxed at 39 percent." Buffett complained
that his income from investments is taxed
at a lower rate than his secretary's wages.
And that was before the 1997 and 2003
capital gains tax cuts went into effect.

$ **ELIMINATE ITEMIZED DEDUCTIONS.** For those
clamoring for tax simplification, here it
is: Eliminate all the deductions, including
the home mortgage interest deduction,
state and local taxes, medical expenses,
and health care. The personal and
dependent exemptions would remain to
ensure a minimum threshold for when
taxes kick in. Eliminating all the complex
deductions would save taxpayers
millions of hours and dollars spent
preparing their taxes, while generally
maintaining progressivity.

$ **PROGRESSIVE TAX RATES.** With the elimination of itemized deductions, we could institute a genuinely progressive rate structure. The bottom tax rate should be dropped to about 5 percent and the top tax rate should be raised to 70 percent on incomes in excess of $2 million. There should be a dozen rate steps in between to ensure that people with incomes of different circumstances would not pay the same rate. All income brackets would be indexed to inflation to prevent "bracket creep," which pushes people into higher tax brackets simply because of inflation.

$ **REMOVE THE CAP FROM SOCIAL SECURITY TAXES.** Impose Social Security withholding on all wages and salaries, rather than capping it at $90,000, the amount of the ceiling in 2005. This would allow the current rate of 6.2 percent to be lowered to 5.3 per-

cent.[58] End Social Security payments to people with other pension and income sources that exceed $100,000 a year after they have received the benefits that they have directly paid in. This will protect the universality of Social Security, guarantee its financial solvency for the next genera-tion, and reduce the enormous bite it takes out of the wages of low- and middle-income workers. Young workers should not have to subsidize wealthy retirees beyond their actual contributions, adjusted for inflation.

$ **TAX SECURITIES AND OPTION TRADING.** Impose a 1 percent excise tax on the value of all securities and options transactions. This would both reduce speculation and allow taxes to be lowered on wage-earn-ers. The brokerage firms that are regu-lated by the Securities and Exchange Commission should pay for its operation.

TAX POLICIES AIMED AT ADDRESSING THE OVER-CONCENTRATION OF WEALTH.

Inherited economic power is as inconsistent with the ideals of this generation as inherited political power was inconsistent with the ideals of the generation which established our Government.
—FRANKLIN D. ROOSEVELT

The most controversial proposals contained in this primer are those that redistribute concentrated wealth. These will be considered confiscatory if we don't make a strong moral and economic argument that the rules of the economy originally "distributed" the wealth in an unjust way.

As we drift toward becoming more of a plutocracy, with big-money interests writing the rules in our democracy, we should defend and expand the estate tax and institute wealth taxation. The establishment of the estate tax was a moral issue for President Theodore Roosevelt who, in 1906, viewed it as strengthening the national community through greater political and economic equality. He viewed the transfer of substantial wealth from one generation to the next as not doing any "real service" for inheritors and posing "a great and genuine detriment to the community at large."59

$ MAINTAIN STRONG ESTATE AND INHERITANCE TAXES. Government policies should facilitate the transfer of family assets from one generation to the next. But we should also be concerned about excessive wealth transfers and their distorting impact on the economy, democracy, and culture. At very high levels, particularly in households in the top 0.5 percent with assets in excess of $10 million, the transfer of wealth represents a transfer of power, not simply the means to lead a decent life.

The estate tax raised $30 billion in 2002 from people who have seen their assets triple in the last decade, those in the richest 1 percent. This amount of revenue will rise substantially with the enormous intergenerational transfer of wealth occurring in the coming decades. Under the 2001 Bush tax cut, the estate tax is currently being phased out, with exemptions rising from $1.5 million in 2005 to $3.5 million in 2009 (double these amounts for couples). The estate tax will be fully repealed in 2010. But unless Congress acts to make the repeal "permanent," the estate tax will return in 2011. The estate tax should be reformed, but not repealed.

$ WEALTH TAXATION. The overconcentration of wealth and power presents such a significant challenge that wealth taxation should be considered. European countries with wealth taxes include Austria, Denmark, Finland, Germany, Luxembourg, the Netherlands, Norway, Spain, Sweden, and Switzerland. With the exception of Spain, most of these wealth taxes have been in place for at least sixty years. While there are no direct wealth taxes in the United States, wealth is subject to estate taxes and taxes on capital gains.

The Billionaire Backlash: Preserve the Estate Tax

On Valentine's Day 2001, a front-page article in the *New York Times* sent a tremor through America's political elite. A prominent group of millionaires and billionaires had publicly launched a petition in opposition to wholesale repeal of the estate tax, our nation's only tax on accumulated wealth.

The initial supporters included financier George Soros, actor Paul Newman, art patron Agnes Gund, several members of the Rockefeller family, and other business leaders. Investor Warren Buffett chose not to sign the statement because he felt it did not go far enough in defending the estate tax—but went publicly on the record opposing repeal.

The effort, organized by the Boston-based Responsible Wealth, caught people's imagination and interest. There are now thousands of people who have signed this petition—and over 2,200 of them are people who will someday owe the estate tax.[60] They believe in mending it, not ending it:

reforming the tax, but not abolishing it. It is not surprising that the "billionaire backlash," as *Newsweek* called it, captured widespread attention, not only in the United States but around the world. If there were ever a "man bites dog" news story, this was it. An organized "backlash" of wealthy people, combined with the newsworthy and eternal themes of death, loss, legacy, taxation, wealth, and power, made for an irresistible story.

Why do they support it? "The estate tax is a perfectly fair and reasonable tax on those who've disproportionately benefited from growing wealth in our society," said Bill Gates Sr., a leader of the effort. "Without the estate tax," observed Warren Buffett, "you in effect will have an aristocracy of wealth, which means you pass down the ability to command the resources of the nation based on heredity rather than merit."[61]

Edward Wolff proposes a wealth tax (based on the Swiss model) in his book *Top Heavy*, with progressive tax rates, the highest of which is well under 3 percent. Most households would fall entirely below the wealth-tax threshold.[62] While it would be challenging to agree on an appropriate form of wealth taxation for the United States, a more significant challenge may be constitutional. The Sixteenth Amendment, which originally established the income tax, may not provide the constitutional authority for a wealth tax.[63]

Action Box: Fair Taxation

Americans for a Fair Estate Tax

c/o OMB Watch
1742 Connecticut Avenue NW
Washington, DC 20009
Tel: (202) 234-8494
Fax: (202) 234-8584
E-mail: ombwatch@ombwatch.org
Web: www.ombwatch.org/
estatetax/

Americans for a Fair Estate Tax
(AFET) is a broad-based
nonpartisan coalition of nonprofit
groups, including civic, labor,
social-justice, faith-based, and
environmental organizations,
as well as organizations providing
human services.

Center on Budget and Policy Priorities

820 1st Street NE, #510
Washington, DC 20002
Tel: (202) 408-1080
Fax: (202) 408-1056
E-mail: center@cbpp.org
Web: www.cbpp.org

The Center conducts research and
analysis to inform public debates
over proposed budget and tax

policies, and to help ensure that
the needs of low-income families
and individuals are considered
in these debates.

Citizens for Tax Justice

1311 L Street NW, 4th Floor
Washington, DC 20005
Tel: (202) 626-3780
Fax: (202) 638-3486
Web: www.ctj.org

Citizens for Tax Justice is a nonpartisan, nonprofit research and
advocacy organization dedicated
to fair taxation at the federal, state,
and local levels. Its website
includes good web links to state
and local fair-tax organizations.

Fair Taxes for All

c/o PFAW
2000 M Street, Suite 400
Washington, DC 20036
Tel: (202) 467-4999
Web: www.fairtaxes4all.org

Fair Taxes for All is a national
coalition of over 250 organizations
working to defend the progressivity of the federal tax system.

Tax Policy Center

Web: www.taxpolicycenter.org

The Tax Policy Center is a joint
program of the Urban Institute
and the Brookings Institution.
It provides independent
analyses of current and longer-
term tax issues and communi-
cates its analyses to the public and
to policy makers in a timely and
accessible manner.

United for a Fair Economy

29 Winter Street
Boston, MA 02108
Tel: (617) 423-2148
Fax: (617) 423-0191
E-mail: info@faireconomy.org
Web: www.faireconomy.org

UFE works to promote fair tax
policies through education,
advocacy, media work, and
support to local organizing
efforts. It publishes a tax-
organizing kit.

Fighting Corporate Welfare

One of the policies that contribute significantly to the unfair initial distribution of wealth is corporate welfare. Subsidies and tax loopholes for large corporations and the wealthy are embedded in our federal tax code. Since 1994, coalitions of environmentalists, libertarians, progressives, and good government organizations have failed to dislodge any significant amount of these subsidies. Meanwhile, in 2004, Congress passed a package of over $150 billion in *new* corporate tax cuts including new corporate welfare.

A number of basic reforms dealing with corporate welfare at the federal level might assist the struggle. They include

$ **ACCURATE INFORMATION ABOUT AMOUNTS OF CORPORATE WELFARE AND BENEFICIARIES.** The federal government should consolidate information about corporate-welfare programs, expenditures, and recipients so that we can ascertain its real costs. This should include reporting on the amount of corporate welfare going to individual corporations each year. A number of states, including Massachusetts, have disclosure laws requiring the state to prepare an annual "tax expenditure" budget calculating the revenue that is lost from tax breaks and loopholes.

$ **ASSESS ECONOMIC IMPACT OF SUBSIDIES.** Corporate welfare should be subject to the same scrutiny and cost-benefit analysis as other aspects of the federal budget. The economic impact, effectiveness, and efficiency of corporate subsidies should be evaluated on an ongoing basis. These could also include environmental and other social-impact assessments.

$ **ESTABLISH BIPARTISAN COMMISSION TO CUT CORPORATE WELFARE.** Corporate welfare is insidious and will be difficult to extricate from the federal budget. Getting rid of "pork" in the budget is difficult because politicians are elected to "bring home the bacon" to their constituents. Each provision has its congressional defenders and special-interest lobbyists. In order to alleviate such pork-barreling, Congress could use the military-base-closing model. Military bases, like corporate welfare, have strong political support, even when they are completely obsolete and wasteful. So in 1997, Congress established a bipartisan "base-closing commission" that put a package of recommendations before Congress, preventing amendments to save particular bases. Corporate welfare opponents could establish a similar commission to put forward a package of $100 billion in corporate-welfare cuts for a single up or down vote.

$ **COMPLEMENTARY REFORMS THAT WILL REDUCE CORPORATE WELFARE.** Larger reforms—lobbying restrictions, campaign-finance reform, tax simplification—will ultimately reduce and eliminate much of the pork for corporations that now exists in the tax code. From an educational and political point of view, it is important to keep corporate welfare in the public spotlight, particularly given the hypocrisy of continuing to slash federal assistance to the poor while shoveling billions in unproductive subsidies to major corporations.

AT THE LOCAL LEVEL

At the local level, coalitions have worked to block municipalities and states from giving away public property, money, tax breaks, and regulatory powers. This is difficult when politicians risk their future electability if they challenge corporate welfare. Nonetheless, more people are asking, "What is our community getting in exchange for these subsidies?"[64] More communities are passing ordinances to hold corporations accountable. According to Greg LeRoy, founder of Good Jobs First,

> The new laws consist of both "sticks" and "carrots," and they reflect a growing national consensus for a halt to the state-eat-state civil war for jobs. The sticks include anti-piracy rules, high disclosure and citizen participation requirements, and the ultimate accountability requirement: "clawbacks" or money-back guarantees against nonperformance. The carrots include requirements that, to obtain subsidies, companies create full-time jobs with prevailing wages and health care, that companies reduce toxic emissions and cooperate with environmental groups, and that defense contractors form labor-management alternative use committees for economic conversion.[65]

$ DISCLOSURE AND REPORTING. Laws could require state and local jurisdictions to disclose the cost and types of subsidies that go to private enterprises. This would enable more public input and scrutiny of development subsidies and consideration of comparative uses of funds. They could require companies to report on the impact of past subsidies.

$ PERFORMANCE GOALS. Subsidy agreements could include specific objectives such as retention and creation of a certain number of jobs at a certain pay level with benefits. It could measure level of employee involvement and investment in employee training, skills upgrading, and lifelong learning.

$ "CLAWBACKS." Subsidy agreements, sometimes called "clawbacks," between communities and corporations frequently spell out the requirement that corporation must pay the community back should it fail to live up to its performance goals and conditions. These goals and conditions could include obligations that the company maintain jobs and operations in the jurisdiction and create a certain number of new jobs. Penalties for failure could include partial or total payback with interest, or alternative sanctions, such as raising interest rates on a subsidized loan or partial payback.

$ FEDERAL ANTIRAIDING LEGISLATION TO STOP LOCAL CORPORATE WELFARE. Today, North Carolina could put together a package of development subsidies including tax abatements, infrastructure improvements, and job training funds—and lure a company from Connecticut to move its operations. One federal policy that might cool some of the war between the states would be a law prohibiting local jurisdictions from directly or indirectly using federal funds, like community development block grants, to lure a company from another state.

Reprinted with permission.

Action Box: Corporate Welfare

Citizens for Tax Justice

1311 L Street NW, 4th Floor
Washington, DC 20005
Tel: (202) 626-3780
Fax: (202) 638-3486
Web: www.ctj.org

Citizens for Tax Justice is a non-partisan, nonprofit research and advocacy organization dedicated to fair taxation at the federal, state, and local levels. Its website includes good web links to state and local fair-tax organizations.

Good Jobs First

1311 L Street NW
Washington, DC 20005
Tel: (202) 626-3780
Fax: (202) 638-3486
E-mail: goodjobs@ctj.org

Good Jobs First is a national organization that provides timely, accurate information to the public, the media, public officials, and economic development profession-als on state and local corporate subsidies. It works with a broad spectrum of local organizations as they seek to ensure that corporate subsidies go only to businesses that provide decent wages and are good corporate citizens.

Friends of the Earth

1025 Vermont Avenue NW, Suite 300
Washington, DC 20005
Tel: (202) 783-7400
Fax: (202) 784-0444
Web: www.foe.org

Friends of the Earth is a national environmental organization dedicated to preserving the health and diversity of the planet for future generations. It has tracked corporate welfare and its impact on environmental and social concerns.

The Institute for Local Self Reliance

1313 Fifth Street SE
Minneapolis, MN. 55414-1546
Tel: (612) 379-3815
Fax: (612) 379-3920
Web: www.ilsr.org

ILSR is a nonprofit research and educational organization that provides technical assistance and information on environmentally sound economic-development strategies. Since 1974, the Institute has worked with citizen groups, governments, and private businesses in developing policies that extract the maximum value from local resources.

Public Citizen

1600 20th Street NW
Washington, DC 20009
Tel: (202) 588-1000
Web: www.citizen.org

Public Citizen was founded in 1971 by Ralph Nader to be a consumer watchdog organization in Washington, D.C. It works for safer drugs and medical devices, cleaner and safer energy sources, a cleaner environment, fair trade, and a more open and democratic government.

United for a Fair Economy

29 Winter Street
Boston, MA 02108
Tel: (617) 423-2148
Fax: (617) 423-0191
E-mail: info@faireconomy.org
Web: www.faireconomy.org

UFE puts the spotlight on income and wealth inequality and the concentration of corporate power—and provides tools to grassroots organizing efforts to close the economic divide.

Reforming Monetary Policy and the Federal Reserve

Issues of equity and social cohesion [are] issues that affect the very temperament of the country. We are forced to face the question of whether we will be able to go forward together as a unified society with a confident outlook or as a society of diverse economic groups suspicious of both the future and each other.

—William McDonough, former chairman of Federal Reserve Bank of New York.[66]

Through its control over the levers of monetary policy, the Federal Reserve has more power to touch the lives of ordinary people in America than our democratically elected public officials. The Fed plays a key role in whether we have jobs, access to home ownership, what interest rate we pay on our variable-rate mortgages, and whether we can pay off our credit card balances.

With so much power over our lives, what can we do to ensure that the Fed is accountable to the concerns of ordinary people? The governance structure of the Federal Reserve has been organized to supposedly insulate it from politics, but also by law it must have representatives of the broader public interest. But, as Fed-watcher William Greider writes, "it is fatuous to pretend that the Federal Reserve can somehow be insulated from politics."

It's bombarded constantly with pleas and demands and unsolicited advice from select interests. Private and semi-private dialogues about monetary policy go on continuously between the Fed, financial markets, banks, brokerages, and other major players, both foreign and domestic. The only players left out of the conversation are the American people and, to a large extent, their elected representatives.[67]

EXPANDING CITIZEN ACCOUNTABILITY OVER THE FEDERAL RESERVE. The Fed is not set up for ordinary citizen participation, but there are ways that citizens can begin to exercise power toward the Fed, primarily through coalitions. Leverage points include the selection process for chairman and appointments to regional Federal Reserve boards, Congressional hearings covering the Fed's full-employment mandate under the Humphrey-Hawkins law, and through the creation of advisory boards to monitor certain aspects of the Fed's performance.

Every four years, the president of the United States gets to nominate the chairman of the Federal Reserve. Both Presidents Clinton and Bush chose to renominate the Reagan nominee, Alan Greenspan, signalling their of allegiance to Wall Street and conservative monetary policy. In 2008 and 2012, there will be opportunities to draw public attention to the policies of the Fed and the political climate in which the Fed chair is chosen. Presidential candidates should be publicly pressed for their views on Federal Reserve policy and leadership.

The composition of regional boards is an important issue in which citizen advocates can push for a greater diversity of perspective. Bankers and CEOs of large corporations, with a sprinkling of entrepreneurs, labor leaders, and community-development practitioners, heavily dominate the seats on the twelve regional boards. Community representatives are generally isolated and need support and accountability to advance the interests of workers, home buyers, small businesses, and consumers. See the "Fed Vacancies" section on the website of the Financial Market's Center to learn more about how to get involved in selecting Federal Reserve board members.

Each year, the chairman of the Federal Reserve is required to report to Congress about the impact of Federal Reserve policies on its legal mandate to promote full employment. This is a rare opportunity to press elected officials to hold Fed leadership accountable.

DISTRICT ORGANIZING. The Federal Reserve has divided the country into twelve districts, each with its own Federal Reserve Bank and governing board. Local Fed branches are responsible for monitoring economic conditions in their regions, moving currency in and out of circulation, and supervising and regulating banks. This includes ensuring compliance with the federal Community Reinvestment Act, which requires banks to meet the credit needs of the communities from which they draw deposits.

In the Fifth Federal Reserve District, also known the Richmond Fed, which includes Maryland, West Virginia, Virginia, North Carolina, and South Carolina, a coalition of labor and community activists has begun organizing to enhance the Fed's accountability to local residents. The coalition includes people from affordable-housing organizations, trade unions, public and private community-development agencies, and small-business development organizations. Its organizing work has focused on the three areas of Fed reform: governance, support for community development, and monetary policy.[68]

$ GOVERNANCE. The Fifth District Initiative is pressing to diversify the interests and perspectives represented on the boards of directors of the Richmond Fed and its branches. The law does require consumer and labor representation on Reserve Bank boards. By watchdogging the appointment process, nominating candidates, and meeting with them regularly, they aim to shape the outlook of Fed policy. District activists have organized tours for the Richmond Bank's president and senior staff to see local community conditions and successful community-development projects in Virginia and South Carolina.

$ COMMUNITY ECONOMIC DEVELOPMENT. District activists have pushed the Richmond Fed to be more involved in community development and reinvestment in the district. This would include broadening financing for affordable housing and small-business development. The formation of a Community Development Advisory Council has become a mechanism for greater accountability.

$ MONETARY POLICY. Coalition members have pressured the Richmond Bank to adopt more community- and worker-friendly perspectives in its monetary policy. They have suggested broader indicators to measure the economic health of the district's economy, including access to credit for businesses in low-income communities, poverty rates, economic security of workers, emergency shelter requests, and more. They developed a survey and methodology for the Richmond Bank, including interviews with 150 to 200 organizations such as unions, religious congregations, credit counseling organizations, small-farm organizations, employment-training firms, and minority- and women-owned business associations.

Action Box: Federal Reserve

Financial Markets Center

P.O. Box 334

Philomont, VA 20131

Tel: (540) 338-7754

Fax: (540) 338-7757

E-mail: info@fmcenter.org

Web: www.fmcenter.org

The Financial Markets Center is an independent, nonprofit institute that provides research and education resources to grassroots groups, unions, policy makers, and journalists interested in the Federal Reserve System and financial markets. It seeks to promote democratic values, hold public institutions accountable, and improve living standards for ordinary citizens.

As citizen activists, we face the challenge that the Federal Reserve seems immune to pressure from the voices of ordinary working Americans, farmers, and consumers. Yet the history of the Fed and its existing structure underscore that this institution was intended to serve broader interests than it does today. As with all the action steps outlined in this primer, we need to reassert our democratic entitlement to broader control over the Federal Reserve and its policies.

Alternatives for a Fair Economy

An essential part of building a fair economy and reducing inequality is to create a parallel economy that works to meet people's real security needs in the context of the predatory global market economy. This is sometimes referred to as "building the new economy in the shell of the old." There is a tremendous amount that has been written on this topic; what follows will be a cursory summary. The principal pitfall in this arena is that it can lead to a withdrawal from the larger policy battles for a fair economy. For example, starting a local currency or cooperative to meet the needs of a small constituency must work in tandem with efforts to reform the rules of the national and global economy.

One simple way to think about gaining control over a local economy is to figure out what the factors of production are and how local ownership or control can be enhanced. The traditional economic model refers to land (or natural wealth), labor (workers), and capital (credit, finance, accumulated labor power in the form of money). Capitalism has been concerned with the project of extracting value from the earth and human laborers for the owners of capital. Capital accumulation (great wealth) comes from successfully getting more work out of people than you pay them and consuming more of the earth's resources than you put back. Obviously, this leads to human impoverishment and environmental ruin, which is why we are in this predicament.

Building an environmentally and socially sustainable economy means building economic institutions that do not exploit the earth and fairly allocate the fruits of labor to those who do the work. Like a farmer who returns manure and crop residue to rebuild the soil, we must recognize that extracting natural wealth without returning natural wealth leads to environmental ruin. It's the compost theory of sustainable economics.

A community that does not control its natural-resource base, its flow of credit, or the sources of its jobs is like a bucket with holes. Investment or purchases flow in, but because land, housing, jobs, and finance capital are absentee-owned, the community is unable to retain the value created. It becomes a colony, exporting the value of its natural resources and labor to absentee owners.

LAND, LABOR, AND CAPITAL. In each of these areas, there is a history of social movements— institutions, experiments, and practices—that give us a strong vision and practical experience upon which to build a fairer economy. Organizing

these institutions goes hand-in-hand with a political program that prevents or limits absentee-owners of capital from extracting the wealth created by people and natural resources from a locality. Without such a program, these alternative economic institutions will remain marginal and will ultimately be overwhelmed or destroyed by powerful corporate interests. The new global economy is built upon the notion of the unfettered ability of capital to extract resources and labor power from anywhere on the planet. The rules of the game are to crush local and national efforts to get sovereignty over their economies.

LAND, HOUSING, AND NATURAL RESOURCES. In the United States, there are efforts to build a third sector of socially owned housing—in the form of home ownership through community land trusts, limited-equity housing cooperatives, mutual housing associations, and co-housing communities committed to preserving affordable access to housing.

The community land trust movement, which is concerned not only with land conservancy but also with housing, agriculture, and other land use, is reframing the terms of our present speculative housing market, where it is assumed that land and housing are commodities. Community land trusts remove land and housing from the speculative market and ensure that they remain affordable for successive generations of homebuyers and land-users.

In the area of farmland and food production, CSAs (Community Supported Agriculture) have emerged in a number of regions of the country.

Food consumers purchase shares in advance of the harvest season, providing up-front capital to farmers and pooling the risk and rewards associated with farming. Shareholders get a weekly share allocation of produce every week. There are over 1,000 CSAs operating in the United States and Canada, providing produce to over 75,000 households.

CSAs were started in Japan in the late 1960s by women's organizations seeking to bridge food production and consumers and "put the farmer's face on food." In the United States, where most food products travel an average of 1,300 miles to consumers and most states import 85 to 90 percent of their food, CSAs keep food dollars in the local economy and contribute to the maintenance and establishment of regional food production.[69]

LABOR AND PRODUCTION. Expanding worker ownership of enterprise has been one of the strategies to increase local control over jobs. Worker ownership can range from Employee Stock Option Plans (ESOPs), which give workers a shareholder interest in corporations but not necessarily control, to 100 percent worker-owned firms.

As discussed in the section on building assets, expanding ownership is one way to address inequalities in wealth ownership. "Over the last several years, the percentage of national income attributable to labor has steadily declined while the percentage attributable to capital has steadily increased," maintains Corey Rosen, executive director of the National Center for Employee Ownership. "If everyday employees are going to be able to share in eco-

nomic growth, it is going to be through becoming capital owners, not just owners of their labor."[70] This is good news, though the benefits of employee asset-ownership are not equally distributed throughout the workforce, even within worker-owned firms. One hundred percent worker-owned enterprises provide the additional benefit of more opportunities for true workplace democracy.

Another way to retain value and jobs in a community is to increase social ownership or municipal ownership of enterprises. A local community-development corporation could be a substantial owner of a for-profit enterprise, ensuring community accountability.

COMMUNITY CONTROL OVER CAPITAL

The history of efforts to gain control over community credit is fascinating and inspiring. The earliest credit unions were efforts on the part of local communities to pool capital for investment. Community development–oriented banks, credit unions, and community loan funds are now part of an infrastructure of credit institutions owned and controlled by people in a local economy.

Communities have organized to hold banks accountable to their localities through the Community Reinvestment Act. This becomes all the more important as banks merge and financial-service companies become more concerned about their wealthy clients rather than the credit and banking needs of working-class communities.

There are now over 225 community-development credit unions around the United States, organized to serve the credit needs of low- and moderate-income communities and their depositors. Some have spun off youth branches, overseen by boards of young people. These credit unions manage over $2 billion in funds and fill the gap where traditional banks fail to lend.[71]

In the last decade, a new financial sector has emerged: community-development financial institutions. These include community-development loan funds and investment programs that target the investments of individuals, religious organizations, foundations, and other institutions to locally controlled community-development projects such as worker-owned businesses, affordable housing, and consumer cooperatives. One of the first community-development loan funds, the Institute for Community Economics Revolving Loan Fund, has now made over 400 loans totaling $35 million to community organizations in thirty states and facilitated the development of more than 3,850 housing units.[72] The entire sector now manages over $6 billion in funds.[73]

LOCAL CURRENCIES. Efforts to create locally based currencies and bartering can help protect a local economy from the external fluctuations of global capital markets. In a number of regions, communities have organized alternative currency systems backed by something of real value in the local community, like cord wood.

SHORTER WORK TIME. Ever since industrialization transformed the nature of work, there has been a struggle for reduced work hours. As described earlier, there has been a steady increase in work hours in the United States corresponding to an increase in economic inequality. The gains of increased productivity of the last two decades have been translated into corporate profits rather than increased leisure for workers. The driving force behind declining free time and the expansion of mandatory overtime is that employers find it less costly to add hours than to increase the fixed costs of new employees. Still, a third of employees surveyed in the United States and Canada enjoy overtime because it enables higher rates of consumption and material standards of living.

One remedy to the increasing number of work hours needed to make ends meet would be to reduce the hours of the work week while maintaining a constant wage level. This would accomplish multiple social and economic goals. In 1998, the French government initiated the thirty-five-hour work week, advocating that "productivity gains should be earmarked for a shorter working week rather than for wages." The government helps with a social security allowance designed to reduce the cost of labor. Italy also legislated a reduction of the work week in March 1998.

The shorter work week immediately translates into expanded jobs for underemployed people. While some reduction in work hours is the result of technology, several studies estimate that 50 to 80 percent of reduced work hours translate into new jobs. The Canadian Auto Workers estimate that 5,000 jobs were created or saved as a result of their 1993 contract shortening work time at three big auto plants.[74]

The Wheel of Shared Prosperity

Political participation rises

Power shifts to ordinary people

- Cooperation
- Social cohesion
- Interdependence
- Celebration of diversity

- Meaningful elections
- Strong unions
- More time for democracy

Rule changes benefit everyone

Broadly shared prosperity

TOWARD A HIGH-ROAD ECONOMY

There are inspiring examples of community-based economic development efforts that strengthen communities and build economic security for all (see Further Reading). These high-road strategies should be encouraged in our economy, rather than discouraged. But they will not succeed without broader changes in the structure of the national and global economy. For a fair economy to grow and gain steam, participants in homegrown development efforts will need to be actively leading the charge.

Action Box: Fair Economy

Institute for Community Economics

57 School Street
Springfield, MA 01105
Tel: (413) 746-8660
Fax: (413) 746-8862
E-mail: iceconomic@aol.com
Web: www.iceclt.org

ICE is a national technical-assistance and lending organization that works with community land trusts and other community-based organizations working to get control over land, housing, and the local economy.

Center for Labor and Community Research

3411 West Diversey Avenue, Suite 10
Chicago, IL 60647
Tel: (773) 278-5418
Fax: (773) 278-5918
E-mail: info@clcr.org
Web: www.clcr.org

CLCR's mission is to assist labor, communities, and business to pursue the high road of economic development guaranteeing the building of a strong, participative, and productive economy; social justice; and the equitable distribution of wealth.

National Federation of Community Development Credit Unions

120 Wall Street, 10th floor
New York, NY 10005
Tel: (212) 809-1850
Fax: (212) 809 -3274
Web: www.natfed.org

The National Federation works to build a network of strong, sustainable, community-owned financial institutions. It was founded by the credit unions that serve low-income communities.

National Center for Employee Ownership

1201 Martin Luther King Jr. Way
Oakland, CA 94612
Tel: (510) 272-9461
Fax: (510) 272-9510
E-mail: nceo@nceo.org
Web: www.nceo.org

The National Center for Employee Ownership is a private, nonprofit membership and research organization that serves as the leading source of accurate, unbiased information on employee stock ownership plans (ESOPs), broadly granted employee stock options, and employee participation programs.

Conclusion

We hope we have made the case that the United States would be a far more democratic, prosperous, and caring nation if we narrowed the vast canyon between the very wealthy and everyone else. This book has attempted to assist those who care about the consequences of growing inequality to be more effective in their communication with others, in their educational work, organizing, and advocacy. As time passes, the numbers in this book may become dated, but unfortunately, the fundamental problem of dramatic social stratification will likely remain for some time.

It is important that each of us realize that we have "standing" and the right to speak out about the economy. We may not be trained economists, nor read the business news every day, but we each have moral and political standing with which to challenge the values of our polarizing unbridled market economy.

It is important to be conversant with the facts and data of the current economic reality. But it is equally essential to articulate a new set of values and criteria for judging the success of our economy. These values become the bedrock of our critique of an economy with growing inequality and our vision of a fair economy.

The values of the so-called new economy posit that the individual is on his or her own, out in the marketplace selling labor. We are told to no longer expect things like job security, health insurance, and retirement security. Nor should we look to the government as a safety net; rather we should be privatizing our financial security in the marketplace. In fact, the *new economy* is premised on a certain level of insecurity—and this supposedly serves as a useful motivator and catalyst for individuals to work harder.

People have internalized the values of this new unbridled market economy as the norms in our culture. Individual achievement, privatized security, cutthroat competition, and lean and mean production are permeating all human interactions and institutions. This is the triumph of the values of the market over other human and environmental values. As theologian Harvey Cox wrote in a 1999 article in the *Atlantic Monthly* titled "The Market as God," the devotion to the religion of the market trumps all other religious and social values.[1]

The religion of the market places the highest value on the role of the individual and individual achievement. In contrast, community values recognize the importance of the individual in a community, and celebrate our fundamental interdependence. The values of the market operate on the notion of winners and losers. The values of a human economy recognizes the worth and dignity of all people and believe that everyone has a fundamental right to participate in the economy and the decisions that affect it. The market economy measures its success by growth and outputs, and uses indicators like the gross domestic product and the expansion of wealth in the stock market as yardsticks. A sustainable economy measures success by the quality of life for all humans and the impact on the natural environment.

In their 1986 Pastoral Letter on the Economy, the U.S. Roman Catholic bishops judged the moral dimensions of an economy with three questions: What does the economy do for people? What does it do to people? And how do people participate in it?

"The economy is a human reality: men and women working together to develop and care for the whole of God's creation. All this work must serve the material and spiritual well-being of people."[2] The Roman Catholic faith is one of many religious and cultural traditions that put forward a set of values counter to the values of the market. These values are our foundation for building a fair economy.

As the twenty-first century unfolds, the pace of change may seem slow. Conditions of economic inequality and polarization may worsen before they get better. We trust, however, that the seeds of the social movement being sown today will blossom. We are at an early stage of movement formation. We each must find our role and devote part of our waking hours to agitating for change. It took a long time for things to become this bad; it will take some time for them to improve.

History is full of examples of ordinary people joining together to change their fate against the odds. The end of apartheid in South Africa and the Berlin Wall coming down are just two recent historical examples. We encourage you to think of yourself as part of a fair-economy movement, to become involved in building a fairer economy for all. An important role will be to keep the faith, to hold and share the belief that change is possible. Social movements rely on such messengers— people who hold the vision and the struggle, the setbacks and the good news.

Speak out. Take action from the values that you know to be true. Expect change. Prepare to make history.

Appendix: We Are United for a Fair Economy and Class Action

United for a Fair Economy

Founded in late 1994, United for a Fair Economy is a national, independent, nonpartisan, nonprofit organization. UFE raises awareness that concentrated wealth and power undermine the economy, corrupt democracy, deepen the racial divide, and tear communities apart. We support and help build social movements for greater equality.

Program Areas

UFE works in three major program areas. Each area draws on our popular education, innovative messaging research, and media capacity in its work. Members of Responsible Wealth, a project of United for a Fair Economy, add the voice of business leaders and affluent individuals to all of UFE's work.

TAX EDUCATION PROGRAM. UFE helps local, state, and national groups defend progressive taxation and influence tax and budget issues. We help strengthen the capacity of state coalitions that have a strategic opportunity to affect tax reform. We continue the fight to retain a reformed estate tax, and actively participate in building a permanent national movement infrastructure to address the assault on progressive taxation at all levels.

RACIAL WEALTH DIVIDE EDUCATION PROGRAM. UFE is undertaking a major educational and outreach effort to address the racial disparities of wealth. We are researching, writing, and publishing a book about the racial wealth divide aimed at a wide audience, and are developing popular educational materials and workshops using the information in the book. We will deepen our ties to media sources that reach ethnic groups and communities of color, and organize workshops adapted to their concerns.

GLOBAL ECONOMY PROGRAM. UFE helps community, labor, and religious audiences understand growing inequality in the global economy. We provide popular education programs on globalization to community-based organizations.

Class Action

Class Action was founded in 2002 to raise consciousness about the issues of class and money and their impact on our individual lives, our relationships, organizations, institutions, and culture. We aim to heal the wounds of classism, support the development of cross-class alliance-building, and support the movement of resources to where they are most needed to create equity, justice, and sustainability for all.

Main Programs and Activities

CONSCIOUSNESS-RAISING AND EDUCATION ABOUT CLASS. Class Action sponsors workshops to create open spaces for people to better understand their own and others' experiences with class and classism in all aspects of their lives. We also conduct workshops that focus on the intersections of identity including Gender and Class and Race and Class. People from across the class spectrum participate in these workshops. We also facilitate longer-term cross-class dialogue groups composed of people from across the class spectrum to delve deeply into what class has meant for each of them so they can be more powerful and effective in their daily lives.

MEDIA AND PUBLIC EDUCATION. Class Action works to reach the general public by engaging with the public about the nature of classism in U.S. society. We work for a dramatic increase in the use of the word "classism," reflecting a growing understanding of the nature of class and class oppression, in daily print, electronic commentary, radio interviews, television interviews, and periodicals. We use our website to share information, resources, articles, and links concerned with class. We use radio talk shows, media interviews, and book tours as a way to further magnify our message. We publish books, articles, pamphlets, and other resources on issues of class and classism.

CROSS-CLASS ALLIANCE-BUILDING. Class Action helps social-change organizations to address their class cultures and biases, so as to be able to engage in cross-class coalitions and alliance-building to more effectively accomplish their goals. We engage in organizational consulting and donor fund-raiser dialogue. Learn more about our work at www.classism.org.

Further Reading

Economic Inequality

Joel Blau. *Illusions of Prosperity: American Working Families in an Age of Economic Insecurity.* New York: Oxford University Press, 1999.

Chuck Collins, Betsy Leondar-Wright, and Holly Sklar. *Shifting Fortunes: The Perils of the American Wealth Gap.* Boston: United for a Fair Economy, 1999.

Dollars and Sense and United for a Fair Economy, editors. *The Wealth Inequality Reader.* Boston: Dollars and Sense, 2004.

James K. Galbraith. *Created Unequal: The Crisis in American Pay.* New York: Free Press/Century Fund, 1998.

James Heintz and Nancy Folbre, Center for Popular Economics, National Priorities Project, and United for a Fair Economy. *The Field Guide to the U.S. Economy,* revised edition. New York: The New Press, 1999.

Robert Kuttner. *Everything for Sale: The Virtues and Limits of Markets.* New York: Alfred A. Knopf, 1997.

Frank Levy. *The New Dollars and Dreams: American Incomes and Economic Change.* New York: Russell Sage Foundation, 1998.

Lawrence Mishel, Jared Bernstein, and John Schmitt, Economic Policy Institute. *The State of Working America 1998–99.* Ithaca, New York: Cornell University Press, 1999.

Kevin Phillips. *Wealth and Democracy: A Political History of the American Rich.* New York: Broadway Books, 2002.

Sam Pizzigati. *Greed and Good: Understanding and Overcoming the Inequality That Limits Our Lives.* New York: Apex Press, 2004.

Robert Pollin and Stephanie Luce. *The Living Wage: Building a Fair Economy.* New York: The New Press, 1998.

Holly Sklar. *Chaos or Community? Seeking Solutions, Not Scapegoats for Bad Economics.* Boston: South End Press, 1995.

Edward N. Wolff. *Top Heavy: The Increasing Inequality of Wealth in America and What Can Be Done About It.* New York: The New Press, 1996.

William Wolman and Anne Colamosca. *The Judas Economy: The Triumph of Capital and the Betrayal of Work.* Reading, Massachusetts: Addison-Wesley Publishing, 1997.

Asset Building

Bruce Ackerman and Anne Alstott. *The Stakeholder Society.* New Haven: Yale University Press, 1999.

Peter Barnes. *Who Owns the Sky? Our Common Assets and the Future of Capitalism.* Washington, D.C.: Island Press, 2001.

Michael Sherraden and Neil Gilbert. *Assets and the Poor: A New American Welfare Policy.* Armonk, New York: M.E. Sharpe, 1991.

Worker Ownership

Frank T. Adams and Gary B. Hansen. *Putting Democracy to Work: A Practical Guide for Starting Worker-owned Businesses.* Eugene, Oregon: Hulogosi Communications, 1987.

Jeff Gates, *The Ownership Solution: Towards a Shared Capitalism for the Twenty-first Century.* Reading, Massachusetts: Addison-Wesley Publishing, 1998.

Jeff Gates. *Democracy at Risk: Rescuing Main Street from Wall Street.* Cambridge, Massachusetts: Perseus Books, 2000.

Consumerism and Consumption

John De Graaf, David Wann, Thomas H. Naylor, David Horsey, and Scott Simon. *Affluenza: The All-Consuming Epidemic.* San Francisco: Berrett-Koehler, 2002.

Robert Frank. *Luxury Fever: Why Money Fails to Satisfy in an Era of Excess.* New York: Free Press, 1999.

Jessie O'Neill. *The Golden Ghetto: The Psychology of Affluence.* Center City, Minnesota: Hazelden, 1997.

Juliet B. Schor. *The Overspent American: Upscaling, Downshifting, and the New Consumer.* New York: Basic Books, 1998.

Democracy and Inequality

G. William Domhoff. *Who Rules America? Power and Politics in the Year 2000.* Mountain View, California: Mayfield Publishing Company, 1998.

William Greider. *Who Will Tell the People: The Betrayal of American Democracy.* New York: Simon and Schuster, 1993.

Labor

Kate Bronfenbrenner, Sheldon Friedman, Richard W. Hurd, Rudolph A. Oswald, and Ronald L. Seeber, editors. *Organizing to Win: New Research on Union Strategies.* Ithaca, New York: ILR Press/Cornell University Press, 1998.

Richard Freeman, editor. *Working Under Different Rules.* New York: Russell Sage Foundation, 1994.

Kim Moody. *Workers in a Lean World: Unions in the International Economy.* New York: Verso, 1997.

R. Emmett Murray. *The Lexicon of Labor.* New York: The New Press, 1998.

Poverty

Osha Gray Davidson. *Broken Heartland: The Rise of America's Rural Ghetto*. Iowa City: University of Iowa Press, 1996.

Diane Dujon and Ann Withhorn. *For Crying Out Loud: Women's Poverty in the United States*. Boston, Massachusetts: South End Press, 1996.

Mark Robert Rank. *One Nation, Underprivileged: Why American Poverty Affects Us All*. New York: Oxford University Press, 2004.

David Shipler. *The Working Poor: Invisible in America*. New York: Alfred A. Knopf, 2004.

William Julius Wilson. *When Work Disappears: The World of the New Urban Poor*. New York: Vintage, 1996.

Race and Inequality

Rebecca Adams, Rose Brewer, Betsy Leondar-Wright, Meizhu Lui, and Barbara Robles. *The Color of Wealth: The Story Behind the U.S. Racial Wealth Divide*. New York: The New Press, 2006.

Dalton Conley. *Being Black, Living in the Red: Race, Wealth, and Social Policy*. Los Angeles and Berkeley: University of California Press, 1999.

Chester Hartman. *Double Exposure: Poverty and Race in America*. Armonk, New York: M.E. Sharpe, 1997.

Melvin L. Oliver and Thomas M. Shapiro. *Black Wealth/White Wealth: A New Perspective on Racial Inequality*. New York: Routledge, 1995.

Thomas Shapiro. *The Hidden Cost of Being African American: How Wealth Perpetuates Inequality*. New York: Oxford University Press, 2004.

William Julius Wilson. *The Bridge Over the Racial Divide: Rising Inequality and Coalition Politics*. Berkeley: University of California Press, 1999.

Gender and Inequality

Randy Pearl Albelda and Chris Tilly. *Glass Ceilings and Bottomless Pits: Women's Work, Women's Poverty*. Boston: South End Press, 1997.

Teresa L. Amott and Julie A. Matthaei. *Race, Gender, and Work: A Multicultural Economic History of Women in the United States*. Boston: South End Press, 1991.

Diane Dujon and Ann Withhorn, editors. *For Crying Out Loud: Women's Poverty in the United States*. Boston: South End Press, 1996.

Tax Policy and Corporate Welfare

Donald L. Barlett and James B. Steele. *America: Who Really Pays the Taxes*. New York: Touchstone, 1994.

Jeffrey H. Birnbaum and Alan S. Murray. *Showdown at Gucci Gulch: Lawmakers, Lobbyists, and the Unlikely Triumph of Tax Reform*. New York: Random House, 1987.

William H. Gates and Chuck Collins. *Wealth and Our Commonwealth: Why America Should Tax Accumulated Fortunes*. Boston: Beacon Press, 2002.

David Cay Johnston. *Perfectly Legal: The Covert Campaign to Rig Our Tax System to Benefit the Super Rich and Cheat Everyone Else*. New York: Portfolio, 2003.

Greg LeRoy. *No More Candy Store*. Washington, D.C.: Grassroots Policy Project, 1995.

Steven R. Weisman. *The Great Tax Wars*. New York: Simon & Schuster, 2002.

Mark Zepenauer. *Take the Rich Off Welfare*. Boston: South End Press, 2004.

Corporate Power

Richard J. Barnet and John Cavanagh. *Global Dreams: Imperial Corporations and the New World Order*. New York: Simon & Schuster, 1994.

Kevin Danaher. *Corporations Are Gonna Get Your Momma*. Monroe, Maine: Common Courage Press, 1996.

Charles Derber. *Corporation Nation*. New York: St. Martin's Press, 1998.

Murray Dobbin. *The Myth of the Good Corporate Citizen: Democracy Under the Rule of Big Business*. Toronto: Stoddard, 1998.

Richard Grossman and Frank T. Adams. *Taking Care of Business: Citizenship and the Charter of Corporations*. Cambridge, Massachusetts: Charter, Ink., 1995.

David Korten. *When Corporations Rule the World*. West Hartford, Connecticut: Kumarian Press, 1996.

David Korten. *The Post-Corporate World: Life After Capitalism*. Co-published by San Francisco: Berrett-Koehler Publishers and West Hartford, Connecticut: Kumarian Press, 1998.

John Stauber and Sheldon Rampton. *Toxic Sludge is Good for You*. Monroe, Maine: Common Courage Press, 1995.

History

Lawrence Goodwyn. *The Populist Moment: A Short History of the Agrarian Revolt in America*. New York: Oxford University Press, 1978.

Howard Zinn. *A People's History of the United States*. New York: HarperCollins, 1980; revised edition, 1995.

Globalization

William Greider. *One World, Ready or Not: The Manic Logic of Global Capitalism*. New York: Simon & Schuster, 1997.

Joshua Karliner. *The Corporate Planet: Ecology and Politics in the Age of Globalization*. San Francisco: Sierra Club Books, 1997.

David Korten. *Globalizing Civil Society: Reclaiming Our Right to Power*. New York: Seven Stories Press, 1998.

Jerry Mander and Edward Goldsmith, editors. *The Case Against the Global Economy and For a Turn Toward the Local*. San Francisco: Sierra Club Books, 1996.

Ralph Nader, editor. The Case Against Free Trade: Gatt, Nafta and the Globalization of Corporate Power. Berkeley: North Atlantic Books, 1993.

Business Practices

Jack Beatty. *The World According to Peter Drucker*. New York: Free Press, 1998.

Derek Bok. *The Cost of Talent: How Executives and Professionals Are Paid and How It Affects America*. New York: Free Press, 1993.

Economic Alternatives

Christopher Gunn and Hazel Dayton Gunn. *Reclaiming Capital: Democratic Initiatives and Community Development*. Ithaca, New York: Cornell University Press, 1991.

Peter Medoff and Holly Sklar. *Streets of Hope: The Fall and Rise of an Urban Neighborhood*. Boston: South End Press, 1994.

Michael H. Shuman. *Creating Self-Reliant Communities in a Global Age*. New York: Free Press, 1998.

Media

Robert McChesney. *Corporate Media and the Threat to Democracy*. New York: Seven Stories Press, 1997.

Norman Solomon and Jeff Cohen. *Wizards of Media Oz: Behind the Curtain of Mainstream News*. Monroe, Maine: Common Courage Press, 1997.

Philanthropy

Chuck Collins and Pam Rogers, with Joan Garner. *Robin Hood Was Right: Giving Your Money for Social Change*. New York: W.W. Norton, 2000.

Mark Dowie. *American Foundations: An Investigative History*. Cambridge, Massachusetts: MIT Press, 2001.

Tracy Gary and Melissa Kohner. *Inspired Philanthropy*. San Francisco: Jossey-Bass, 2002.

Class and Classism

David Brooks. *Bobos in Paradise: The New Upper Class and How They Got There*. New York: Simon & Schuster, 2000.

Benjamin Demott. *The Imperial Middle: Why Americans Can't Think Straight About Class*. New York: William Morrow & Co., 1990.

Barbara Ehrenreich. *Fear of Falling: The Inner Life of the Middle Class*. New York: Pantheon, 1989.

bell hooks. *Where We Stand: Class Matters*. New York: Routledge, 2000.

Paul Fussell. *Class: A Guide Through the American Status System*. New York: Summit Books, 1983.

Lewis H. Lapham. *Money and Class in America: Notes and Observations on the Civil Religion*. New York: Random House, 1988.

Alfred Lubrano. *Limbo: Blue-Collar Roots, White-Collar Dreams*. Hoboken: John Wiley & Sons, 2004.

Stephen McNamee and Robert Miller Jr. *The Meritocracy Myth*. Lanham, Maryland: Rowman & Littlefield, 2004.

Robert Perrucci and Earl Wysong. *The New Class Society: Goodbye American Dream*, 2nd edition. Lanham, Maryland: Rowman & Littlefield, 2002.

Lillian B. Rubin. *Worlds of Pain: Life in the Working-class Family*. New York: Basic Books, 1992.

William Ryan. *Equality*. New York: Vintage Books, 1982.

Richard Sennett and Jonathan Cobb, *The Hidden Injuries of Class*. New York: W.W. Norton, 1993.

Studs Terkel. *Working: People Talk About What They Do All Day and How They Feel About What They Do*. New York: The New Press, 1997.

Felice Yeskel and Betsy Leondar-Wright. "Classism Curriculum Design." In *Teaching for Diversity and Social Justice*, edited by Marianne Adams, Lee Anne Bell, and Pat Griffin, 233. New York: Routledge, 1997.

Michael Zweig. *The Working Class Majority: America's Best Kept Secret*. Ithaca, New York: Cornell University Press, 2000.

Cross-Class Dynamics

David Croteau. *Politics and the Class Divide: Working People and the Middle-Class Left*. Philadelphia: Temple University Press, 1995.

Betsy Leondar-Wright. *Class Matters: Cross-Class Alliance Building for Middle Class Activists*. Gabriola Island, British Columbia: New Society Publishers, 2005.

Fred Rose. *Coalitions Across the Class Divide*. Ithaca, New York: Cornell University Press, 2000.

Linda Stout. *Bridging the Class Divide and Other Lessons for Grassroots Organizing*. Boston: Beacon Press, 1996.

Notes

Introduction: Economic Boom for Whom?

1. "Changes in Household Wealth in the 1980's and 1990's in the U.S.," in Edward N. Wolff, Editor, *International Perspectives on Household Wealth*, Elgar Publishing Ltd., forthcoming.

2. Joel Blau, *Illusions of Prosperity: American Working Families in an Age of Economic Insecurity* (New York: Oxford University Press, 1999).

3. Louis Uchitelle, "The American Middle, Just Getting By," *New York Times*, 1 August 1999. Marc Miringoff and Margue-Luisa Miringoff, *The Social Health of the Nation* (New York: Oxford University Press, 1999).

4. Robert W. McChesney, *Corporate Media and the Threat to Democracy* (New York: Seven Stories Press, 1997). Westinghouse bought CBS in 1995 and then announced plans to sell off the industrial and energy businesses and concentrate on broadcasting. Westinghouse changed its name to CBS Corporation in December 1997. CBS Corporation completed spinoffs of its industrial businesses in March 1999. It is not quite accurate to say that Westinghouse owns CBS, as CBS Corporation is now a broadcasting giant along the lines of Time Warner or Disney.

5. Lawrence Mishel, Michael Ettlinger, and Elise Gould, "Less Cash in Their Pockets," Economic Policy Institute, 21 October 2004. At: http://www.epinet.org/content.cfm/bp154.

6. Wallace Peterson, *The Silent Depression* (W.W. Norton, New York, 1994), 18–20.

7. Ibid.

8. Productivity gains discussed in: Economic Policy Institute, *The State of Working America, 1998–1999* (Ithaca, N.Y.: Cornell University Press, 1999), 127, 153–55. Productivity went up 33 percent between 1983 and 1998.

9. This is not to imply that the post-World War II years were a great time for everyone in the United States. Obviously, it was a time of great racial discrimination. But, as we describe later, the prosperity of these years was shared more. This was in part because of the cold war compact that saw U.S. businesses share the bounty of global domination and imperialism with their workers.

10. The Gallup Organization, "American Public Opinion About the Economy," http://www.gallup.com/poll/focus/sr040217.asp. 17 February 2004. According to this survey, 33 percent thought the economy was excellent while 21 percent thought it was poor.

11. Remarks by Chairman Alan Greenspan, "The Mortgage Market and Consumer Debt," at America's Community Bankers Annual Convention, Washington, DC, 19 October 2004. Can be found at: http://www.federalreserve.gov/boarddocs/speeches/2004/20041019/default.htm. Also see: Louis Uchitelle, "The Stronger It Gets, The Sweatier the Palms," *New York Times*, 21 March 1999.

12. Kevin Phillips, *Wealth and Democracy: A Political History of the American Rich* (New York: Random House, 2002). See pp. 122–123. Phillips writes that the "precise official markers do not exist," but that an informed guess would put the zenith of American wealth inequality at around 1901 or 1902.

13. National Conference of Catholic Bishops, *Economic Justice for All: Pastoral Letter on Catholic Social Teaching and the U.S. Economy* (Washington, DC: U.S. Catholic Conference, 1986).

I. The Dangerous Consequences of Growing Inequality

1. Robert J. Samuelson, "It's Not As Bad As You Think," *Newsweek*, 8 January 1996. Adapted and excerpted from Robert J. Samuelson, *The Good Life and Its Discontents: The American Dream in the Age of Entitlement 1945–1995* (New York: Times Books, 1996).

2. U.S. Bureau of the Census, Statistical Abstract of the United States: 1999 (119th Edition) Washington, DC (U.S. Government Printing Office) Table 662, 418. For non-agricultural wage and salary employees. Yearly hours arrived at by multiplying weekly hours by 50 weeks. See also Gary Cross, "Who Has the Time? It's Work, Work, Work," *Boston Globe*, 8 July 2001.

3. Lawrence Mishel, Jared Bernstein, and Heather Boushey, *The State of Working America, 2002/2003* (New York: Cornell University Press, 2003), 100.

4. Ibid.

5. Pat Wechsler, "Its 8 P.M., and Mom's Out Trading," *BusinessWeek*, 14 June 1999.

6. Kathleen Reagan, "The Illusion of Family Leave in America: Millions of Families Cannot Benefit From This Federal Law," *The Boston Parents Paper*, May 1999, 16–18.

7. Council of Economic Advisors, "Families and the Labor Market, 1969–1999: Analyzing the Time Crunch," Washington, DC, 1999.

8. Barbara Downs, "Fertility of American Women: June 2002," Current Population Reports (Washington, DC: U.S. Census Bureau, 2003), 20–548.

9. As of 2001, the legally mandated vacation days in the following Western European countries are: Sweden 32, Denmark 30, France 30, Austria 30, Spain 30, Ireland 28, Netherlands 25. Although not legally mandated, the average yearly vacation in Italy and France are 42 and 35 days respectively. See data from the Economic Policy Institute World Almanac as indicated on the Timesizing Wire website at http://www.timesizing.com/1vacatns.htm. See also Gary Cross, "Who Has the Time? It's Work, Work, Work," *Boston Globe*, 8 July 2001.

10. Communications, Energy and Paperworkers Union of Canada, "Reduction of Workweek," convention document, November 1994. See their work on "shorter work week" at http://www.cep.ca/swtime_e.html.

11. Douglas Clement, "European Vacation: There's a simple reason Americans work longer hours than Europeans," Federal Reserve Bank of Minneapolis, December 2003. Referring to statistics from the International Labor Organization.

12. Robert D. Putnam, *Bowling Alone: The Collapse and Revival of American Community* (New York: Simon and Schuster, 2000). Also see Putnam, "Bowling Alone: America's Declining Social Capital," *Journal of Democracy*, January 1995. Much of Putnam's research is rooted in a major study on social capital and democracy in Italy: Robert Putnam, Roberto Leonardi, Raffaella Y. Nanetti, *Making Democracy Work: Civic Traditions in Modern Italy* (Princeton, N.J.: Princeton University Press, 1994).

13. Families USA, "Health Care: Are You Better Off Today than You Were Four Years Ago," September 2004.

14. "Numbers of Americans With and Without Health Insurance Rise, Census Bureau Reports" (Washington, DC: United States Department of Commerce News, 30 September 2003). 2004 statistic from Jeanne Lambrew, "45 Million Uninsured Americans," Center for American Progress, 26 August 2004.

15. Mike Bergman, "United States Department of Commerce News" (Washington, DC: United States Census Bureau, 30 September 2003).

16. Vanessa Fuhrmans, "Fewer Workers Have Health Benefits," *Wall Street Journal*, 3 August 2004. Also see: John Holahan, "Changes in Employer-Sponsored Health Insurance Coverage," Urban Institute, 17 September 2003.

17. "National Compensation Survey: Employee Benefits in Private Industry in the United States, March 2003," U.S. Department of Labor, Bureau of Labor Statistics, April 2004.

18. "Numbers of Americans With and Without Health Insurance Rise."

19. Bradley Dakake and the state PIRG Consumer Team, "Deflate your Credit Card APR," (Boston, MA: MASSPIRG), 27 March 2002. See http://www.masspirg.org.

20. William Branigin, "U.S. Consumer Debt Grows at Alarming Rate: Debt Burden Will Intensify When Interest Rates Rise," *Washington Post*, 12 January 2004.

21. CNNMoney, "Late payments at 5-year high: Past-due credit card debt highest since 1997, while bad debts soar to 11-year peak," 29 April 2004. See http://www.freerepublic.com/focus/f-news/674898/posts.

22. U.S. Bureau of the Census, *Statistical Abstract of the United States: 1998*, 118th edition, Washington, DC (U.S. Government Printing Office), Table 822, 523.

23. Statistics for 1989–94 taken from: U.S. Bureau of the Census, *Statistical Abstract of the United States: 1996* (Washington, DC: U.S. Government Printing Office), table 847; statistics for 2002 taken from Administrative Office of the U.S. Courts; statistics for 2003 taken from: William Branigin, "U.S. Consumer Debt Grows at Alarming Rate: Debt Burden Will Intensify When Interest Rates Rise," *Washington Post*, 12 January 2004.

24. U.S. Department of Commerce, Bureau of Economic Analysis, "Personal Savings as a Percentage of Disposable Income." In February 2000, the Commerce Department began using a narrower definition of income that slightly magnified the savings rate decrease. Note the report by John Ruser, Adrienne Pilot, and Charles Nelson, "Alternative Measures of Household Income," Bureau of Economic Analysis, May 2004, indicating that in December 2003, personal savings as a percentage of disposal personal income was 1.3 percent. See http://www.bea.gov.

25. Brian Bremmer, "Japan's Dangerous Savings Drought," *BusinessWeek*, 9 June 2003. See also "Germany, Monthly Economic Report," British Embassy Berlin, February 2004. http://www.britishebotschaft/de/en/embassy/eu/pdf/MERFeb_04.pdf.

26. Gordon Matthews, "Drop in Savings Rate Isn't For Lack of Trying," *American Banker*, 12 November 1996. This article summarizes the report by Federal Reserve analysts Lynn Elaine Browne and Joshua Gleason: "The Saving Mystery, or Where Did the Money Go?" *New England Economic Review*, September–October 1996.

27. In 1998 approximately 25 percent of employees participate in defined benefit pension plans; nearly 30 percent are in defined contribution pension plans. See Mishel, Bernstein, and Heather Boushey, *State of Working America, 2002–2003*. (Ithaca: Cornell University Press) 2003. p. 148.

28. Economic Policy Institute, "Non-Standard Work, Substandard Jobs: Flexible Work Arrangements in the U.S." (Washington, DC: Economic Policy Institute, August 1997). Also see: Susan N. Houseman, "Temporary, Part-Time, and Contract Employment in the United States: A Report on the W.E. Upjohn Institute's Employer Survey

on Flexible Staffing Policies" (Kalamazoo, MI: W.E. Upjohn Institute for Employment Research, November 1996; revised June 1997).

29. Mishel, Bernstein, and Boushey, *State of Working America, 2002–2003*, 255.

30. In 2001, Federal government provided $56 billion in federal aid, $33 billion was in the form of loans (the other portion included grants, tax credits, tax-advantage savings, etc.) Source: "Private and Public Contributions to Financing College Education," Congressional Budget Office, http://www.cbo.gov/showdoc, January 2004.

31. Joshua Wolf Shenk, "In debt all the way up to their nose rings," (*U.S. News and World Report*, 9 June 1997.)

32. Nellie Mae, "The College Board," as reported in *Boston Globe*, 23 October 1997 and Dr. Sandy Baum and Marie O'Malley, "College on Credit: How Borrowers Perceive Their Educational Debt, Results on the 2002 National Student Loan Survey," (Nellie Mae), 6 February 2003. This information can be found at http://www.nelliemae.com/library/research_10.html. The data indicates that while the average student debt is $18,900, the average debt for students who attend a four year private college is $21,200.

33. Pell Institute Statistics on Opportunity in Higher Education. 2004. See http://www.pellinstitute.org/statusreport/5b_Indicators_cvrsTxt.pdf.

34. U.S. Department of Commerce, Bureau of the Census, Current Population Survey, October 1998. From "Percentage of high school completes ages 16–24 who were enrolled in college after completing high school, by type of institution, family income, and race/ethnicity: October 1972–1996."

35. Richard Morin, "Misperceptions Cloud Whites' View of Blacks," *Washington Post*, 11 July 2001. See also U.S. Bureau of the Census, "Hispanic Population in the United States," March 2002 Current Population Survey, June 2003. (Source: U.S. Census Bureau, Annual Demographic Supplement to the March 2002 Current Population Survey) 20–545.

36. For a terrific survey of economic literature on the link between inequality and poor economic performance, see James R. Repetti, "Democracy, Taxes and Wealth," *New York University Law Review*, June 2001. Also see Ravi Batra, *The Great Depression of 1990* (New York: Dell Publishing, 1988). Batra chronicles the correlation between concentrated wealth and economic depressions going back several centuries.

37. Associated Press, "Jones Apparel to Buy Barney's for $294 M," *Boston Globe*, 12 November 2004, p. C4.

38. Henry Ford, *Henry Ford: Today and Tomorrow* (Special Edition, 1926: reprint, 1998) 152–153.

39. "Holiday Finale Disappoints Retailers —Again," *Wall Street Journal*, 26 December 1997.

40. Jeff Gates, *The Ownership Solution: Towards a Shared Capitalism for the 21st Century* (Reading, Mass.: Addison-Wesley, 1998), 6.

41. *Random House Webster's Unabridged Dictionary*, 2d edition, (New York, Random House, 1998).

42. John Stauber and Sheldon Rampton, *Toxic Sludge is Good For You* (Monroe, Maine: Common Courage Press, 1995).

43. Michael Kranish, "Tougher Drunk Driving Rule Ran Into Roadblock in Congress," *Boston Globe*, 22 May 1998. See also Michael Kranish, "Rep. Neal is Point Man in Push to Halve Federal Beer Tax," *Boston Globe*, 21 July 1998.

44. Center for Responsive Politics. See http://www.opensecrets.com.

45. The Center for Responsive Politics, "2004 Election Outcome: Money Wins," 3 November 2004.

46. Center for Responsive Politics, "04 Elections Expected to Cost Nearly $4 Billion," 21 October 2004.

47. U.S. Census Bureau, "Voting and Registration in the Election of November 2000," p.20–542. Table B. February 2002. Information from the U.S. Census Bureau, Current Population Survey, November 2000.

48. Andy Serwer, "The Waltons: Inside America's Richest Family," *Fortune*, 15 November 2004.

49. Jim Hopkins, "Wal-Mart Heirs Pour Riches into Reforming Education," *USA Today*, 11 March 2004.

50. B.P. Kennedy, I. Kawachi, R. Glass, D. Prothrow-Stith, "Income Distribution, Socioeconomic Status, and Self-rated Health in the United States: Multilevel Analysis," Harvard School of Public Health, December 1997.

51. Richard Wilkinson, *Unhealthy Societies: The Afflictions of Inequality* (London: Routledge, 1996), 102.

52. There is a concerted challenge to the argument that inequality has an impact on public health. See Nicholas Eberstadt and Sally Satel, *Health and the Income Inequality Hypothesis: A Doctrine in Search of Data* (Washington, DC: AEI Press, American Enterprise Institute, 2004).

53. Information about Kerula from Wikipedia, http://www.kikipedia.org/wiki/Kerala.

54. Sam Pizzigati, "In India's Kerula, a Little Equality Works Wonders," *Too Much* (New York and Boston: Council on International and Public Affairs and United for a Fair Economy, Spring 1996); and Patrick Heller, *The Labor of Development: Workers and the Transformation of Capitalism* (Ithaca, N.Y.: Cornell University Press, 2000).

55. "Two Americas," *Taipan Newsletter*, Fall 1994, 1217 Saint Paul St., Baltimore, Md. 21202.

56. Jeff Gates, *The Ownership Solution* (Reading, Mass: Addison-Wesley, 1998), 207–208.

57. Income breakdown by quintile can be found in the United States Census Bureau, Current Population Survey, Table H-2. See http://www.bls.census.gov/cps/ads/sdata.htm.

58. Mutual Fund Education Alliance as cited in Herb Ezell, "Americans Have Reasonable Idea of College Costs," *Atlanta Constitution*, 31 May 1998.

59. Philip J. Longman, "The Cost of Children," *US News and World Report*, 30 March 1998, 50.

60. Derek Bok, *The Cost of Talent* (New York: The Free Press, 1993), 246.

61. Haya El Nasser, "Gated Communities more popular, and not just for the rich," *USA Today*, 15 December 2002. Quoting interview with Edward J. Blakely.

62. Edward J. Blakely and Mary Gail Snyder, *Fortress America: Gated Communities in the United States* (Washington, DC: Brookings Institution Press, 1997), 44.

63. Christopher Parkes, "A Look Behind the Fortress Gates," *The Financial Post*, 24 September 1997, p. 61.

64. Fern Shen, "Middle Class Homing In On Gated Enclaves," *Washington Post*, 14 April 1997, B1.

65. U.S. Department of Justice, Bureau of Justice Statistics, "Nation's Prison and Jail Population Exceeds 2 Million Inmates for First Time," 6 April 2003.

66. U.S. Department of Justice, Bureau of Justice Statistics, "Prison and Jail Inmates at Midyear 2002," 6 April 2003 and "Criminal Offender Statistics," 14 January 2004. See also Federal Bureau of Prison Statistics, "Federal Bureau of Prison Quick Facts, February 2004," 7 February 2004. Also see: Justice Policy Institute Study, as reported by Jesse Katy, *Los Angeles Times*, "A Nation of Too Many Prisoners?" 15 February 2000; and Louise D. Palmer, "Number of Blacks in Prison Soars," *Boston Globe*, 28 February 1999. Also Fox Butterfield, "Number of Inmates Reaches Record 1.8 Million," *New York Times*, 15 March 1999.

67. BC & A International, "Second Chance Program – Executive Summary," August 2003. See http://www.penalrehab.org/whitepapers/bcanda/1/.

68. U.S. Department of Justice, Federal Bureau of Prisons, "Operations Memorandum," Number 015–2993, 25 September 2003.

2. The Picture: Growing Economic Insecurity and Inequality

1. U.S. Bureau of the census, March 2004, Current Population Survey, Table F-3. See also Robert Greenstein and Isaac Shapiro, "The New Definitive CBO Data on Income an Tax Trends" (Washington, DC: Center on Budget and Policy Priorities), 23 September 2003. Data from Congressional Budget Office, "Effective Federal Tax Rates, 1997–2000,) August 2003.

2. Lawrence Mishel, Jared Bernstein, Sylvia Allegretto, *The State of Working America, 2004–2005*. (Economic Policy Institute, forthcoming from ILR Press, an imprint of Cornell University Press), p. 62, Table 1.10. Also see: Isaac Shapiro and Robert Greenstein, *The Widening Income Gulf* (Washington, DC: Center on Budget and Policy Priorities, September 1999), 1–10.

3. Ibid., table 1.12. Income breakdown by quintile can be found in the United States Census Bureau, Current Population Survey, Table H-2.

4. "Executive Pay: Special Report," *BusinessWeek*, 19 April 2004.

5. U.S. Census Bureau, *March 2001 Census, Current Population Survey*, Tables F-1 and F-3. Income ranges in 2001 dollars.

6. Ibid.

7. U.S. Census Bureau, *Current Population Survey, Historical Income Tables*, Tables P-Ia (White 1968), P-Ib (African American 1968 and 2001), and P-Ie (White 2001). Parity comparison from United for a Fair Economy, *The State of the Dream 2004: Enduring Disparities in Black and White* (15 January 2004). See http://www.racialwealthdivide.org/stateof.html.

8. U.S. Census, "Mean Income Received by Each Fifth and Top 5 Percent of Black Families," from *March 1998 Current Population Survey*.

9. William Julius Wilson, *When Work Disappears* (New York: Vintage Books, 1996), 195.

10. Ibid., 195.

11. Louis Uchitelle, "Gaining Ground on the Wage Front," *New York Times*, 31 December 2004. Citing new Bureau of Labor Statistics data analyzed by the Economic Policy Institute.

12. Lawrence Mishel, Jared Bernstein, and John Schmitt, *The State of Working America, 1998–99* (Ithaca, N.Y.: Cornell University Press, 1999), 134.

13. "Executive Pay: Special Report," *BusinessWeek*, 20 April 1998, 58. 2003 data from "Executive Pay: Special Report," *BusinessWeek*, 19 April 2004.

14. "Executive Pay: Special Report," *BusinessWeek*, 19 April 1999.

15. Institute for Policy Studies and United for a Fair Economy, "Executive Excess 2004: Campaign Contributions, Unexpensed Stock Options and Rising CEO Pay," (IPS/UFE, 2004). See http://www.faireconomy.org/prss/2004/EE2004_pr.html.

16. Ibid.

17. "Forbes 400," *Forbes*, 11 October 2004, 114.

18. Micheal Jordan at his peak earning years brought in about $100 million a year. It would take him 480 years to earn the $48 billion of net worth that Bill Gates had in 2004. "Forbes 400," *Forbes*, 11 October 2004, p. 104.

19. AFL-CIO, "Too Close for Comfort" (Washington, DC: AFL-CIO), April 1999. This report uses data from the Investor Responsibility Research Center.

20. Mishel, Bernstein, and Allegretto, *The State of Working America*, 2004–2005, 285.

21. "Changes in Household Wealth in the 1980's and 1990's in the U.S.," Edward N. Wolff, editor, *International Perspectives on Household Wealth* (Northhampton, MA: Elgar Publishing Ltd., forthcoming), table 7.

22. Mel Oliver and Tom Shapiro, *Black Wealth, White Wealth* (New York: Routledge, 1995). Also see: Dalton Conley, *Being Black, Living in the Red: Race, Wealth and Social Policy* (Berkeley: University of California Press, 1999).

23. Rebecca Adams, Rose Brewer, Betsy Leondar-Wright, Meizhu Lui and Barbara Robles, *The Color of Wealth: How Government. Widened the Racial Wealth Divide* (New York: The New Press, 2006).

24. Arthur B. Kennickell, "A Rolling Tide: Changes in the Distribution of Wealth in the U.S., 1989–2001," Levy Economics Institute, November 2003, Table 26.

25. For in-depth discussion of wealth inequality, see Chuck Collins, Betsy Leondar-Wright, Holly Sklar, *Shifting Fortunes: The Perils of the Growing American Wealth Gap* (Boston: United for a Fair Economy, 1999). See also, Edward N. Wolff, *Top Heavy: The Increasing Inequality of Wealth in America and What Can Be Done about It* (New York: The New Press, 1996).

26. Wolff, *Top Heavy*, 78–79.

27. Mishel, Bernstein, and Allegretto, *The State of Working America*, 2004–2005, 282.

28. "Changes in Household Wealth in the 1980's and 1990's in the U.S."

29. Mishel, Bernstein, and Allegretto, *The State of Working America*, 2004–2005.

30. Economic Policy Institute, March 1999. See also, Mishel, Bernstein, and Schmitt, *The State of Working America*, 1998–99. (Ithaca, N.Y.: Cornell Unversity Press, 1999) 127, 153–55. Originally discussed in Chuck Collins, Betsy Leondar-Wright, and Holly Sklar, *Shifting Fortunes: The Perils of the Growing American Wealth Gap* (Boston: United for a Fair Economy, 1999).

31. "Changes in Household Wealth in the 1980's and 1990's in the U.S." See also Kelly D. Smith, "New Nasdaq Survey Finds Investing Population Has Doubled in Seven Years," CNN Money News, 22 February 1997. This information was based on a telephone survey of 1,200 adults. As of January 2001, the last completed Federal Reserve Survey of Consumer Finances, 51.9 percent of households owned stock directly or indirectly—including through a mutual fund, individual retirement account, or defined contribution pension.

32. Aaron Bernstein, "A Sinking Tide Does Not Lower All Boats," *BusinessWeek*, 14 September 1998.

33. "Changes in Household Wealth in the 1980's and 1990's in the U.S."

34. Mishel, Bernstein, and Schmitt, *The State of Working America* 1998–99, 267.

35. Mishel, Bernstein, and Allegretto, *The State of Working America*, 2004–2005, 287.

36. Thomas J. Stanley and William D. Danko, *The Millionaire Next Door* (New York: Pocketbooks, 1998).

37. "The Forbes 400," *Forbes*, 11 October 2004.

38. Ibid.

39. Lester Thurow, *The Future of Capitalism: How Today's Economic Forces Will Shape the Future* (New York: William Morrow, 1996).

40. United for a Fair Economy, "Born on Third Base: The Source of Wealth of the 1997 Forbes 400," (Boston: United for a Fair Economy, October 1997). See http://www.faireconomy.org/press/archive/Pre_1999/forbes_400_study.html. 2004 figures based on "The Forbes 400." *Forbes*, 11 October 2004.

41. "Forbes 400," *Forbes*, 11 October 2004.

42. For more on the role of society's investment in creating private wealth, see Chuck Collins, Scott Klinger and Mike Lapham, "I Didn't Do It Alone: Society's Contribution to Individual Wealth and Success," Responsible Wealth, 2004. See http://www.responsiblewealth.org/press/2004/NotAlone_pr.html.

43. United Nations Development Program, 1999. There is no more recent report on this. See Mueller's Poverty of Nation's List at http://www.egroups.com/list/poverty-nations.

44. "Forbes 400," *Forbes*, 11 October 2004, 160.

45. United for a Fair Economy, "Born on Third Base: The Source of Wealth of the 1997 Forbes 400," (Boston: United for a Fair Economy, October 1997). See http://www.faireconomy.org/press/archive/pre_1999/forbes_400_study.html. 1999 figures based on "The Forbes 400." *Forbes*, 28 September 1999.

46. Net worth estimates from the "Forbes 400," *Forbes*, 11 Oct. 2004.

3. The Causes of Inequality

1. Some of these arguments are made in Michael Cox and Richard Alma, *Myths of Rich and Poor: Why We're Better Off Than We Think* (New York: Basic Books, 1999).

2. James K. Galbraith, *Created Unequal: The Crisis in American Pay* (New York: Twentieth Century Fund and the Free Press, 1998), 5.

3. Lawrence Mishel, Jared Bernstein, Sylvia Allegretto, Economic Policy Institute, *The State of Working America*, 2004–2005. (Ithaca, NY: ILR Press, an imprint of Cornell University Press). See section on international comparisons, 381–420.

4. Center for Responsive Politics, *A Brief History of Money*

in Politics: Campaign Finance and Campaign Finance Reform in the United States (Washington, DC: Center for Responsive Politics, 1995).

5. U.S. Representative Romano Mazzoli (D-Ky.) as quoted in Martin Schram, Speaking Freely: Former Members of Congress Talk About Money in Politics (Center for Responsive Politics, Washington, DC, 1995), 63.

6. The Campaign Finance Institute estimates that the total amount of donations under $200 made to presidential candidates rose from $54 million in 2000 to $205 million in 2004. See http://www.cfinst.org. See Albert R. Hunt, "McCain-Feingold Did Its Job," Wall Street Journal, 18 November 2004.

7. Public Campaign, "The Color of Money: Campaign Contributions and Race," (Washington, DC: Public Campaign, September 1998). Also see John Green, Paul Herrnson, Lynda Powell and Clyde Wilcox, "Individual Congressional Campaign Contributors: Wealthy, Conservative, and Reform Minded," (Chicago: The Joyce Foundation, June 1998). See http://www.publiccampaign.org

8. Testimony from Campaign Finance Investigation, Chaired by Senator Fred Thompson (R-Tenn.), 18 September 1997, as reported in Federal News Service.

9. Sarah Anderson and John Cavanagh, "Corporate vs. Country Economic Clout: The Top 100" (Washington, DC: Institute for Policy Studies, 2002). See http://www.ips-dc.org/projects/global_econ/idex.htm.

10. Institute for Policy Studies, The Top 200 (Washington, DC: Institute for Policy Studies, 2002).

11. Hoover's Online, "World Bank Development Indicators." (Note: We used FY 2003 data because the fiscal year ends in January.) See http://www.hoover.com.

12. Sandra Sugawara, "Merger Wave Accelerated in '99," Washington Post, Friday, 31 December 1999.

13. For an overview of the negative effects of this merger see: United for a Fair Economy, Great Expectations: Corporate Greed in the MCI WorldCom Merger (Boston: United for a Fair Economy, March 1998). See also: Jeff Keefe, Monopoly.com: Will the WorldCom-MCI Merger Tangle the Web? (Washington, DC: Economic Policy Institute, 1998) and Dan Schiller, Bad Deal of the Century: The Worrisome Implications of the WorldCom-MCI Merger (Washington DC: Economic Policy Institute, 1998).

14. Shawn Young, "MCI's Roberts Sold Stock at Discount to Merger Value," Wall Street Journal, 14 November 1997.

15. MCI and WorldCom, Amendment No. 2 to SEC Form 8-K, filed 28 January 1998 (8-K Amend. No. 2), 22–23. For stock option information, see MCI and WorldCom, Joint Proxy Statement/Prospectus, 22 January 1998, 63. See also: Joanne S. Lublin, "MCI Offers Managers Hefty Bonuses to Retain Them Prior to Its Merger," Wall Street Journal, 25 November 1997, B9.

16. Mike Mills, "WorldCom Would Shift MCI's Focus; Bidder Plans to Shed Residential Service," Washington Post, 3 October 1997.

17. "Up to 1,500 Posts to Be Cut in Routine Restructuring," Wall Street Journal, 22 December, 1997. Additional job losses and their impact on minority communities in Rainbow/PUSH Coalition, Petition to Deny, in the Matter of Applications of WorldCom, Inc., and MCI Communication Corporation for Transfer of Control of MCI Communications Corporation to WorldCom, Inc., CC Docket No. 97–211, 5 January 1998.

18. Comments of Communication Workers of America, in the Matter of Applications of WorldCom, Inc., and MCI Communication Corporation for Transfer of Control of MCI Communications Corporation to WorldCom, Inc., CC Docket No. 97–211, 5 January 1998.

19. Christopher Stern, "WorldCom, Executives Settle Employees' Suit," Washington Post, 7 July 2004.

20. "MCI Just Can't Escape Its Past," AccountancyAge.com, 8 July 2003. Online at http://www.accountancyage.com/TakingStock/1134489.

21. Charles Derber, Corporation Nation: How Corporations are Taking Over Our Lives and What We Can Do About It (New York: St. Martin's Press, 1998), 4–5.

22. Constance L. Hays, "Math Book Salted With Brand Names Raises New Alarm," New York Times, 21 March 1999.

23. The math book is Mathematics: Applications and Connections (McGraw-Hill, 1995 and 1999 editions) as reported in Constance L. Hays, "Math Book Salted With Brand Names Raises New Alarm," New York Times, 21 March 1999.

24. See the discussion of the drug Taxol, later in this book and in Mark Zepezauer, Take The Rich Off Welfare (Cambridge: South End Press, 2004).

25. Jill Smolowe, "A Healthy Merger?," Time magazine, 15 April 1996.

26. Gary Strauss, "Sweet Exit Deals Get Sweeter. Today's executives hit pay dirt when their golden parachutes open," USA Today, 1 April 1999.

27. Evanston Tribune, 27 September 1996.

28. David Gross and Normandy Brangan, "Out-of-Pocket Spending on Health Care by Medicare Beneficiaries Age 65 and Older: 1999 Projections," American Association of Retired Persons, December 1999. See www.research.aarp.org/health/ib41_hspend.html.

29. "Program Information on Medicare, Medicaid, SCHIP, and Other Programs of the Centers for Medicare & Medicaid Services," Section III, B5, 10, Office of Research and Development, June 2002. Data from Bureau of Labor Statistics, Consumer Expenditure Survey, 1999–2000.

30. Michael Casey, "The AMA Jumps on the Union

Bandwagon," *Managed Care Newsperspectives*, 1 July 1999.

31. Richard Grossman and Frank Adams, *Taking Care of Business: Citizenship and the Charter of Incorporation* (Cambridge, Mass.: Charter Ink, 1993). See the more recent reader: Dean Ritz, ed., *Defying Corporations, Defining Democracy: A Book of History and Strategy* (New York: Apex Press, 2001).

32. Ibid. See also, Adolf A. Berle and Gardiner C. Means, *The Modern Corporation and Private Property* (New York: Macmilliam, 1933); and Martin Sklar, *The Corporate Reconstruction of American Capitalism, 1890–1916, The Market, The Law and Politics* (New York: Cambridge University Press, 1988).

33. Charles Derber, *Corporation Nation* (St. Martins Press, 1998), 129.

34. "Trends in Union Membership," AFL-CIO as cited from the U.S. Department of Labor, Bureau of Labor Statistics, 2004. See http://www.aflcio.org.

35. Bureau of Labor Statistics, February 2004. See http://www.bls.gov/schedule/archives/all_nr.html#union2.

36. AFL-CIO, "Grocer Workers Expand Their Fight for Health Care," 18 December 2003.

37. "Why It Pays to Be Union!," International Union of Operating Engineers as cited from the Bureau of Labor Statistics, 2002.

38. Lawrence Mishel with Matthew Walters, "How Unions Help All Workers," (Washington, DC: Economic Policy Institute, August 2003). See www.epinet.org/content.cfm/briefingpapers_bp143.

39. Ibid.

40. AFL-CIO Analysis of the Current Population Survey, Supplement of Employee Benefits, April 1993. As cited in AFL-CIO, *Communities at Work: The Role of Public Officials in Restoring Workers' Right to Organize* (Washington, DC: AFL-CIO, 1996). See http://aflcio.org.

41. Industrial Union Department, AFL-CIO, 1998.

42. See Peter Bruce, "On the Status of Workers' Rights to Organize in the United States and Canada" and Richard N. Block, "Reforming U.S. Labor Law and Collective Bargaining: Some Proposals Based on the Canadian System," *Restoring the Promise of American Labor Law*, ed. Sheldon Friedman, Richard W. Hurd, Rudolph Oswald, and Ronald L. Seeber (Ithaca, NY: ILR Press, 1994).

43. Tom Geoghegan, *Which Side Are You On?* (New York: Farrar, Straus and Giroux, 1991), 273–82.

44. Cornell University School of Industrial and Labor Relations as cited by the AFL-CIO in Voices@Work program information, 1999.

45. Kate Bronfenbrenner, "Uneasy Terrain: The Impact of Capital Mobility on Workers, Wages and Union Organizing," a report for the U.S. Trade Deficit Review Commission, 6 September 2000. Available at http://www.americanrightsatwork.org/resources/studies.cfm.

46. AFL-CIO "Federal Government Wins Court Case Against Avondale on Safety Records" AFL-CIO press release, 13 January 1998.

47. Associated Press, "Shipyard Ordered to Rehire Workers," 12 July 2001. See "Avondale's Price for Union-Busting: $5.4 million-plus," at http://www.aflcio.org/aboutunions/ns07192001.

48. Robert D. Putnam, *Bowling Alone: The Collapse and Revival of American Community* (New York: Simon and Schuster, 2000). Robert D. Putnam, "The Strange Disappearance of Civic America," *The American Prospect*, Winter 1996. See also Putnam, "Bowling Alone: America's Declining Social Capital," *Journal of Democracy*, January 1995.

49. Father Leo J. Penta, "Organizing and Public Philosophy: Fifty Years of the Industrial Areas Foundation," IAF Reflects, August 1990 as reported in Greider, *Who Will Tell the People: The Betrayal of American Democracy* (New York: Simon & Schuster, 1992), 223.

50. William Greider, *Who Will Tell the People*, 245–69.

51. Ibid, 20.

52. William Wolman and Anne Colamosca, *The Judas Economy: The Triumph of Capital and the Betrayal of Work* (Reading, Mass.: Addison-Wesley Publishing, 1997).

53. Clearing House Interbank Payment System. Website: http://www.chips.org. The overwhelming majority of currency transactions are conducted in U.S. dollars. The amount may be shrinking because the number of banks participating in CHIPS is shrinking. We have seen citations that $2 trillion a day flows in international currency exchanges. In Doug Henwood's *Wall Street*, he cites the Bank for International Settlements located in Switzerland as the source of the $2 trillion-a-day number.

54. U.S. Labor Department, *By the Sweat and Toil of Children* (March, 1999) as reported by Associated Press, "Global Child-Labor Abuses Reported," (Washington, DC: U.S. Department of Labor), *Boston Globe*, 26 March 1999.

55. Kate Bronfenbrenner, *The Effects of Plant Closing or Threat of Plant Closing on the Right of Workers to Organize* (Ithaca, N.Y.: Cornell University, 1996). This was included in a report, *Plant Closings and Labor Rights*, published by the Labor Secretariat of the North American Commission for Labor Cooperation, and on its website, http://www.naclc.org.

56. U.S. Census Bureau, Foreign Trade Statistics, "U.S. International Trade Goods and Services Highlights: Goods and Services Deficit Increases in 2003." http://www.census.gov/indicator/www/ustrade.html, 13 February 2004.

57. The United States is more accurately leading the charge.

58. U.S. Department of Labor. See also: Lori Wallach and

Michelle Sforza, "The Ten Year Track Record of the North American Free Trade Agreement: U.S. Workers' Jobs, Wages and Economic Security" (Washington, DC: Public Citizen at http://www.citizen.org/publications/ NAFTA_10_jobs.pdf.

59. Robert Scott, "The High Price of 'Free' Trade: NAFTA's Failure Has Cost the United States Jobs Across the Nation," Economic Policy Institute, 17 November 2003. See http:// www.epinet.org/content.cfm/briefingpapers_bp147.

60. Ibid.

61. Jeff Gerth, "Where Business Rules: Forging Global Regulations That Put Industry First," New York Times, 9 January 1998.

62. Tony Clarke and Maude Barlow, The Multilateral Agreement on Investment and the Threat to Canadian Sovereignty (Toronto: Stoddard, 1997). See action section about organizations working on globalization.

63. Reginald Dale, "The NGO Specter Stalks Trade Talks," International Herald Tribune, 5 March 1999.

64. "NAFTA Lawsuits Cloud MAI Discussions," Parliamentary Bureau, 24 August 1998.

65. Colin Nickerson, "Canada Rescinds Ban on Gas Additive, to Pay U.S. Firm $10M," Boston Globe, 21 July 1998. Also Andrea Durbin and Mark Valliantos, "Winners Take All," Dollars and Sense magazine, May/June, 1997.

66. John Witte, The Politics and Development of the Federal Income Tax (Madison, Wisc.: University of Wisconsin Press, 1985).

67. Donald L. Barlett and James B. Steele, America: Who Really Pays the Taxes (New York: Simon and Schuster, 1994), 14–15.

68. See report on the right-wing anti-tax movement by People for the American Way, "Upper Brackets: The Right's Tax Cut Boosters," at http://www.pfaw.org, search: "Upper Brackets."

69. United for a Fair Economy, "Shifty Tax Cuts" (June 2004). See http://www.faireconomy.org/press/2004/shiftytaxcuts_ pr.htm.

70. Joel Friedman, "The Decline of Corporate Income Tax Revenues," Center on Budget and Policy Priorities Report, 24 October 2003, http://www.cbpp.org/10-16-3tax.htm.

71. Casandra Q. Butts, "The Corporate Tax Dodge," Center for American Progress. 10 April 2004. See http://www. americanprogress.org

72. See Robert S. McIntyre and T.D. Coo Nguyen, "Corporate Income Taxes in the Bush Years," September 2004. Jointly published by the Citizens for Tax Justice and the Institute on Taxation and Economic Policy. See http://www.ctj.org. Also see David Cay Johnson, "Corporations' Taxes are Falling Even as Individuals' Burden Rises." New York Times, 20 February 2000.

73. Robert S. McIntyre and T.D. Coo Nguyen, "Corporate Income Taxes in the Bush Years," September 2004. Jointly published by the Citizens for Tax Justice and the Institute on Taxation and Economic Policy. See http://www.ctj.org.

74. Citizens for Tax Justice, "Who Pays?" 2004. See http:// www.ctj.org.

75. Citizens for Tax Justice, "Details on Bush Tax Cuts," Fall 2003. See http://www.ctj.org.

76. Kevin Phillips, Wealth and Democracy (New York: Random House, 2002). See pp. 47–68.

77. William Lazonick, Competitive Advantage on the Shop Floor (Cambridge, Mass.: Harvard University Press, 1990). Provides extensive discussion of Ford Motor experience throughout book.

78. Robert Pollin and Stephanie Luce, The Living Wage: Building a Fair Economy (New York: The New Press, 1998). See also Laura Owen, "Worker Turnover in the 1920s: The Role of Changing Employment Policies," from The Journal of Economic History, issue no. 55, 231–46.

79. Bennett Harrison, Lean and Mean: The Changing Landscape of Corporate Power in the Age of Flexibility (Basic Books, 1994).

80. Information from the Manpower web site: http://www. manpower.com.

81. "Temps Fact Sheet," Temp Worker Justice Week, October 2002. See information on the Fair Jobs web site: http://www.fairjobs.org/week/facts.htm.

82. Jeffrey Wenger, "Share of Workers in Non-Standard Job Declines," (Washington, DC, Economic Policy Institute, 2003). See http://www.epinet.org/content.cfm/ briefingpapers_bp137.

83. Susan N. Houseman, "Temporary, Part-Time, and Contract Employment in the United States: A Report on the W.E. Upjohn Institute's Employer Survey on Flexible Staffing Policies (Kalamazoo, MI: The W.E. Upjohn Institute on Employment Research, June 1997).

84. Economic Policy Institute and Women's Research and Education Institute, "Nonstandard Work, Substandard Jobs: Flexible Work Arrangements in the United States," (Washington, DC: Economic Policy Institute, August 1997).

85. Ibid., 16.

86. Jeffrey Wenger, "Share of Workers in Non-Standard Job Declines," (Washington, DC, Economic Policy Institute, 2003).

87. Mishel, Berstein and Boushey, The State of Working America, 2002–2003. (Ithaca: Cornell University Press, 2003), 253.

88. Wenger, "Share of Workers in Non-Standard Job Declines."

89. Economic Policy Institute and Women's Research and Education Institute, "Nonstandard Work," 39.

90. "Privatization: Fraud and Cost Over-Runs," in The Labor Institute, Corporate Power and the American Dream (New York:

Apex Press, 1997).

91. Doug Saunders, "For-Profit U.S. Schools Sell Off Their Textbooks," Toronto Globe and Mail, 30 October 2002.

92. Challenger, Gray and Christmas, Inc., report on layoffs as cited in Jennifer Laabs, "Job Cuts Reach Record Levels for 1998," Workforce Magazine, 1 February 1999.

93. David Sirota, Christy Harvey and Judd Legum, "Bush Said His Tax Cuts Would Create 1,836,000 New Jobs By Now – He is 1,615,00 Short of His Goal," Center for American Progress, 11 January 2004. See http://www.american-progress.org. Data from the U.S. Department of Labor, Bureau of Labor Statistics, "National Employment, Hours and Earnings."

94. Survey data by International Survey Research Corporation, reported by New York Times, 27 February 1997.

95. The living wage is determined by dividing $18,100 (HHS poverty level for a family of four) by 2080 (52 weeks x 40 hours).

96. William Greider, Secrets of the Temple: How the Federal Reserve Runs the Country (New York: Simon & Schuster, 1987) 11–29.

97. Doug Henwood, Wall Street: How It Works and for Whom (London: Verson, 1997).

98. For an excellent discussion of the "nonaccelerating inflation rate of unemployment (NAIRU)" see Chapter 10, "The NAIRU Trap," in James K. Galbraith, Created Unequal: The Crisis in American Pay (New York: Twentieth Century Fund, 1998), 171–182.

99. Kenneth Jackson, Crabgrass Frontier: The Suburbanization of the United States (New York: Oxford University Press, 1985), 190–209.

100. Donald L. Barlett and James B. Steele, "What Corporate Welfare Costs You," Time, 9 November 1998.

101. "Surge in Corporate Welfare Drives Corporate Tax Payments Down Near Record Low," Citizens for Tax Justice, 17 April 2002. See http://www.ctj.org/html/corpo402.htm.

102. Mark Zepezauer, Take the Rich Off Welfare (Cambridge, MA.: The South End Press, 2004). Zepezauer includes a wide range of subsidies for the rich and corporations, totaling $815 billion a year.

103. Updated figures from Office of Management and Budget, Fiscal Year 2004 Budget of the United States (Washington, DC: Government Printing Office, 2003).

104. Ibid. Also see Mark Zepezauer, Take The Rich Off Welfare (Cambridge: South End Press, 2004).

105. "Corporate Welfare Hit List," Public Citizen. See their web site at: http://www.citizen.org/congress/corwel/cuts.html.

106. C. Ford Runge, John A. Schnittker, and Timothy J. Penny, "Ending Agricultural Entitlements: How to Fix Farm Policy," Progressive Policy Institute, 1 May 1996. See

http://www.ppionline.org. See analysis of new farm bills at the Environmental Working Group, http://www.ewg.org. See Mark Zepezauer, Take The Rich Off Welfare (Cambridge: South End Press, 2004), chapter on agribusiness subsidies.

107. David Cay Johnston, Perfectly Legal: The Covert Campaign to Rig Our Tax System to Benefit the Super Rich and Cheat Everyone Else (New York: Portfolio, 2003), 296.

108. Sarah Newport, et al., Green Scissors 1999 (Washington, DC: Friends of the Earth, 1999). See http://www.foe.org/res/pubs/index.html.

109. Ibid., p. 9.

110. "Public Handouts Enrich Drug Makers, Scientists: Public Research/Private Profit," three part series, Boston Globe, 5, 6, and 7 April 1998.

111. Greg Leroy, "Race, Poverty and 'Economic Development' Gone Haywire," 13 Poverty and Race, no. 3, May/June 2004. See also Good Jobs First, http://www.goodjobsfirst.org, and new book, Greg LeRoy, The Great American Job Scam (San Francisco: Berret Koehler, 2005).

112. Keon Chi, in two reports from the Council of State Governments: "The States and Business Incentives: An Inventory of Tax and Financial Incentives," 1989, and "State Business Incentives," in State Trends Forecasts (Washington, DC: Council of State Governments, June 1994).

113. Wall Street Journal, 28 September 1998.

114. Donald L. Barlett and James B. Steele, "What Corporate Welfare Costs You," Time, 9 November 1998.

115. Joanna Cagan and Neil deMause, Field of Schemes: How the Great Stadium Swindle Turns Public Money Into Private Profit (Monroe, ME: Common Courage Press, 1998).

116. Rick Horrow, "Across America, Cities Dream (Lucrative) Stadium Dreams," Sun-Sentinel (Fort Lauderdale, FL), 4 February 1998.

117. Roger G. Noll and Andrew Zimbalist, Sports, Jobs, & Taxes: Are New Stadiums Worth the Cost? (Washington, DC: Brookings Institution Press, 1997). Also see Andrew Zimbalist, May the Best Team Win: Baseball Economics and Public Policy (Washington, DC: Brookings Institution Press, 2003).

118. Alex Marvez, "Taxing Fans' Patience; By Rejecting Increase, Voters Prove Winning Isn't Everything In Pittsburgh," Rocky Mountain News, 7 December 1997.

119. Molly Ivins with Lou Dubose, Shrub: The Short But Happy Political Life of George W. Bush (New York: Random House, 2000), 41.

120. James Dao, "In Washington, A Delay on the Road to Baseball's Return," New York Times, 10 November 2004. See: http://www.nodctaxesforbaseball.org.

121. Adrian Fenty and Davidi Catania, "In a Bargaining Position On Baseball," Washington Post, 11 July 2004.

122. Charlie Derber, The Wilding of America (New York: St. Martin's Press, 1996).

123. Institute for Policy Studies and United for a Fair Economy, "CEOs Win, Workers Lose 1999: the 1990s –A Decade of Greed," August 1999. See http://www.faireconomy. org/press/2004/EE2004_pr.html for most recent "Executive Excess" report.

124. Institute for Policy Studies, with assistance from Ralph Estes of the Stakeholders Alliance. Methodology: $10,712 (lowest wage for workers) x 25=$267,800 (amount above which corporations could not claim a deduction under the proposed law). $2.2 million (average executive salary and bonus for top two executives at the 365 companies included in the *BusinessWeek* survey) -$267,800=$1,932,200 (unallowable corporate deduction) x 35 percent (maximum corporate tax rate)=$676,270 (taxpayer savings per executive) x 365 companies x 2 executives =$493,677,100 in taxpayer savings.

125. "Forbes 400," *Forbes*, 11 October 2004, 180.

126. Jack Beatty, *The World According to Peter Drucker* (New York: The Free Press, 1998).

127. "Corporate Governance Background Report F: Executive and Director Compensation 1994," Investor Responsibility Research Center, F-47.

128. Joann Muller, "Employees, in Snub to Wall Street, to Purchase Dynatech Corp," *Boston Globe*, 23 December, 1997.

4. Building a Fair Economy Movement

1. Labor quotes from "LaborNet," a website maintained by IGC: http://www.igc.org/labornet.

2. C. Vann Woodward, *Tom Watson: Agrarian Rebel* (London: Oxford University Press, 1938), 135.

3. Howard Zinn, *A Peoples History of the United States* (New York: HarperCollins, 1980).

4. Quoted from C. Vann Woodward, *Tom Watson*.

5. Lawrence Goodwyn, *Democratic Promise: The Populist Moment in America* (New York: Oxford University Press, 1976), xxi.

6. Sam Pizzigati, *The Maximum Wage* (New York: Apex Press, 1992). See also Sidney Ratner, *American Taxation: Its History as a Social Force in Democracy* (New York: W.W. Norton, 1942).

7. Edward N. Wolff, *Top Heavy*, 78–79.

8. Upton Sinclair, "End Poverty in California," *Literary Digest*, 13 October 1934. See also: Upton Sinclair, *I, Candidate for Governor: And How I Got Licked* (Berkeley and Los Angeles: University of California Press, 1934).

9. Eight million billion in 1935 is equivalent to $96,583,941 in 1999, using the online inflation calculator sponsord by the American Institute for Economic Research.

10. T. Harry Williams, *Huey Long* (New York: Random House, 1969), 693–95.

11. Arthur M. Schlesinger, Jr., *The Coming of the New Deal:*
The Age of Roosevelt (Houghton Mifflin, Boston, 1958), 1-23.

12. Taylor Branch, *Parting the Waters* (New York: Touchstone, 1989).

13. Earl M. Page, "The Fuel Melting Incident" in *Fermi-I: New Age for Nuclear Power*, ed. E. Pauline Alexandersen (LaGrange Park, Ill.: The American Nuclear Society, 1979).

14. Bill Moyer, "Map Training Manual" (1990) and "Practical Strategist" (Social Movement Empowerment, 1990). See archives about Moyer's work at: www.nonviolance.org.au.

15. Berit Lakey, et al., *Grassroots and Nonprofit Leadership: A Guide for Organizations in Changing Times* (Gabrioloa Island, British Columbia: New Society Publishers, 1995).

16. See Chuck Collins and Pam Rogers, *Robin Hood Was Right: A Guide to Giving Your Money for Social Change* (New York: W.W. Norton, March 2000).

17. Lawrence Goodwyn, *Democratic Promise: The Populist Moment in America* (New York: Oxford University Press, 1976), 34; a poetic description of a populist encampment.

18. Gwendolyn Parker, "George W. Bush's Secret of Success," *New York Times*, 25 May 1999.

5. Actions to Close the Economic Divide

1. On 12–13 March 1999, Texas A&M and the Bush Presidential Library sponsored a conference, "Increasing Income Inequality in America." Charles Murray presented a paper on "IQ, Success in Life, and Inequality: The Ambiguous Merits of Meritocracy"; Marvin Kosters presentated a paper, "Government Policy and Wage Inequality: Regulation, Incentives, and Opportunities"; William Cline of the Institute of International Finance presented "Trade, Immigration, and Wage Distribution"; and James P. Smith of the RAND Institute presented "Why is Wealth Inequality Rising?" (unpublished papers).

2. George Seldes, *The Great Thoughts* (New York: Ballantine Books, 1986), 166.

3. Elaine Bernard, *Why Unions Matter* (Open Magazine Pamphlet Series, Westfield, N.J., May 1996).

4. "Union Coverage Rates and Trends," Labour Relations Agency of the Government of Newfoundland and Labrador. Data from Labour Force Survey, Statistics Canada. Information online at http://www.gov.nl.ca/lra/ statistics/unionrates.htm.

5. See Richard Freeman, *Working Under Different Rules* (New York: Russell Sage Foundation, 1994).

6. Charles Derber, *Corporation Nation* (New York: St. Martin's Press, 1998), 252.

7. See Center for Working Capital: http://www.centerfor-workingcapital.org.

8. James Madison, Federalist Paper No. 57, *The Federalist*

Papers (New York: Penguin Books, 1961), 351.

9. Quoted in Eric Schmitt, "Senate Debates Campaign Bill, But Two Sides Remain Divided," *New York Times*, 27 September 1998.

10. Campaign Finance Institute, "The $100 Million Dollar Exemption: Soft Money and the National Party Conventions," July 2004. Available at http://www.cfinst.org/eguide/partyconventions/financing/cfistudy.html.

11. "New Legislation Introduced to Tighten Regulations on Nonparty Groups," Brookings Institution, Round-up of Campaign Finance Stories, 22 September 2004.

12. For contacts at state and local campaigns, contact Public Campaign. Visit their web site at http://www.publiccampaign.org/states/index.htm.

13. Center for Responsive Politics, *Money in Politics: Reform, Principles, Problems and Proposals by the Center for Responsive Politics* (Washington, DC: Center for Responsive Politics, 1996). Summarized by Jenny Ladd in an unpublished paper, "Money in Electoral Politics" from Responsible Wealth Working Papers, United for a Fair Economy, 1 December 1997.

14. Hoover Institute, "Public Policy Inquiry, Campaign Finance, Current Structure," at http://www.campaignfinancesite.org/structure/terms/p.html. See also Public Campaign's national web site, especially the section "The States Take the Lead," at http://www.publiccampaign.org/statereform.html.

15. For more information on the Clean Election Campaigns in Massachusetts see the Mass Voters for Fair Elections website: http://www.massvoters.org.

16. See http://www.publiccampaign.org to find state level organizations. Also see: Meg Gage, *The Funders Handbook on Money and Politics* (Amherst, Mass.: The Piper Fund,1997).

17. See New Party's web site at http://www.newparty.org.

18. Charles Derber, *Corporation Nation*, 244.

19. David Korten, *When Corporations Rule the World* (West Hartford, Conn.: Kumerian Press, 1996), and Richard Grossman and Frank Adams, *Taking Care of Business: Citizenship and the Charter of Incorporation* (Cambridge, Mass.: Charter Ink, 1995).

20. In 1977, the Rev. Leon Sullivan, a member of the General Motors board of directors, proposed a series of principles suggesting how U.S. corporations should do business in apartheid South Africa. These included treating African workers the same at their American counterparts. See http://www.revleonsullivan.org.

21. There is evidence that since the INFACT campaign ended, Nestlé reverted back to some of their shady practices.

22. "The Social Investment Forum 2003 Report on Responsible Investing Trends," (Washington, DC: Social Investment Forum, 4 December 2003).

23. For a good summary of Sarbanes-Oxley corporate reforms, see the American Institute of Certified Public Accountants: http://www.aicpa.org/info/sarbanes_oxley_summary.htm.

24. David C. Korten, *The Post-Corporate World: Life After Capitalism* (copublished by Berrett-Koehler Publishers, San Francisco; and Kumarian Press, West Hartford, Conn., 1998).

25. Ralph Nader, "On the Corporate Crime Campaign Trail," from his column, "In the Public Interest," *San Francisco Bay Guardian*, 27 October 1998.

26. The case against Unocal is being coordinated by the National Lawyer's Guide in California and the International Law Project for Human, Economic, and Environmental Defense. Contact: 8124 W. Third St. Suite 201, Los Angeles, CA. 90048 USA. See http://www.heed.net/doc1.html.

27. Russell Mokhiber, "Death Penalty for Corporations Comes of Age," *Business Ethics*, November/December 1998.

28. Nader, "On the Corporate Crime Campaign Trail."

29. Based on author Chuck Collins' interviews with participants of the Bejing's Women's Conference, 1996.

30. Citizens Trade Campaign, "Fact Sheet on Africa Trade Bills," May 1999. See http://www.citizenstrade.org.

31. Patrick J. Buchanan, *The Great Betrayal: How American Sovereignty and Social Justice are Being Sacrificed to the Gods of the Global Economy* (Boston: Little, Brown and Company, 1998). 282–326.

32. See John Cavanagh, et. al., *Alternatives to Economic Globalization: A Better World is Possible* (Berrett-Koehler Publishers, 2004).

33. Steven Greenhouse, "Activism Surges at Campuses Nationwide, and Labor Is at Issue," *New York Times*, Monday, 2 March 1999.

34. See http://www.jubileedebtcampaign.org/uk

35. "Ten Questions About Jubilee 2000," from Jubilee 2000 in the United Kingdom. Their website is http://www.jubilee2000.uk.org.

36. Susan George, *The Debt Boomerang: How Third World Debt Harms Us All* (London: Pluto Press, 1997).

37. Jeff Sachs, "Self-Inflicted Wounds," *Financial Times*, 22 January 1999. See also Jeff Sachs and Steven Radalet, "What Have We Learned, So Far, From the East Asian Financial Crisis," unpublished paper, Harvard Institute for International Development, 1998.

38. The Tobin tax, named after James Tobin, the Nobel Laureate economics professor from Yale who first proposed it, is a 0.25 percent tax on the purchase of national currencies. It is not a large amount, but it is considerably more than the margins upon which currencies are often traded. Imposition of such a tax would moderate currency speculation as it would take larger fluctuations for buying and selling to be worthwhile. The tendency would be to encourage money to stay in one place for periods long enough to do some good.

39. Jared Bernstein and John Schmitt, "The Sky Didn't Fall: An

Evaluation of the Minimum Wage Increase" (Washington, DC: Economic Policy Institute, October 1996). See http://www.epinet.org.

40. For a good survey of the impact of minimum wage legislation, see Robert Pollin and Stephanie Luce, *Toward a Living Wage: Building a Fair Economy* (New York: The New Press, 1998. This is the first significant documentation of this emerging movement.

41. While neither a journalistic account of local victories nor a handbook for winning campaigns, *The Living Wage Building a Fair Economy* (New York: The New Press, 1998) is a level-headed response to many of the key arguments that local activists encounter when advocating for a living wage.

42. Living Wage Resource Center, http://www.livingwage campaign.org, November 2004.

43. Diana Pearce and Jennifer Brooks, with Laura Henze Russell, *The Self-Sufficiency Standard for Massachusetts* (Washington, DC: Wider Opportunities for Women, September 1998).

44. Chuck Collins, Scott Klinger and Karen Kraut, "Choosing the High Road: Businesses That Pay a Living Wage and Prosper," Responsible Wealth and United for a Fair Economy, March 2000. Download report at http://www.responsi-blewealth.org/living_wage/choosing/html.

45. Preamble Center, "Corporate Irresponsibility: There Ought to Be Some Laws," July 1996. Polling conducted by Ethel Klein, EDK Associates and Guy Molyneux of Peter D. Hart Associates.

46. Institute for Policy Studies, with assistance from Ralph Estes of American University. As cited in "CEOs Win, Worker's Lose," *Fourth Annual Executive Compensation Survey* (Boston, Mass.: United for a Fair Economy; Washington, DC: Institute for Policy Studies, May 1997).

47. John Witte, *The Politics and Development of the Federal Income Tax* (Madison: University of Wisconsin Press, 1985), 125.

48. Sam Pizzigati, "America Needs More Than a Raise" in *Working USA* (Armonk, N.Y.: M.E. Sharpe, September-October 1997).

49. "Surge in Corporate Tax Welfare Drives Corporate Tax Payments Down to Near Record Low," Citizens for Tax Justice) 17 April 2002.

50. Michael Sherraden and Neil Gilbert, *Assets and the Poor: A New American Welfare Policy* (Armonk, N.Y.: M.E. Sharpe, 1991).

51. Jeff Gates, *The Ownership Solution* (Reading, MA: Addison-Wesley,1998), 185–212.

52. Press release, "ESOPs, Stock Options, and 401 (k) Plans Now Control 8.3% of Corporate Equity" (Oakland, CA: The National Center for Employee Ownership, 1998); 2004 information estimates 8.8 million ESOP participants with an estimated $400 billion in assets; analysis of amount per non management worker conducted by Chris Mackin of Ownership Associates and Chuck Collins of United for a Fair Economy.

53. Peter Kardas, Adria Scharf, and Jim Keogh, "Wealth and Income Consequences of Employee Ownership: A Comparative Study from Washington State," Washington State Community, Trade and Economic Development, November 1998.

54. David Cay Johnston, *Perfectly Legal: The Covert Campaign to Rig Our Tax System to Benefit the Super Rich and Cheat Everyone Else* (New York: Portfolio, 2003), 134–135.

55. Ibid., p. 296.

56. See the work of the Center on Budget and Policy Priorities to promote state earned income credits. Joseph Llobrera and Bob Zahradnick, "A Hand Up: How State Earned Income Tax Credits Are Helping Working Families Escape Poverty in 2004," published by the Center on Budget and Policy Priorities on 14 May 2004. See: http://www.cbpp.org/pubs/eitc.htm.

57. From campaign statements of the 1999 Steve Forbes for President Campaign, as cited on their website http://www.forbes2000.org.

58. Proposal introduced by Senator Edward Kennedy in February 1998.

59. See William H. Gates and Chuck Collins, *Wealth and Our Commonwealth: Why America Should Tax Accumulated Fortunes* (Boston: Beacon Press, 2003).

60. We are still enlisting individuals to sign this petition at http://www.responsiblewealth.org.

61. David Cay Johnston, "Dozens of Rich Americans Join In Fight to Retain the Estate Tax," *New York Times*, 14 February 2001.

62. Wolff, *Top Heavy: The Increasing Inequality of Wealth in America and What Can Be Done About It* (New York: The New Press, 1996), 33–59.

63. The Sixteenth Amendment to the Constitution, passed in 1913, states that "Congress shall have the power to collect taxes on income, from whatever source derived, without apportionment the several States, and without regard to any census or enumeration." Prior to this, the powers of taxation were limited. A direct tax would be a tax on real or personal property, imposed solely by reason of its being owned by the taxpayer. In contrast indirect taxes are levied on an event, like the transmission of property. The Sixteenth Amendment allowed income taxes to be legal as indirect taxes that did not have to be apportioned among the states. The estate tax is actually an excise tax on the transfer of property at death. A net-worth tax, a form of direct taxation, would be barred unless it was directly apportioned among the states according to population.

Thanks to attorney Roy Ulrich in his unpublished memorandum on this matter prepared for Citizens for Tax Justice and Professor Edward Wolff.

64. Michael M. Phillips, "Localities Force Firms to Keep Promises," *Wall Street Journal*, 29 June 1996.

65. Greg LeRoy, "Good Jobs First: For Corporate Accountability and Family Wage Jobs," unpublished report.

66. Quoted from Jeff Gates, *The Ownership Solution*, 5.

67. William Greider, testimony before Congressional Banking Committee, 7 October 1993.

68. Information on the Fifth District Initiative is listed on the website of the Financial Markets Center at http://www.fmcenter.org.

69. Information about Community Supported Agriculture (CSAs) from the Extension Program of the University of Massachusetts, 29 July 1997. See http://www.umassvegetable.org

70. Corey Rosen, "ESOPs, Stock Options, and 401(k) Plans Now Control 8.3% of Corporate Equity" (Oakland, CA: The National Center for Employee Ownership, 1997). See http://www.nceo.org.

71. Data from the National Federation of Community Development Credit Unions: http://www.natfed.org/i4a/pages/index.cfm?pageid=256.

72. Institute for Community Economics, ww.iceclt.org.

73. CDFI Coalition of Community Development Financial Institutions, http://www.cdfi.org.

74. Canadian Auto Workers, "Big Three Bargaining Backgrounder Issues" October, 1996.

Conclusion

1. Harvey Cox, "The Market as God: Living in the new dispensation," *Atlantic Monthly*, March 1999.

2. National Conference of Catholic Bishops, *Economic Justice for All: Pastoral Letter on Catholic Social Teaching and the U.S. Economy* (Washington, DC: U.S. Catholic Conference, 1986).

Index

Also Available from The New Press

DOUG HENWOOD

AFTER THE NEW ECONOMY

The Binge . . . And the Hangover That Won't Go Away

(PB, 1-56584-983-3, 304 pages)

Economist Doug Henwood scrutinizes the 1990s and brilliantly dissects the so-called new economy.

BETH SHULMAN

THE BETRAYAL OF WORK

How Low-Wage Jobs Fail 30 Million Americans

(PB, 1-56584-733-4, 272 pages)

How the United States turns its back on the working poor.

MEIZHU LUI, BARBARA ROBLES, BETSY LEONDAR-WRIGHT, ROSE BREWER, AND REBECCA ADAMSON

THE COLOR OF WEALTH

The Story Behind the U.S. Racial Wealth Divide

(PB, 1-59558-004-2, 320 pages)

Written by five leading experts on the racial wealth divide, this is a uniquely comprehensive multicultural history of American wealth.

SUSAN LINN

CONSUMING KIDS

The Hostile Takeover of Childhood

(HC, 1-56584-783-0, 304 pages)

A shocking expose of the $15 billion marketing maelstrom aimed at our children and how we can stop it.

EDITED BY JULIET B. SCHOR AND DOUGLAS B. HOLT

THE CONSUMER SOCIETY READER

(PB, 1-56584-598-6, 528 pages)

The definitive reader on the nature and evolution of consumer society.

SARAH ANDERSON AND JOHN CAVANAGH, WITH THEA LEE

FIELD GUIDE TO THE GLOBAL ECONOMY

Revised and Updated

(PB, 1-56584-956-6, 160 pages)

An eye-opening guide to the myths and realities of the international economy.

PRISCILLA MUROLO AND A.B. CHITTY

FROM THE FOLKS WHO BROUGHT YOU THE WEEKEND

A Short, Illustrated History of Labor in the United States

(PB, 1-56584-776-8, 384 pages)

An engrossing history of American labor that captures the full sweep of working people's struggles.

MEDARD GABEL AND HENRY BRUNER

GLOBAL INC.

An Atlas of the Multinational Corporation

(PB, 1-56584-727-X, 176 pages with 200 full-color maps, charts, and graphs throughout)

A unique and startling visual representation of the rise of the global corporation.

SASKIA SASSEN

FOREWORD BY K. ANTHONY APPIAH

GLOBALIZATION AND ITS DISCONTENTS

Essays on the New Mobility of People and Money

(PB, 1-56584-518-8, 288 pages with 7 black-and-white charts)

Groundbreaking essays on the new global economy from one of the leading experts on globalization.

RICHARD G. WILKINSON

THE IMPACT OF INEQUALITY

How to Make Sick Societies Healthier

(HC, 1-56584-925-6, 368 pages)

How inequality—more than destroying health and social status—affects the very way people view their lives.

R. EMMETT MURRAY

THE LEXICON OF LABOR

More Than 500 Key Terms, Biographical Sketches, and Historical Insights Concerning Labor in America

(PB, 1-56584-456-4, 208 pages)

An innovative and informative mini-encyclopedia of work and workers in America.

ROBERT POLLIN AND STEPHANIE LUCE

THE LIVING WAGE

Building a Fair Economy

(PB, 1-56584-588-9, 272 pages)

A comprehensive examination of the economic concept that has yielded dramatic results across the nation.

ANDREW ROSS

LOW PAY, HIGH PROFILE

(PB, 1-56584-893-4, 272 pages with 31 black-and-white photographs)

Anti-sweatshop activist and commentator Andrew Ross presents case studies from around the world to showcase the success and strength of the fair labor movement.

GEORGE MONBIOT

MANIFESTO FOR A NEW WORLD ORDER

(HC, 1-56584-908-6, 288 pages)

A global perspective on the current state of democracy, from the most realistic utopian of our time.

HOWARD ZINN

A PEOPLE'S HISTORY OF THE UNITED STATES

Abridged Teaching Edition, Revised and Updated

(PB, 1-56584-826-8, 640 pages)

Zinn's original text available specifically for classroom use, including exercises and teaching materials to accompany each chapter.

STEPHEN J. ROSE

SOCIAL STRATIFICATION IN THE UNITED STATES 2000

The New American Profile Poster: A Book-and-Poster Set

(PB, 1-56584-550-1, 48 pages with one full-sized poster)

A book and poster set on American comparative wealth, based on the most recent census data.

EDWARD WOLFF

TOP HEAVY

The Increasing Inequality of Wealth in America and What Can Be Done About It

(PB, 1-56584-665-6, 128 pages)

Compelling evidence on the growing gap between America's rich and poor.

JAMES HEINTZ, NANCY FOLBRE, CENTER FOR POPULAR ECONOMICS

THE ULTIMATE FIELD GUIDE TO THE U.S. ECONOMY

A Compact and Irreverent Guide to Economic Life in America

(PB, 1-56584-578-1, 224 pages with illustrations, charts, tables)

An accessible, concise reference that provides a comprehensive and informative overview of the U.S. economy.

WILLIAM K. TABB

UNEQUAL PARTNERS

(PB, 1-56584-722-9, 288 pages)

An eye-opening primer on some of the less explored aspects of globalization.

RANDY ALBELDA, NANCY FOLBRE, AND THE CENTER FOR POPULAR ECONOMICS

THE WAR ON THE POOR

A Defense Manual

(PB, 1-56584-262-6, 144 pages)

An incisive look at self-perpetuating poverty in America.

LORI WALLACH AND PATRICK WOODALL, PUBLIC CITIZEN

WHOSE TRADE ORGANIZATION?

The Comprehensive Guide to the WTO

(PB, 1-56584-841-1, 416 pages)

A meticulous chronicle of how the WTO has eroded democracy around the world.

STUDS TERKEL

WORKING

People Talk about What They Do All Day and How They Feel about What They Do

(PB, 1-56584-342-8, 640 pages)

A timeless snapshot of people's feelings about their working lives, consisting of over 100 interviews.

To order, call 1-800-233-4830

To learn more about The New Press and receive updates on new titles, visit www.thenewpress.com.